A PORTRAIT OF AN JON HOLMES IDIOT AS A YOUNG MAN

PART MEMOIR, PART EXPLANATION
AS TO WHY MEN *ARE SO RUBBISH*

Copyright © Jon Holmes 2015

The right of Jon Holmes to be identified as
the author of this work has been asserted in accordance with the
Copyright, Designs and Patents Act 1988.

This edition first published in Great Britain in 2015 by
Orion
an imprint of the Orion Publishing Group Ltd
Carmelite House, 50 Victoria Embankment
London, EC4Y 0DZ
An Hachette UK Company

1 3 5 7 9 10 8 6 4 2

A CIP catalogue record for this book is available
from the British Library.

Trade Paperback ISBN: 978 1 4091 2977 6

Typeset by Input Data Services Ltd, Bridgwater, Somerset

Printed and bound by CPI Group (UK) Ltd, Croydon, CR0 4YY

The Orion Publishing Group's policy is to use papers that are natural,
renewable and recyclable and made from wood grown in sustainable forests.
The logging and manufacturing processes are expected to conform to
the environmental regulations of the country of origin.

Every effort has been made to fulfil requirements with regard to
reproducing copyright material. The author and publisher will be
glad to rectify any omissions at the earliest opportunity.

www.orionbooks.co.uk

This book is for Maisie and Isla,
who will never be allowed to read it.

CONTENTS

INTRODUCTION

To the Devil, a daughter.

Due to a misunderstanding on the part of all involved parties as to exactly what constituted 'going into labour', when our first child was born my wife and I made it to the hospital with just moments to spare. There was no time for gas and air, certainly very little chance of filling a birthing pool, and barely a moment for me to shout 'shitting hell!' while doing 140 mph through the streets of Canterbury, in Kent, at three o'clock in the morning. Quite by accident, most of the breathing, painful bits, swearing and yelling had been done at home, the latter mostly directed at me, largely because I'd thought it a good idea to time the contractions via an app on my phone and had managed to get it staggeringly, impressively wrong.

'According to the app,' I kept saying to my wife as she huffed, puffed and profaned on all fours, 'the contractions are still quite far apart.'

My wife's scepticism, by which I mean anger, was exacerbated only by me confidently explaining that I couldn't be wrong, because all I had to do was press a button at the start and end of each contraction. It was hardly rocket science. Hell, it wasn't even rocket salad, yet somehow I still got it way off and, having narrowly avoided a newborn baby's first experience of the world being the footwell of a car, we arrived at the birth unit only to be immediately hooked up to machines with varying levels of nursing staff peering intently between my wife's legs.

'Baby's coming right now,' one said.

And so it began.

'Gas and air!' screeched my wife.

'No time, baby's here,' said the midwife. 'Push.'

There was agony, more shouting, gore, blood and things that the human eye should never ever see happening to bed sheets, as if Eli Roth, rather than a midwife, was directing proceedings. Clearly, I was aware that midwives are trained professionals who are taught to pull babies out of people willy-nilly, day in day out, but to my inexpert eye it was carnage. And then it happened. In the midst of all the bleeping and shrieking, I was dimly aware that the midwife had called a trainee over to show her the ropes of whatever it was that was coming out of my wife. I was, like most cowardly men, stationed firmly at the northern end, because I had taken one look and seen enough of what was happening in the southern sector to know that it was best avoided.

'Push!' people were now shouting.

'Fuck off!' my wife was bellowing. And then suddenly a head began to appear.

'Crowning,' said the midwife, and pulled the trainee closer still so that she could get a better view of what was going on. I too took the opportunity to glance down at the action, knowing I was about to see the miracle of life being brought into this world. The fragility of human existence entering this realm in the shape of a child, our child, *my* child – a tiny bundle of pink happiness, slicked wet with the natural processes of nature. It is the most wondrous thing that a human being can bear witness to.

And it was then that I noticed that the trainee midwife was wearing a low-cut gown. She was bent over, staring intently at my wife's vagina, and I could see straight down her top. All the way down, almost to her waist, and she was wearing nothing underneath but a lacy bra. My child was being born, yet here I was, being distracted by the attractive breasts of a trainee midwife.

I am a man. Despite this, I felt bad, and so later I consulted various male friends as to what they would have done in the same situation. My research revealed one common denominator: each and every one of them concurred that they would have done pretty much the same thing. I offer this only as proof, if proof were needed, that men are pretty much fucked up.

And it's why I was glad, moments later, that I was holding a girl.

Some weeks after this, I and the family Holmes were at the post-natal clinic where I was asked to fill in countless boxes on myriad medical forms detailing whether or not this crying creature that I'd co-created was likely, at any time in the future, to be hit by heart disease, diabetes, an early death, or all three due to some underlying hereditary condition. The problem was, I didn't know. And that's because I have simply no idea who my parents are.

'This form,' said the nice lady, 'is an essential document that will let everyone know what may lie in store for little Maisie in the future.'

'Hmm.' I said. 'I can't fill this in.'

'Do you need a pen?' she asked, reaching into her drawer.

I needed a lot more than a pen. I couldn't fill in the form because I have no idea whether my grandad had diabetes, or if my mother and father's hearts were alive or dead.[1] I know nothing of them, not even their names, and what's more I have nothing to go on, save for a teddy bear that my mum bought for me before she gave me up for adoption at two weeks' old. Yet what I will be forever carrying with me are whatever medical time bombs she and my unknown father kindly bequeathed to me, and while I am, arguably, (thanks to genetics and good old-fashioned DNA) a cocktail of my missing parents' looks and personality, the answer to the question of who I am – who I *really* am, the person I've become – lies with a childless young couple who walked through a door one day, picked an unwanted baby out of a line-up, and then took it home to set about the tricky task of turning it into a person.

---

1 And it's just this kind of lack of medical history coupled with the fact that I actually wasn't even originally even called 'Jon Holmes', that creates a situation pretty much guaranteed to confuse the hell out of the staff at the post-natal clinic. I don't blame them either, because who would want to have to write 'N/A' on a piece of paper that could have such profound consequences on the lives of my daughters? (I should mention that we now have two of them. The beautiful Isla was born in 2012. I was forbidden to use the app.)

I may not ever be able to pass on anything about me via any kind of important form, but I can hand my daughters a document of who I am.

This is it.[2]

ONE

... in which I am 1.

'You can watch *The Six Million Dollar Man* until he does something bionic, and then you can go to bed,' said the lady who wasn't my mum, heading back into the kitchen armed with a tea towel that had various badly reproduced paintings of scenes of the Norfolk Broads on it. Despite not being my mum, she'd been waving the cloth souvenir to emphasise Mum's Law, a little-known branch of theoretical physics that dictates that if, in her opinion, you are too young to stay up and watch Steve Austin jump over a car, then it was time, in my dad's words, 'to go up the wooden hill to Bedfordshire'.[1] Although he wasn't my dad either.

I have no idea who my parents are. I was born at the age of nought in 1969, the year the moon landings represented a giant leap for man, to someone for whom my arrival

---

[1] My dad always said this, and for years I was convinced there was another county at the top of the stairs, the border of which was the top step. As you passed the landing windowsill on the right, home to a thin blue glass vase with a pottery cat clambering over the rim, I had the idea we were entering a different land. I think I was heavily influenced by the work of Enid Blyton and the interchangeable worlds that used to swirl through her seminal work of theoretical aesthetic emotionalism, *The Magic Faraway Tree*. It's £5.24 in paperback on Amazon.

represented an impossible step for a woman. At the arse end of the sixties it was still very much a social stigma to be an unmarried mother, so my unmarried mother was either forced – or chose – to give me up for adoption. I took my own giant leap from birth canal to maternity ward in the county town of Stratford-upon-Avon, Warwickshire, precisely four hundred and five years and one day after the birth, in the same town, of William Shakespeare in a hospital that, back when he was born, was probably all fields piled high with dead people infected with the bubonic plague. Improvements in Stratford-upon-Avon's Healthcare Authority over the intervening years meant that I was born entirely plague-free and yet, despite this, the tiny 4lb me was quickly whisked away from a mother who I never saw or heard from again. Even if I were to pass my birth mother in the street I wouldn't recognise her, although, to be fair, I've only ever realistically seen her fleetingly, and from one angle, so unless she reassumes that position in the street, which seems unlikely, then I'd say I'm not in with a very good chance of picking her out of a crowd. Plus, I have as much recollection of the birth as I do the conception, which was quite possibly the last time either of us had anything to do with my natural father. All that remains of her – all that she left me with – was a small box of baby clothes, some knitted toys she'd made for me while she was pregnant, and a teddy bear, which I still have. It came home with me when I was adopted by a young married couple called Dorothy and Leslie Holmes, of Nuneaton, Warwickshire, who couldn't have children of their own.

*

If my formative years were a series of scenes painted on the souvenir tea-towel of life, then this is one that sticks in my mind. I was six, well into my tenure as a child, and *The Six Million Dollar Man* was a staple of 1975 Saturday teatime television, sharing space with Bruce Forsyth's *Generation Game* and *New Faces*, a shiny floor talent show that sucked in singers and other entertainers and crushed them to shit, like some kind of reverse musical event-horizon, gobbling up a star.[2] This was how and when Showaddywaddy was discovered. It was also perfectly acceptable to black up. These were dangerous times.[3]

I remember this particular day because it was just after tea, and we'd all been to my nana and grandad's house (on Dad's side), where I'd spent the afternoon eating new-fangled prawn cocktail Skips[4] and falling into their pond. *The Six Million Dollar Man* was a favourite, so with Mum doing the drying up in the kitchen and my dad disappearing, like clockwork, upstairs to Bedfordshire for a post-tea poo, I was safe in the knowledge that I, and I alone, would be the only one to know when Steve Austin had committed his first

---

2 Bruce Forsyth and ITV talent shows passing for Saturday evening entertainment? I know, it's unthinkable in modern times, of course, but it actually happened.

3 See also *Jim'll Fix It*, *The Rolf Harris Show* and Dave Lee Travis on Radio 1.

4 Prawn cocktail-flavour Skips were launched on an unsuspecting public in 1974. Back then, a prawn cocktail was seen as the height of social sophistication, along with Black Forest gateaux and wife swapping. Prawn cocktail Skips were fucking horrible then and they're fucking horrible now. You may as well eat a bit of polystyrene packaging that you've found on the floor and then rubbed on a fish.

bionic act. This way, I would squeeze extra time out of the day and no one would be any the wiser.

Within a minute of the opening credits, the Bionic Man jumped over a car. I was so excited by this spectacle that I immediately ran into the kitchen to tell my mum what I had witnessed, because it was, I told her breathlessly, *the most AMAZING thing that I had ever seen in my life*. She looked at me as only mothers can, and put down the tea towel. In slow motion, just like Steve Austin's car-jump had been, I saw bits of fabric Norfolk scrunch themselves into a pile on the draining board, and the sickening understanding of what I had just done dawned heavily on my six-year-old self. Standing in a seventies' Nuneaton kitchen, in a house built by my dad's own fair hand, I realised a lunching awareness that was with nothing short of horror that I had become the author of my own demise. Hoist by a petard made of childish excitement and all-action television, I was in immediate danger of going to bed and I needed to act fast. I started to say that I'd made a mistake, and that what Steve Austin had done didn't count as bionic because bionic was really when he picked a car up, rather than jumped over it, but Mum, with the plates from the Findus crispy pancakes and chips still dripping on the Formica, turned me round, switched off the television and marched me up the infamous wooden hill faster than *The Six Million Dollar Man* could have ever dreamed of. As we passed the border into Bedfordshire, she called out to my dad.

'Are you still in there, Les?'

'Yes,' came the muffled reply.

'Well, if you use all the loo roll,' she said, 'don't just leave the empty tube on the holder for once. And use air freshener.'[5]

Oh yes, in 1975 my parents and I were living the high life, yet given that I already knew that they weren't actually my parents and that I was only brought to live with them in their house a month after I was born (even if at this stage I didn't understand why), I guess we weren't doing too badly.

In the bathroom, my protestations were falling on not deaf, but certainly indifferent, ears. By now, I'd given up on the Bionic Man and was trying a new tactic.

'Can I stay up and watch *The Pink Panther Show*?'

'*The Pink Panther* was on before the Bionic Man,' said my mum, displaying a hitherto unseen grasp of TV scheduling. 'You watched it while you were having your tea. Now, clean your teeth.'

'I love *The Pink Panther*. It's my favourite,' I bleated hopelessly through toothpaste. But I knew the battle had been won. And not by me.

'You haven't done the top ones,' said my mum, and assumed control of the toothbrush. My Saturday was all but over.

---

5 The toilet was adjacent to, but separate from, the bathroom. When my dad had built the house he must have been taking into consideration his own predilection for going for a long poo at children's bath time. This allowed the two things to take place simultaneously, rather than one action having to wait for/rely on the timing of the other. He's a clever man, my dad. He had foresight. Although not so much that he'd had the prescience to build more than one bathroom; say a downstairs one or an en-suite, for instance – this was the seventies – downstairs and en-suite toilets were quite literally distant pipe dreams.

The Pink Panther Show was surely a rival in any seventies' child's affections for *The Six Million Dollar Man*. It was a cartoon spin-off from the Peter Sellers' films, in which, confusingly, the pink panther was a diamond, rather than a pink panther.[6] Yet its magical theme tune drew me in, begging, as it did, even the most casual viewer to 'Think of all the animals you've ever heard about, like rhinoceroses and tigers cats and mink.' Back then, I hadn't ever heard of a mink, but nevertheless I spent quite a long time drawing one, imagining it to be somewhere between a Yorkshire terrier and a basilisk. I knew full well what a Yorkshire terrier was, because my parents had one (called Bobby) that had openly resented my arrival, and I knew what a basilisk was because I had seen one in a book of *Fabulous Animals*.[7] 'There are lots of funny animals in all this world,' the theme song went on to remind us, 'But have you ever seen a panther that is pink? Think. A panther that is positively pink'. The answer to this question was a resounding 'no'. Pink Panthers were up there with the elusive mink as far as I was concerned, and despite several childhood trips with Mum and Dad to Twycross Zoo, I had failed to find either. What I had seen there though, was a poster that idly wondered whether one,

---

6 The Peter Sellers' *Pink Panther* films about a diamond called the Pink Panther had an animated pink panther in their title sequences, which wasn't a diamond but was also an actual pink panther. The panther (the actual panther, not the diamond) then got its own spin-off series. There were a lot of drugs around at this time.

7 The book in question was based on a 1975 children's TV series of the same name, which saw David Attenborough prowling round a studio made up to look like a museum, talking about unicorns, dragons and mermaids. It was to my young eyes, as the title suggests, fabulous.

as a conscientious zoo-goer, had ever considered adopting an otter.

The process of adopting animals was, and still is, far easier than that of adopting a child. For a start, it doesn't matter if you're gay (although it probably did in the seventies), plus there's the added advantage that any animal that you do adopt won't necessarily come and live with you. Instead of having to bring up an otter on a diet of Findus crispy pancakes and limited access to Saturday evening television, your only real commitment is a one-off payment or a small monthly stipend in return for which you get a certificate and the warm glowing feeling that comes with the knowledge that you've contributed to the general well-being of a semi-aquatic mammal. It's alive and it's yours, but the bonus is that you don't even ever have to meet it, let alone have to shell out on a Mr Frosty[8] for it for Christmas. Standing well below the height of the ticket counter in my cagoule and wellies, looking at the adoption poster while my dad handed over money and my mum fussed about a guide leaflet, I was certainly aware that I wasn't an otter, yet understanding why my birth mum didn't want me and two complete strangers did, took a little more time to figure out.

*

8 Despite having a name like a supernatural serial killer from a Stephen King novel, Mr Frosty was a plastic snowman who, when you poured ice into a hole in his head and turned a handle, would dispense slush from his stomach. One was then encouraged to flavour this resulting mess with brightly coloured, possibly toxic, liquid poured out of a penguin, and then eat it. Actually, come to think of it, that sounds exactly like a supernatural serial killer from a Stephen King novel.

From the earliest age I knew I was adopted. My adoptive parents had been married in September 1963 and had spent some years trying to conceive with no luck. They first met at the Co-op Hall, Nuneaton's glittering nightspot of choice, in 1962, where their young eyes had met over a skiffle band and (in my dad's case) untold quantities of Marston's Bitter. Through the haze of this he also saw a then unknown Beatles playing in support of Tanya Day And The Vampires[9] shortly before the venue played host to an equally unknown Rolling Stones, who played a children's party there in November 1963 and were pelted with cream cakes by unappreciative toddlers.[10] All of this excitement obviously took its toll on my dad's sperm, because four years and several trips to a specialist later, he was diagnosed with a low count and the decision was taken to adopt a baby.

'I'm sorry, Dorothy, but my sperm is rubbish,' my dad told my mum over a breakfast of oatcakes and a boiled egg. Obviously, I'm paraphrasing as I wasn't there. To be honest, I've also invented the scenario of the oatcakes and the egg, but he's always liked both, so it's safe to assume.

'Never mind, dear,' she replied. 'What do you think about adoption?'

'Where would we keep an otter?'

'No, Les, a child,' replied my mum, 'I've always thought that if we couldn't have a baby ourselves, then we should adopt.'

---

9 Nope, me neither.

10 This famous Nuneaton incident is even recorded by Bill Wyman in his autobiography *Stone Alone*. Presumably they were playing new material, and the six-year-olds just wanted to hear the hits.

'Girl or boy?' asked my dad, because in those days you could choose.[11]

'Boy,' said my mum firmly. Both she and Dad were sibling-free and as my mum had always wanted an elder brother, she wanted a baby boy. Such was her logic. 'And you don't keep the otter. You just get a certificate.'

'Fine,' said my dad. 'Pass the jam.'

And so it was that in the summer of '67 they threw themselves into the adoption process. Two years, various forms, letters, social workers and home visits later they found themselves in the small office of a midwife in a Mother and Baby Home in Stratford-upon-Avon, looking down at a parentless baby. I was four weeks old and possessed, apparently, of both the biggest brown eyes and sorest bottom of any baby my mum had ever seen. And for all of us, it was love at first sight.

'What's wrong with his bottom?' said my dad, eyeing my arse suspiciously.

'Be quiet, Les,' said my mum. 'But yes,' she said to the lady in charge, 'what's wrong with it?'

Subsequent lines of inquiry led to the revelation that, to try to keep me alive without a breast to have a crack at, the staff at the hospital had decided to feed me nothing but condensed milk from a tin. And just in case this heady concoction of homogenised liquid wasn't sweet enough already,

---

11 You could, too. There was a baby surplus because back then unmarried mothers received nothing in the way of benefits, very little help and complete ostracism from their uptight families. Single pregnant girls were often sent away to have the baby, which was then taken from them at birth. Love may well have been free in the 1960s, but you paid a high price for it.

they'd put sugar in it. To be frank, I was lucky that I wasn't shitting Milkybars.

'We need to get this baby out of here if only to stop it from exploding,' my mum told my dad.

'He's tiny,' said Dad, leaning over my top end, rather than be party to the red-raw destruction at the other.

'Yes,' said my mum. 'And he needs us.'

'Do you know what?' said my dad, twenty-nine years old and beaming like the one working headlamp on his Hillman Super Minx, 'When we get him home, he's going to look really funny wearing my flat cap.'

And so it was that I was chosen. Like the little bald boy in *The Golden Child* with Eddie Murphy, I was The Chosen One. Sadly, unlike the little bald boy in *The Golden Child* with Eddie Murphy, I couldn't bend metal with my mind or bring dead insects back to life by touching their wings with magic but, on the plus side, I hadn't been captured by a monster and hidden away locked in a cage in a remote Tibetan castle. Instead, I was to be taken to Nuneaton, where I would spend the next eighteen years of my life.

This, the story of my discovery, was told to me straight-away from as young as I can remember and, subsequently, the same tale was told for years afterwards to any girlfriends that I brought home, to whom my mum would concentrate the story mainly around the bit about the sore bottom.

'The first time we saw him,' she would say to them with barely concealed glee, 'he had a sore bottom.'

My girlfriend would look uncomfortable.

'Since birth,' she'd continue, 'they'd been feeding him on condensed milk. Condensed milk. From a tin. And they put sugar in it. Can you imagine such a thing?'

My girlfriend would give me a look that suggested she could neither imagine such a thing and nor would she want to, but here she was being forced to imagine it, by a lady that she'd only just met.

'His bum was red raw,' she'd tell them. 'I'd never seen anything like it, had you, Les?'

My dad, whose experience with babies prior to me was nil, would agree that he had not, and then he would go upstairs for a poo.

'Use freshener,' my mum would call after him, and at that point I knew I would never see the girl sitting in our lounge ever again.

TWO

... in which I thank God that my real dad isn't Bono.

The whole 'adoption' thing, to me, has never been that much of an issue, which is, in the main, thanks to my parents making it seem so much like part of everyday life. At school, occasionally, it would crop up. Usually during some kind of highbrow break-time chat about the sociological implications of child rearing in post-war Britain.[1]

'What?' said Paul Bolton, who was in my English class at secondary school. 'You're a fucking orphan?'

'No,' I said, 'I'm not an orphan. You're thinking of Oliver Twist. Or Annie.'

'Who's Annie? Have you got off with her?'

'No. You know, Little Orphan Annie. From *Annie*.'

He paused for a moment, as if to consider the parallels between my young life and that of a depression-era American waif and her benefactor.

---

1 Or during a lull in a conversation about breasts, as was more likely. We were fourteen, and like any fourteen-year-old boys, we talked of very little else. As the Bible tells us, 'When two or three fourteen-year-old boys are gathered together, they are apt to discuss trying to get off with girls. And so it is written.'

'Urgh,' he said. 'You're like a girl called Annie. You're gay.' And then he wandered off to chalk a spunking cock on a wall without once noting the irony.

It's fair to say that people do react strangely when you tell them you're adopted because it's a bit unusual. If it helps, think of it like Mowgli in the film *The Jungle Book* but where Mowgli was not brought up in the jungle by a black (not pink) panther, a special-needs bear, and a suspicious-looking orangutan, but rather in a house in the Midlands by a state-registered nurse and a builder.[2] There had also been the tricky question of my name. As any parent knows, the identification of a child is something not to be undertaken lightly. You are bestowing upon this sensitive human crea-ture something with which it will be saddled in perpetuity, something that will forever be used to address it, cajole it, admonish it, call it hither and mercilessly taunt it, if you pick the wrong one. There was a girl at my school called Gay Wally, and among pupils and staff alike she came to epito-mise the whole 'what were your parents *thinking*?' debate. There was no escape for her.

'What's your name?' she was inevitably asked on the first day. Probably by Paul Bolton.

'Gay.'

'Gay? Gay what?'

'Gay Wally.'

---

2 Although, to be fair, there was a suspicious-looking orangutan involved, because in a rare moment of philanthropy, my dad had adopted one at Twycross Zoo. Although it didn't live with us. Partly because you only get a certificate, but mostly because, for Bobby, the attention-seeking jealous Yorkshire terrier, it would have been the last straw and he would have killed it.

'Hahahahahahahaha. You're Gay, like a Wally,' he'd say, and then draw another cock on a wall. By lunchtime everyone knew and Gay Wally's schooldays were numbered. Back then a fellow pupil's amusing name would travel round a secondary school faster than chlamydia does now. And it was all her parents' fault for not thinking it through.

Everyone gets some kind of nickname at school and, as a parent, it's very easy to accidentally give your offspring's peers an open goal. My nickname was simply 'Holmesy', which was part of the time-honoured tradition of simply adding the letter 'Y' to any given surname for instant nickname gratification. Adding a Y was simple and worked along much the same lines as Pot Noodle or sex with Fishy Fiona from the year above us: it was quick and effective, if not especially satisfying. At least, with regard to the latter, that's if Anthony 'Walshy' Walsh was to be believed, which he wasn't. These were comfortable, simple, classic go-to nicknames, formed in a hurry (among my peers I could also count 'Woody', 'Granty' and 'Stouty') but the best and most rewarding monikers were reserved for people who had something wrong with them, or had a stupid real name bestowed on them by their unthinking parents. Kev, who was Fat, was thus known as 'Fat Kev', John Thomas was quite obviously referred to as 'Cock', Matthew Stirling, who was quite possibly certifiably insane,[3] somehow got labelled

---

3 He had a schoolbag that he insisted was a vampire bat. His speciality was to launch it at people while they were standing against walls in the playground. The resulting impact would smash their noses from the front and bounce their heads off the bricks at the back. He told them that they'd been 'attacked by the bat'.

'Feek', poor Lorna Jenkins had very bad eczema so she was known as 'Jenkins Fever' (children are horrible little fuckers, aren't they?) and, despite having everyday, run-of-the-mill, eminently sensible first names, Wayne Grewcock and Lisa Wankling never even stood a chance. Fishy Fiona was her own fault, a result of bad personal hygiene. In fact, some given names are so bad that they are destined to be changed by deed poll the moment the unfortunate recipients reach eighteen. David Bowie's son Zowie Bowie, for instance, is now called Duncan Jones and Elijah Bob Patricius Guggi Q, spawn of Bono, can only be counting the days. Mind you, his dad is called 'Bono', a man who, lest we forget, once paid for a first-class ticket to fly his hat round world because he'd forgotten it, and therefore can't really be relied on to do anything sensible. I think it's safe to assume that Elijah Bob Patricius Guggi Q is probably having a bit of a hard time at school. And sure enough, where I was concerned, my new parents had a problem.

'We need to give him a name,' my mum told my dad over some more oatcakes.[4]

'He's already got a name,' said my dad.

'Yes,' said my mum. 'But I don't like it.'

Dad was right. The name on the front of this book says Jon Holmes but that's technically not who I first was. I'd arrived into the fledgling Holmes' household with another name entirely.

---

4 My dad loves oatcakes. He's from Stoke-on-Trent. Oatcakes are like catnip to those people. They're sort of flat pancakes made from oatmeal, flour, yeast and bits of old pottery.

'Why not?' said my dad, not unreasonably. 'What's wrong with it?'

'Nothing. Just that now that he's ours, we should give him a name that we've chosen.'

This was perfectly acceptable. In the early seventies you could take an adopted child home and rename it with the kind of easy nonchalance that these days you'd associate with renaming a Word file.

'What about John?' suggested my dad, whose middle name was John.

'Too harsh for a baby,' said my mum, with a quick frown, as though my dad was considering getting his paintbrushes out to paint 'Vlad Dracul' on the end of my cot.

'How is John too harsh?'

'It just is.'

'No it isn't,' countered Dad. 'My dad was called John. And it's my middle name.'

'Be quiet, Les, I'm thinking.'

'What about Les? That's a nice name.'

'Don't be silly.'

Thank heaven for small mercies. At my school, 'Les' would have immediately been translated into the nickname 'Lesbian' and would have drawn playground mockery like homophobic moths to a gay flame.

'What about Jonathan?' she said. 'That's got John in it. And it's a much nicer name for a baby.'

'Perfect,' said my dad, knowing, like any man, both when he was beaten and when to be quiet.

So it was decided. I'd arrived into their lives in a brown carrycot with the name of Sean Richard Smith and I was now lying in it, post-breakfast, as Jonathan Richard Holmes. Mum was pleased because Jonathan 'had John in it' which in turn was an Anglicised equivalent of the Irish 'Sean' so some of my original identity had been kept, and Dad was happy because he could eat his oatcakes in peace. Mum was doubly content with her choice, as the meaning of 'Jonathan' is 'God has Given',[5] whereas Sean means 'God's Gracious Gift'[6] so, overall, she'd found a happy symbiosis in her nomenclature. Likewise, they kept my middle name intact as a nice touch, though my surname had to be changed for legal reasons.[7]

Of course, it's entirely random chance that I became Jon(athan) Holmes as the next family through the door of the Stratford maternity home that day could have been called 'Hitler' for all I knew and I could just as easily have been called Jonathan Hitler, which may well have taken the playground name calling to the next level. Growing up, I was only too aware that things could have been very different, and my entire life was wholly dependent on where I had been placed, and with whom. Who knows where I'd be or what I'd be doing if I'd been allowed to stay with my birth mother. And occasionally, usually when drunk, I have

---

5 In the 1970s there was no name with the meaning 'Gift From Stratford-upon-Avon Mother and Baby Maternity Home'.

6 My mum is big on God. More about this later.

7 Later in life, when I was old enough to understand that my birth mother had entirely coincidentally given me an entirely different name from the one I was walking around with, it prompted a brief identity crisis. To solve this, I told myself I was a spy and even went as far as finding my dad's passport and altering the details to match my 'spy name' of Sean Richard Smith with a Berol felt-tip pen. He wasn't best pleased, but he has only himself and my mother to blame.

the sobering thought that, simply by a quirk of timing and fate, I could have ended up being someone else entirely. Irrespective of nature, one day either side of my parents walking through the door that day could have seen me nurtured by anyone from millionaire yacht owners to breadline barge owners to anyone in between, such as someone who ran a family-owned pedalo business.[8] I could even have been scooped up by a passing, adoption-crazed Madonna, longing to take this poor abandoned child home to suckle at her conical teat, although given that Madonna would have been eleven at the time and lived in Michigan, the chances of her passing through Stratford on one of her humanitarian child rescue missions is improbable at best. And anyway, I was the wrong colour.

In recent years, it's arguably been Madonna and her baby-taking Hollywood compatriots that have given adoption a slightly embarrassing public face. Madonna went off to Malawi to do her child shopping, Angelina Jolie came back from Ethiopia with a tan and a toddler, Ewan McGregor and his wife went slightly left field by opting for Mongolian, and in 2006 Meg Ryan popped out for a Chinese. Not only that, but round about the time I was first learning to say my new name, the actress Mia Farrow, who has four biological children, turned the notion of adoption up a few notches and set out on a path to reach out around the world and take on eleven more, one of whom, Soon-Yi, as a teenager,

---

8 Thinking about it, the authorities probably wouldn't have given a child to anyone who'd written 'pedalo' on their form, lest it be a typo.*

*For 'Paedo'. Come on, this is just Chapter Two. Do try to keep up.

then had an affair with Mia's partner Woody Allen. Shortly afterwards, Woody and Soon-Yi married and adopted two children themselves. Given this kind of mental family skeleton, life in Nuneaton as the newest member of the Holmes family was going to have to go some way to keep up. Which, forty-one years later, it did, in quite spectacular fashion. But we'll get to that. Yes, they were adopting me, but by default I was adopting the entire history – and future – of the Holmes family.

THREE

. . . in which I fail to listen properly.

My first birthday sort of passed me by without me noticing. I mean, I'm sure I noticed at the time, but none of the details have stayed with me and I have no real memory of what happened. While this may be unhelpful when writing a memoir (of sorts), it is hardly news. No one remembers their first birthday, they are the anniversary equivalent of listening to the Radio 1 Breakfast Show; you're aware that *something* must have happened, but you certainly can't recall anything of any note and, during it, more than one person was probably sick.[1]

So I have no recollection of mine whatsoever and neither do you of yours. And this is selfish, given the effort that most first-time parents go to for their offspring's inaugural celebration. When, four years ago at the time of writing, our eldest

---

[1] Message to any listeners of the Radio 1 *Breakfast Show*: I am led to believe that the word 'sick' can, nowadays, actually mean 'good'. This is a young people's thing. 'That gig last night was well sick' they say, having seen a Rizzle Kicks, whatever that is. Young people! Stop changing the definitions of words. We didn't do that. We didn't go into school going 'Did you hear Noel Edmonds on Radio 1? It was well diarrhoea.' Well, we did, but back then it meant what it was supposed to.

daughter Maisie turned one, all manner of lavish plans were put in place, plans which were so rich with detail they would have prompted even the most methodical of mice and/or men to comment on how well they were organised. As a new father, the big question of what we were going to do to mark this birthday seemed to me to be a rhetorical one. Mainly because I am a man and therefore I wasn't listening.

'Where shall we have the party?' said my wife one evening out of the blue, about six months before the actual date.

'Mmm?' I said, because I wasn't listening.

'Are you listening?'

'Yes.'

'Then where?'

At this point, as a man, you have a choice. You have now arrived at the moment in a conversation when it has become abundantly clear to both parties that you haven't been listening to whatever it is that you are supposed to be listening to. I was dimly aware that there had been a sort of background sound while I was concentrating on an episode of *24* I'd taped,[2] but had no idea what it was. The question is: is it worse to have not been listening to what could have been quite a long (if one-sided) conversation and then pretend

---

2 Being 2010, of course, I'd 'taped' nothing of the sort. Now we all live in the future where videotape is a thing of the past. Recordable DVD has also come and gone, and in our house we're plugged into the modern world by means of an old-fashioned SkyBox. Yet whatever the delivery medium, the notion that we 'tape' things has stuck. Saying, 'Sorry I wasn't listening, I'm watching a series-linked episode of *24* that I've digitised on to an internal hard drive by dint of the hardware making sequential changes in the direction of magnetisation represent binary data bits' just, (in my experience) causes a further row.

you've been listening all along but are now risking getting caught out on, or is it better to come clean and admit you weren't listening to your wife from the off while she was canvassing your opinion on whether we should have a jungle theme or something to do with princesses? Naturally, I tried to bluff it out.

'Oh, I dunno. What do you think?'

Any man will tell you that that is how it's done. Play for time. Bat the question, to which you have no answer, back, in the hope of getting a few more clues.

'You haven't been listening to a word I've said, have you?'

Come clean. Come clean and you could still get away with this.

'Yes. Of course I've been listening. You asked where and I asked what you thought.' On-screen, Jack Bauer has a Russian assassin tied to a chair and is torturing him by pulling bits of his tummy off with pliers. I'm beginning to know how his victim feels. Yet it's quite an exciting bit of *24*, so now I'm simultaneously trying to concentrate on what Jack Bauer is doing and what my wife is saying.

'Where's the SIM card?' someone growls and I can't remember whether Jack or my wife is looking for a SIM card. Could that have been her original question? On television, Jack produces a knife and disembowels the screaming man to pull a swallowed SIM card out of his guts. Damn. That means it was Jack's question and I'm no closer to knowing what my wife's was. Yet the air of menace she's exuding is not dissimilar to that of everyone's favourite CTU operative when he's in a bad mood. I realise I'm a dead man. I press 'pause' on the SkyBox.

*

This kind of thing happens on a regular basis. Sometimes it can take up to three whole evenings to watch a single fifty-minute-long episode of *The Walking Dead* because I have to pause it every thirty seconds to have a conversation that apparently cannot wait until it is finished. The record as it stands is five nights to get through forty minutes of one episode of *The Killing*. I imagine it would have been even longer if, say, something had to be organised. Something like a first birthday party.

'So what am I talking about?'

OK. Now I'm in trouble. The metaphorical SIM card is now being pulled from my intestines. It's game over.

'I don't know, I was watching this.'

There's a sigh. 'Your daughter's birthday. Should we have a party here or should we hire somewhere? Plus, jungle or Princesses?'

My first thought, as previously discussed, is: 'What's the point of a party for a first birthday? One-year-olds don't remember anything from when they were one. I have no memory of mine and neither does anyone else. Plus her birthday is in January, just after Christmas, so she really isn't going to need any more presents and, let's face it, she won't remember whether she got any or not because she's one and one-year-olds lack the cognitive ability to remember much so really it's just a waste of money why don't we wait until she's old enough to remember such things like when she's about five?' I say precisely none of this out loud.

'Princesses?'

'No. Jungle. And we'll do it here.'

In our house, by the time I get round to being involved in the discussion, it is already over; my input was merely perfunctory and I was only really being consulted out of politeness. I imagine this must be much like how Belgium feels during meetings at the United Nations.[3] Of course there is also every chance that my wife, being a woman, had actually said to me, 'Where shall we have the party?' without any build-up at all, simply having had the conversation leading up to it by herself, in her own head. Among the skills passed down to man by his ancestors – hunting, gathering, making fire – I find that women often expect us to have been handed telepathy too. Perhaps the many theories put about by authors and researchers who believe that the pyramids were built by aliens, and that once we had telepathic powers but lost them, only came up with the concept after discussing first-birthday parties with their wives. It's only a hypothesis, but it's as valid as theirs.

I *do* remember my second birthday, although my memory of it, like so many moments of early childhood, may well not come from inside my own head, but via a series of dog-eared photographs. In them, I am wearing something Godawful that my mum has dressed me in and am blowing the two candles out on a cake that's been fashioned into the shape

---

3 'So the question is, shall we invade Iraq or not? Without documentary evidence of WMDs we could be entering into an illegal war. Belgium, what do you think?'
   'I think we should leave it.'
   'No, we're going in.'
Actual transcript of meeting of the UN General Assembly, April 2003.

of a steam train. It was the seventies, after all, and my mum had seemingly figured that this gave her carte blanche to be creative with a number of Arctic Rolls. There are other children in the background of this memory, but I have no idea who they are. I asked my mum to dig the photograph out and I stared at them, trying to put names to faces almost thirty-three years before Facebook tagging made this sort of thing all modern and easy.[4]

'That was Simon. You remember,' said my mum, pointing at a boy. It wasn't a question; she told me that I remembered, assuming that I must.

I didn't remember.

'And that is Lee. The family moved to the Isle of Wight when he was eight.'

No idea.

'And that's Lindsay. She used to live down the road.'

Ah yes, The Road. Magyar Crescent, where we lived at number sixty-three, was a suburban utopia, just so long as your idea of a suburban utopia is Nuneaton, in Warwickshire. 'Magyar', if you're wondering,[5] is the denonym with which the people of Hungary refer to themselves, being a Finno-Ugric tribal word from the Old Hungarian 'mogyer', although being two years old, I was largely unaware of this at the time. Quite why Nuneaton's town planners had seen fit to name our street after an ancient Finno-Ugric tribe is anyone's guess, but we lived there in the house that, quite literally, Jack built. My dad, as we've learned, was a builder

---

4 Facebook tagging is sick.
5 You're probably not.

and in what could be the world's most romantic gesture, had enlisted the help of my grandad, Jack,[6] to build the house for his new wife and forthcoming (they hoped) family. Thus it was that house I grew up in, aged four weeks to thirteen years, in Magyar Crescent, and we'd have stayed there forever, I imagine, if we hadn't been forced to leave, but we'll get to that later as well.[7]

My dad's other smooth move was to come up with a name for the house and paint it on a large upright stone, which he embedded in the front lawn. He chose 'Mycroft', and before long it seemed fitting that he'd chosen the very same name Sir Arthur Conan Doyle gave to our fictional namesake Sherlock Holmes' elder brother, who didn't seem to like him much, for it was the stone with 'Mycroft' written on it that broke my fall while I was learning to ride a bike, cushioning the subsequent blow to my face with its rough, inflexible surface.

Mycroft wasn't big, but it was detached, which was mainly down to the fact that it had been the very first home on a brand-new plot earmarked for housing back in the sixties. My dad had seen the potential, gone in and built a modest three-bedroom dream house (it had a SEPARATE bathroom and toilet as we learned earlier) for the princely sum of four thousand pounds, which included both construction and the plot of land it was to be built on. It had an open-plan

---

6 His actual name was John, but he was called Jack by everyone who knew him. I have no idea why this was the case.

7 When I say 'forced to leave', I don't mean in the Amityville Horror sense. There were no disembodied demon voices whispering 'Get out' to any of us, nor any plagues of flies, although we did have a wasp's nest in the loft once.

lounge/diner and a sizeable kitchen for the time. I also remember a big garden, horrific carpet, flock wallpaper and polished wooden stairs, down which my mum fell when she was carrying me when I was two months old.

She'd slipped, basically, on polished wood. She was a new mum, cradling a child that she'd promised to care for, and love, and bring up and nurture, and she had even ticked boxes and filled in forms to say so. But then she dropped me down the stairs. It was an accident, yet she was nearly sick with panic. My dad was at work, so it was a visiting Auntie Gladys (who was my mum's aunt and thus my great-aunt) who gave my mum a large brandy, which, given that my mum doesn't drink was absolutely the wrong thing to do, because now not only did she have to negotiate the stairs again, but had to do it while drunk. For my part, I was completely and utterly uninjured because I was straight outta Stratford-upon-Avon, and thus made of sterner stuff.

The house held other dangers: in the lounge, for instance, there was also a perilous brick fireplace which took up one whole wall and was later used as a regular hazard for my sister's teeth. Then there was the glass front door, out of which our collie dog Susie[8] once burst while barking at a postman, only to reappear two hours later, covered in bloodied fur and bits of smashed window. And who could forget the piano stool with the not quite level feet and legs that pitched me backwards one Sunday lunchtime aged nine,

---

8 Susie came along and replaced the dangerous Yorkshire Terrier Bobby, after he died. A moment in my dog-bitten book that could not have been more welcome.

so that the back of my head cracked into the wall, leaving an indentation in the plaster that stayed there until the day we moved out. Given all this, I don't know why my dad didn't go all out and install a deadly cliff face complete with thundering waterfall to push us all into, and simply call the house 'Moriarty'. Certainly it *was* touching of Dad to build this house for my mum, but as romantic gestures go it was up there with some of the more dangerous traps from *Saw*.

My builder dad, like Slash from Guns n' Roses, Robbie Williams and oatcakes, was from Stoke-on-Trent. Unlike (as far as I know) Slash[9] and Robbie Williams, his pottery-town heritage means he retains an unhealthy interest in teapots. He collects them to the point where they still sit on shelves high up near the kitchen ceiling, waiting and watching like spout-based sentinels, reminiscent of a time when Stoke was a thriving manufacturing hub of ceramic earthenware. Meanwhile, Mum was a nurse, something that often came in handy, given the deathtrap my dad had built for us all to live in.

I look back on our time in Magyar Crescent with no small amount of nostalgia-tinged affection. It was where I learned to walk and talk and play and use a rock to bring my bike to

---

9 I have interviewed Slash and I brought up the heritage that he and my father share. We chatted about Guns n' Roses, Slash's audition for the eighties' metal band Poison, and the shop where he found his trademark hat. I then asked him if he was a frequent visitor to Stoke-on-Trent's Pottery Museum, like my dad. He told me that despite having family still in the area, he had never been there. I told him that if he ever found himself in Stoke and was at a loose end, then my dad would happily drive up there to show him around. Slash is yet to call me back.

a halt and where I also become scared of spiders. It's where I learned to bounce on my parents' knees (not to mention down their stairs), it's where I first saw a girl's bottom and comprehensively revealed my talent for not being able to do anything at all practical. My dad would despair of this, often bemoaning my lack of skill when it came to fixing a puncture on my bike. As a builder, he was obscenely hands-on, harbouring an unrivalled aptitude for making and/or mending things. Like his father before him, these skills run through his DNA but, of course, as I was adopted, and possessed not a jot of his deoxyribonucleic acid, he understandably felt that passing these abilities on through nurture rather than nature was the way forward. Fixing stuff, he not unreasonably reasoned in the 1970s and 80s, was a man's job. I watched, open-mouthed, as he conjured childhood magic out of anything and everything; items ranging from Roman shields (for a school project) and a properly constructed tree house (sort of attached to a tree at the bottom of the garden and balanced on a shed) to bows and arrows and go-carts and even realistic swords fashioned from the handle of a toilet brush and a sharpened bit of wood.

I've no idea why Mum let him manufacture weapons, especially given that the house he'd built was already trying to murder us, but let him she did. Perhaps she wanted the practice with bandages for work? As for me, I was, and remain, utterly inept in this area. Putting up a picture is a skill that is beyond the realms of possibility to me. How do you get them straight? If it requires any more than one nail then it's game over for me, not least because either if not both of the nails will bend at an angle on first hammer hit, rather than go into the wall, and then I will lose one. I once bought a laser measuring device on a whim, thinking it would solve my wonky picture problems forever. I have never used it, except as a pretend lightsabre. When I moved into my first house, my dad gave me loads of his old tools as a kind of rite of passage. I think I used his garden rake once, but the novelty didn't last.

Once, during the school holidays, my dad took me to work with him. I wanted to stay at home to read *The Day of The Jackal* which I had found in the library and thought looked interesting but no, I was going to learn a trade. Or at the very least a skill. Something, certainly, of which my dad could be proud. I would have been hovering somewhere around twelve years old when he took me to a building site where his men were working on the site of an old factory, knocking it down to build a new squash court. These days, of course, any Health and Safety Officer worth his (no doubt low-in-sodium) salt would probably commit hari-kari (with an approved sword) over the notion of a small boy being given the run of the kinds of piles of bricks and machinery one finds on a building site, but we already know from his construction of The House of Death that Dad had no time for such frivolity.

'Here,' he said, handing me a brick hammer. 'Cut those bricks in half.'

There was a pile of bricks, a haphazard, pyramidal display of air-dried concrete blocks about twice my height[10] sitting in a sea of sand, quite near to some unsecured scaffolding

---

10 Yes, I know 'which made it, what? Two feet high?' Ha HA.

poles and a full skip. Dad pointed at them, and wandered off to build something, leaving me staring at my impossible task like a ham-fisted boy-version of the miller's daughter (later queen) in 'Rumpelstiltskin', tasked with turning straw into gold. I looked round, but helpful, baby-stealing goblin came there none, so I shrugged and began tapping gently at one of the blocks. Nothing happened so I tried a bit harder and it shattered into bits.

Later, at lunchtime, when I had halved precisely three bricks and turned about twenty more into unusable dust, we stepped into a Portakabin to eat our sandwiches. It was filthy, paint-flecked and sparse. The only heat came from a paraffin heater that, had the Health and Safety Officer not already fainted during the pile of bricks/child interface, would have had him lying in front of the on-site JCB and praying for death's sweet relief. My chief memory is that the size of the tiny space, crammed with sweating, dirty men in hardhats and work boots, was directly inverse to the cacophony of swearing that was on offer. My dad, certainly when at home, was a non-swearer – it was totally frowned upon chez Holmes – and the look in his eyes when he realised I was about to be subjected to a builder's lunch hour was one of panic.

'Who wants a cup of fucking tea?' asked one of the men.

'Three fucking sugars,' said another. 'Yesterday you fucking only fucking put fucking two in it.'

'Fuck off you fucking fucker,' replied the first.

There was already sweat in the room; sweat from a hard morning building whatever it was that they were building, but my dad was beginning to sweat more.

'Fucking skip still hasn't been fucking picked up,' piped up another hardy . . . whatever the building equivalent of a son-of-the-soil is.

'Cunts,' announced another and took a bite of his sandwich.

'What have you fucking got today?' the man with the sweet tooth asked.

'Fucking cheese.'

'Lucky cunt. I've fucking got fucking jam.'

'You cunt.'

It was like the Algonquin Round Table chaired by Malcolm Tucker from *The Thick of It*. I stared, fascinated. I had never heard such swearing and was tremendously excited to hear all this forbidden fruit being noisily and robustly picked in front of my very ears. They made absolutely no concession to the fact that their boss's young son was sitting in there, covered in brick dust and eating a bag of Outer Spacers.[11]

'Fucking cement delivery's late again as well.'

'Cunts.'

'I fucking said to fucking Barry, fucking didn't I, Barry?'

Barry nodded his fucking acknowledgement through a mouthful of fucking sandwich.

'I said "fucking cement fucking delivery's fucking late again".'

'Fucking cunts.'

---

11 A popular corn-based crisp snack of the time, with flavours ranging from the obvious Salt & Vinegar all the way through to the futuristic and experimental Pickled Onion and Hot Dog. Hot Dog-flavour spaceship-shaped crisps! Back then we were honestly living the dream. And they must have been good for you because they cost 5p a packet.

I was staring open-mouthed, half-chewed Outer Spacers dropping into my lap, the crisp dust mixing with that of the bricks.

'What do you fucking reckon, Les?' said the man with the fucking cheese.

To my twelve-year-old ears this was profanity on a whole new level. I knew the words – hell, I'd heard them at school – but this was something else. This was ADULTS saying The Words Which We Dare Not Speak Their Name. No one at school was going to believe this. And now my dad had been dragged into the eye of the swearing storm.

'Les?'

My dad was trapped. When he'd taken me to work with him, hoping to introduce me to a world where men made things and built stuff, he'd clearly clean forgotten about the cheeky lunchtime banter.

'Les? What do you fucking reckon?'

His people were waiting for an answer.

'Cement should be here by three,' he said.

The room froze. No one moved. The atmosphere changed. My dad, my builder dad, had said a sentence without swearing in it. It was like the scene in *An American Werewolf in London* where Jack, the American hitchhiker walks into The Slaughtered Lamb, points at a pentangle and asks 'What's that star on the wall for?' If Brian Glover and Rik Mayall (for it was they in the film) had been playing chess in this Portakabin right now, they too would have stopped and stared. A builder, in the company of other builders, had not sworn and it had caused a moment.

Cheeseface was the first to speak. 'Fucking three?' he said.

'That's this afternoon all fucking fucking-fucked then, isn't it?' said Sweet Tooth.

I realised that it wasn't the swearing that had stilled the room; it was the bad news re the cement delivery. My dad had dodged the fuck-bullet.

'Cunts,' said someone.

So this was my first introduction to the adult world of swearing. At school it would be unthinkable that the working adults – the teachers – would be big swearers. Of course now, in later life, when many of my friends are teachers and, like you, swear with impunity off duty (some of them even going so far as to call the children in their care 'cunts') I realise that as a child myself I was simply living in the expletive-free utopia that surrounds children as far as (most) adults are concerned. Some might argue that this is a class issue; we've probably all heard about someone in leggings from a social underclass hurling abuse at their three-year-old daughter in Aldi along the lines of 'Put the fuckin' nuggets down, Miley, or yer won't be getting yer fuckin' ears pierced for yer fuckin' birthday', yet my parents were resolutely working class and would *never* have been heard doing a swear. So this day, right there in a Portakabin in Tamworth, was an education. I learned all sorts, and also that the word 'fuck' could be used as a noun, verb, adverb or adjective. And it was by no means all I learned, because I also learned that that the people in charge of delivering cement on time are fucking wankers.

'Back to fucking work,' said someone and that was that. There was a downing of crusts and Tupperware and the afternoon had begun. They all filed out, picking up their hats and grumbling. A copy of the *Sun* fluttered to the floor in their wake, falling open at Page Three. My dad stared at it.

'Don't tell your mum about any of this,' he said.

'Can I not do any more bricks, then?'

'Fair enough,' he said. 'Go and sit in the van and read your book.'

He looked disappointed. He glanced at what was left of the bricks and in that moment it was clear that wherever my future was to be, it was not on the building site. He, and his father before him, had grown up here and now it was obvious that I wasn't cut out to follow in the Holmes' family footsteps. He didn't say it out loud, but he looked like he was thinking, 'What if, thirteen years ago, we hadn't picked him? What if, like in the film *Sliding Doors*,[12] we'd simply have adopted the next baby to be put in front of us? Things could have been so completely different. My bricks could be perfectly halved.'

To show willing, I went up to the top of some scaffold-ing[13] with the brick hammer while he showed me how to lay bricks with a trowel. And when he left me for a moment, I took the opportunity to accidentally drop his hammer down the inside of a wall of the half-built squash court, into

---

12 Admittedly he probably wasn't thinking exactly this, mainly because *Sliding Doors* wasn't released until 1998, sixteen years in the future.

13 At this point I think the health-and-safety man would have given up and gone and sat in his van to read *The Day of The Jackal*.

a gap between the double skin of the insulating cavity. It fell about twenty-five feet into a chasm of darkness only a couple of inches wide, never to be seen again. I had effectively walled it in – just as if my day of work experience had been overseen by Edgar Allen Poe.

Presently, my dad came back.

'I dropped your hammer down there,' I said.

'Why?' he asked. Again, not unreasonably.

'Accident.'

'Is your book good?' he said. 'You should go and read it.'

As I climbed down the ladder, he was probably still thinking of Sliding Doors; although it was a good job he hadn't put any in at home, as the dog would've jumped right through them. For years afterwards, as we drove through Tamworth on our way to family holidays in Wales we would pass the now-completed squash courts and, without fail, I would call to my dad from the back seat 'your hammer's in there' and point. It became a thing. We still talk of it now, and while my retired dad is proud of whatever it is I do now in what we laughingly refer to as a career, I still think he'd have preferred it if I could fix a bike puncture and hadn't lost his brick hammer. If you should ever find yourself driving through Tamworth and see the squash court, remember that thanks only to the process of adoption, is there an unseen brick hammer trapped quite literally within its walls, lying dusty in the dark.

FOUR

Here Be Spiders.

So, this isn't the kind of book that's going to unfurl in front of you sensibly, in chronological order. I've already jumped between the ages of nought and twelve within the first two chapters and I'm afraid that from here on in it's not really going to get any more logical. What you're holding in your hands is a sort of papery trawl through the windmills of my mind (or an *electronic* papery trawl through the windmills of my mind, if you're reading this on a futuristic Kindle-type Kindle),[1] a fact which means that it is quite likely to flit all over the place, wildly and erratically, like a moth on meth. I make no apology for this; it's just how it's going to pan out. For instance, in a couple of pages' time we may well fast forward to the time I got forcibly removed from the vicinity of Margaret Thatcher by her security detail, or to the time that an Oscar-nominated screenwriter took me into Graham Norton's toilet and put some scissors in my ear. But first, let's talk about spiders.

A spider is, fittingly, at the centre of my web of early

---

1 Or an electronic papery trawl through the offshore wind turbines of my mind, if you're doubly modern.

memories. In fact, what I'm going to refer to as 'the night of the long spider' may well be my earliest memory of all. I do have another very early one; that of finally being able to reach the door handle on the kitchen door,[2] but that isn't a memory that would go on to affect me in quite the same way as The Night of the Long Spider did. Like Peter Parker, I too came into contact with a spider at a formative age, but where he would go on to develop its powers; able to climb walls, super senses, swinging from skyscraper to skyscraper on his teenage sticky webs,[3] when I encountered one I just cried, wet the bed and set in motion a psychological chain of events that to this day prevent me from ever clearing out a shed or garage.

I often wonder, when faced with a spider, heart rate increasing, sweat forming on my brow, if things could have been different. What if the night in question had run a different course? What if I'd never seen this particular spider? What if it had chosen that particular evening to crawl on a different wall? And of course, what if I hadn't been adopted, chosen from that original baby collection five years previously by the recently wedded Mr and Mrs Holmes? Certainly I wouldn't have been lying in that bed, in that room, in that house, in that town, in that particular thunderstorm and thus may not now be terrified of each and every eight-legged web-peddler that scuttles its way into my life.[4]

---

2 'When was that, Jon? When you were about twenty?' Yes. Another height joke. Very funny.

3 Yeah. Like Freud wouldn't have had a field day with *that*.

4 At time of writing, scientists have revealed that a fear of spiders may be in our DNA; a drawback to early humans, protecting themselves against venomous ones in our evoluntionary history. Fine. Whatever.

It was a Saturday night, of that I am sure. My parents were not big goer-outers when I was young, but on this occasion they'd gone to a dinner and dance and babysitting duties had been turned over to Nana Smith, my mum's mum. Clearly, I was conscious that Mum and Dad were absent, so perhaps, deep down, there was a sense of abandonment, a hangover from what I knew about my adoption. Maybe that's the case, I don't know, I'm not a psychoanalyst[5] but, if I was, I'd probably nod and agree with myself and then charge myself sixty pounds per hour for the privilege of telling myself something that I already knew. Anyway, it's my theory and I'm sticking to it. To add to the drama, it was a stormy night. There was a thunderstorm outside my bedroom window, over which the curtains were not quite pulled tight enough, leaving a small sliver of a gap down the middle. I remember a crash of thunder waking me and I remember a flash of lightning forcing its way in through that gap which in turn forced me to turn over and put my head under the covers to muffle the thunder and put my back to the window. As I lay there, wanting Mummy and Daddy to be there, there was a lull in the storm, and I gingerly poked my head out.

The next flash of lightning lit up the room – and in its terrible illumination I saw it. My bed was against the wall and on it, centimetres from my face, was a great big house spider; a house spider that was suddenly and terrifyingly irradiated in a burst of lightning, its hideous shadow thrown starkly

---

5 Although, handily, my mum now is, and when I asked her about it, she agreed that all of this was eminently possible. And then charged me sixty quid.

across the Anaglypta. And then, as the brief flash subsided, we were plunged back into darkness and I think it was then that I screamed the place down.

It certainly doesn't take Sigmund Freud to figure out what was going on here. My fears of abandonment had manifested themselves into my own private arachnid hell and consequently, to this day, my fear of spiders remains resolute. It developed fairly rapidly after that, and my fear of the little scurrying shits continues unabated. I can tolerate tiny ones, but if anything half a centimetre upwards runs out from under the sofa, I simply cannot cope. Which is why, later, I genuinely bought a gun.

'Do you know anyone who wants to buy a gun?' said my university friend Pete one day, who was training to be a teacher and had presumably been told in class that gun ownership might be a disadvantage on his CV.

'What sort of gun?' I enquired.

'Air pistol. Fires pellets. It's pretty accurate over a distance.'

I was thinking of the house in which I lived. It was 1990, I was a student in Canterbury, and I lived in a hellhole that was prone to spiders. You hear stories about houses that are built on old Indian burial grounds and of the vengeful spirits of long-dead squaws and braves being disturbed enough to come back in spirit form to terrorise the living by stacking chairs up on a kitchen table,[6] or inexplicably moving pictures so that they hang not quite straight. Because of this, I had developed a (yet another unprovable) theory that our

---

6 Like out of the original version of the film *Poltergeist*.

student terraced house in Martyrs Field Road in Wincheap, Canterbury, Kent, had been built on the sacred burial ground of long-dead spiders. It seemed to me they were sending their living, scampering ancestors to wreak terrible revenge by running across the lounge floor while I was trying to watch *Twin Peaks*.[7]

They were regular visitors, and they weren't small either. They were properly enormous house spiders, many of them the size of cats and each, to coin a phrase, meaner than a junk-yard dog. If you've ever seen the John Carpenter remake of *The Thing* (the one from 1982) and the bit when Norris's head comes off, sprouts arachnid legs and then screeches at Kurt Russell's face, well, then they were exactly like that. See also the Facehugger in *Alien*. Except now these creatures were in my house. Over time, a combination of fear, resourcefulness and a keen survival instinct meant that I became a dab hand at killing these monsters from a distance. If both heavy telephone directories and cups of boiling water were weapons (which in my hands, they most certainly were), then I was a master of the art of killing. In just one night I single-handedly smote five of the beasts with a heavy book and hot Cup-a-Soup combination attack, but soon they grew wise to my methods and changed their tactics, taking to sitting in the high corner of my Victorian-ceilinged bedroom, well out of reach of conventional weapons. I needed to change my strategy too, which is why I bought the gun.

---

7 David Lynch's original 1990 televisual epic that really was a box set long before box sets were invented. It's back now, like it's never gone away. Much like my fear of spiders.

Before long, my student bedroom ceiling, with its decorative coving, was a pockmarked, spider-leg-strewn war zone. It looked to the untrained eye like an Artexed Somme. Over time, I became quite the marksman and the monster spiders learned to fear me. I appreciate that if you are an animal rights' enthusiast you are probably recoiling in horror at my brutality, but I just did what had to be done. In my defence, the only reason that I kept a loaded air pistol next to my bed was because I was far too arachnophobic to go anywhere near one of the little fuckers with the traditional anti-spider technique of a glass and bit of card, and was operating on pure adrenalin. Whenever a spider appeared, I simply dropped into combat mode. It was fight or flight.

When I was about eight, a next-door neighbour, Ian, and I were playing a game of Spiderman. This was long before Tobey Maguire or Andrew Garfield donned the arachno-mask; our version of the webslinger had arrived in our consciousness via a US made-for-TV live-action movie that got a theatrical release in the UK in the summer of 1977. It was shit, but if you're eight years old, it most certainly wasn't, and its labyrinthine plot (of a bad guy hypnotising people to make them jump off high buildings while Spiderman attempted to save them) formed the basis of our summer holiday role-play. Several weeks in, it was my turn to be Spiderman (on the grounds that I had new Spiderman pyjamas and was wearing the top as a T-shirt) and we had reached the point in the (our) plot where I had been captured by the Green Goblin (Ian), who had tied me to the door of my dad's shed with a dog lead.

'You are my prisoner, Spiderman!' he shouted through the green towel he'd tied round his head to denote his Goblin-ness. 'I will make the people jump off the buildings and there is nothing you can do to stop me!'

Damn him. I had to save the world, and yet I was trussed up by the wrists with a border collie's choker chain.

'You'll never get away with it, Goblin!' I shouted back. 'Spiderman will stop you!'[8]

'Never!' shouted the Goblin and ran past me into the shed.

Because of the angle I was tied at, I couldn't see what he was doing and as I twisted and turned I could hear him rummaging amongst tools and flowerpots and bits of old mower. And then The Green Goblin emerged from the gloom, brandishing a dibber. It was sort of an old spade handle, minus the blade and sharpened into a point – I think my dad had made it himself and ordinarily used it for making holes to plant bulbs. But what made it terrifying, as he waved it towards my face, was the fact that it had a great big spider on the end of it.

It was actually dead, but it was massive and there's something about dead spiders that's almost as horrific as live ones. Its eight spidery legs were curled under it; each one of those twisted appendages seemingly big enough to have knuckles. It was black and thick and wrong and evil. It was my worst nightmare, and it was coming towards me on the end of a dibber.

----

8 The Green Goblin wasn't actually the villain of 1977's *The Amazing Spiderman* but we liked him best and were only too aware of his evil work. The Green Goblin would tie his nemesis to a shed as soon as look at him.

I knew that if it touched me I would die. The Green Goblin was shouting something about having ultimate control and the ability to hypnotise spiders and could therefore harness their power to defeat Spiderman, but I barely heard him because my primal survival instinct was kicking in. He was going to actually put a spider on my face while I was tied to a door and there was nothing I could do about it. I could see it was balled up, still in a net of its own dusty webbing and I began ferociously screaming 'No! No!', which of course Ian presumed to be part of the game. I began frantically pulling at the dog lead for all I was worth, snaking left and right, trying to stay out of range of the approaching arachnid awfulness, with the Dibber of Death tracking my every move, getting closer and closer. At last, at the point where it was about to touch me, I made one last desperate bid for freedom and pulled the shed door clean off its hinges. The wood split, the door crashed on to the ground, I fell over and The Green Goblin stood open mouthed, looking between me and the shattered shed. Neither he nor I could believe I'd physically pulled a door off its hinges at the age of eight. But with great power comes great responsibility – not to mention a great stoppage of pocket money to pay for a new shed door.

As I grew up with this fear, Mum would try to teach me to deal with it rationally using quite the most irrational technique known to man.

'I,' she would announce, 'am afraid of cows.'

It was well known in our family that Mum didn't like cows, and she would always use the same argument for dealing with the issue.

'I do not like cows,' she would say, 'but I just take a deep breath and tell myself not to be frightened.'

I had an argument too, it went like this: 'Yes, but Mum, when are you ever faced with cows? Actual cows, up close?'

'When we go walking, on holiday,' she said. It was true, on our annual holiday to Wales there was always a countryside walk or two (or nine) involved and, to be fair to her, there are cows in the countryside.

'I don't like the way they look at you,' she said. 'They stare and chew. But you have to learn to get over it if you want to carry on.'

As far as I am concerned, this argument was bollocks.

'Mum, cows are not the same as spiders,' I would say. 'First, you can see a cow from a long way off. If the path goes through a field of cows then you can see them in the distance. In a field. And then choose to avoid them. There is no circumstance I can think of when you'd go upstairs, put your pyjamas on, get into bed and then look up and see a cow on the ceiling. A cow isn't going to walk over your face while you're sleeping. Furthermore, cows lumber, they don't scuttle.'

'Yes, but . . .'

'There is no "but". I don't like spiders and you don't like cows; you have your fear, and I have mine but at least yours doesn't surprise you when you go to have a bath or by climbing out of one of your wellies. What would you do if you were going to bed and there was a cow on the wall?'

'Now you're just being silly.'

'No, I'm not. It's a perfectly valid argument. What would you do if you went to bed and there was a cow in your room?'

She thought for a moment, weighing up her options.

'I'd get your dad to deal with it,' she said.

Which, as a child, is exactly what I tended to do. In 1982 a film called *The Evil Dead* was released on video.[9] I was a bit obsessed with it, not least because it was about to be banned in the then-Government's Great 'Video Nasty' Purge of the Early Eighties,[10] and so I wrote to the distributor – Palace Pictures – and told them of my love for the film and the fact that I was doing a school project on it.[11] They kindly sent back a full synopsis, the theatrical poster and a set of black-and-white production stills and, in return, they received the respect and admiration of a fifteen-year-old boy. The poster went straight on to my bedroom wall, brightening up my bedroom with its lurid depiction of frightened faces, a reel-to-reel tape machine flicking blood, the dead, zombified face of Cheryl the protagonist, and a quote from horror author Stephen King who thought it to be 'the most ferociously original horror film of the year'. It hung proudly alongside full-page adverts for *Driller Killer* torn out of video magazines and a Snoopy sticker on my bedroom door that featured the titular dog dressed as a vampire. But one night, one terrible, terrible night, the poster for *The Evil Dead* began to move of its own accord.

---

9 Hey kids! Video was a sort of tape, a bit like an audio cassette except you could watch the contents. An audio cassette was kind of like an LP except it was . . . er, well, it was a sort of vinyl, erm . . . I dunno. It was like a sort of flat, black mp3. You know what? Forget it.

10 See Chapter Thirteen.

11 A lie. But this sort of lie often worked because in those days there was sympathy towards a child making an effort with school projects. Now, a snot-nosed kid like me would just download a poster and some photos off the Internet and call that 'research'. Lazy little twats.

FIVE

. . . in which I confront my worst fears and then get shot in the face.

Just after I'd turned the light off, there came a noise in the dark and at first I didn't know what it was. I listened, intently; the only sound was the grumbling traffic on the distant Lutterworth Road and my own breathing. The whisper came again. It sounded like someone scrunching paper, ever so slightly. I froze. It was clear from the posters on my walls that I was very much into horror films at this time, and thus, in my mind, both the Driller Killer and the most Evil bits of anyone that was Dead had clearly teamed up to hide in the darkest corners of my room with the sole intention of lurching forward and biting my throat off. The papery scrunching noise came again, and I knew for a fact that I was lying perfectly still listening to a serial killer making an origami machete in the dark. The noise came again. It was coming from the wall next to my bed. Yet all that was on the wall was the poster. There was nothing else there, yet *something* was definitely in here with me.

At that moment, in my head, the Thing in my bedroom with me was everything from Jason in the *Friday the 13th* films, about to reach up from his hiding place beneath my bed, clamp my head to the pillow and drive an arrow upwards through my neck,[1] to the claw of a werewolf, dripping blood on to my nearby Binatone radio cassette player, its ravenous maw aching for the taste of human flesh because it had been driven mad by a ferric C90.[2] Terrified, I reached out from under the duvet and snapped on my bedside light.

Nothing.

There was no sign of anything at all. Not a creature was stirring, not even a mouse – although if it had been a mouse then I'd have been fine with that. I have no problem with mice, rats, snakes, frogs, cows or pretty much anything else.[3] What I did have a problem with, however, was the thing moving behind my *Evil Dead* poster. At first I thought I was seeing things, because it appeared as if the middle of the poster was moving. It was attached to the wall with Blu-Tack,[4] a lump of the grey sticky stuff which I had carefully rolled into balls and applied to each of its four corners in order to attach it to the wall. And, now, like the chest-burster lurking beneath John Hurt's ribcage in *Alien*, something behind it was beginning to stir.

My eyes were drawn to a large moving shape rippling

---

1 In the first *Friday the 13th* film, this is pretty much what happened to a then-unknown Kevin Bacon. If only it had been a snuff movie we'd have all been spared those shit fucking EE mobile phone adverts that he was in.

2 I refer you back to footnote 9 on page 51.

3 Actually I don't like wasps either. Or any large insects. Or werewolves. Or Kevin Bacon's EE adverts. Or, come to think of it, moths. I don't like moths. They make me jump when they flit.

4 Blu-Tack was invented by accident in 1970 and has unique properties: it is completely non-carcinogenic, it can be swallowed without harm, it has a flashpoint of 200°F and, perhaps most significantly, it leaves marks on your bedroom walls that will never come off and that will make your mum angry. It is also grey, not 'blu'.

its way from the middle of the poster out towards the side. Towards me. And straightaway I knew what it was. It was a spider, a spider that was impossibly large. It was moving beneath the surface of the poster like the Loch Ness monster, with its oily coils flowing just below the glassy surface of the lake. I looked frantically around for something to smash it with, a shoe maybe, yet I was in two minds – I didn't want to come face to face with whatever this hell-born creation was, yet I also didn't want to damage my pride and joy, the *Evil Dead* poster that was very much the envy of my friend Nick Roser. I was as torn as I very much didn't want the poster to be, and then, while I was panicking about what to do, the spider came out. I am no expert, but it was definitely about the size of a dog and Not Of This Earth. It was hideous; its legs were the textbook freakishly angled bent ones that big house spiders have and its enormous segmented body was as turgid and as black as Satan's anus. It had come out of its lair behind an *Evil Dead* poster, the protection of which had stalled any footwear-based attack, but now I wished to God I'd struck while the shoe was hot because, now that I'd seen it, I knew I could never forget it as, from across the gulf of my bedside table, it regarded me with envious eyes and slowly, surely, that spider drew its plans against me.

So I did what anyone would do in these circumstances: I shouted for my dad. Yet it was Mum who came in and by the time she'd come upstairs to see what all the yelling was about, I had got out of bed and nervously edged around the room, never taking my eyes off the intruder.

'Why aren't you asleep? What are you shouting about? And why are you standing in the corner?' she said.

'There's a spider,' I managed to say, not taking my eyes off it.

'It's just a spider. I don't like cows and you should do what I do and . . .' Her bovine advice petered out as her gaze fell upon the monster. 'That's quite a big spider,' she said. Which is when she did what anyone would do under these circumstances, and shouted for my dad.

I didn't want to be in there with it, yet of course I was acutely aware of the first rule of coming face to face with a spider: don't look away, do not leave the room because what if, when you look back, it's gone? There's only one thing worse than seeing a spider and that is seeing a spider and then having it disappear, because you know it's alive, you know it is somewhere in the room with you and you know it will come back. And when it does it will wait until you are asleep and lay eggs in your mouth. Dad came up the stairs.

'There's a spider,' said Mum and I in unison.

'It's just a spider,' he said.

Then he saw it.

He wasn't bothered by it.

'Get it,' I said. 'Get rid of it.' And I knew this to be the risky part of the operation, because a spider that knows it is facing its ultimate nemesis of a glass and bit of card, is a spider that will bolt. And then we're right back to the egg/mouth-laying scenario described above. I couldn't watch this. I did not want to see it move. Spiders are horrifying when they move. Dad walked towards it and picked up the glass from my bedside table. Using all of his skill and builder's training and his eye for scale he quickly assessed the situation.

'We're going to need a bigger glass,' he announced and went to find one.

'Why can't we just kill it?'

'You can't kill spiders,' Mum said. But she was wrong – a fact to which the bullet-holed ceiling in my future student house was later to be testament.

The spider crawled slightly. I could take no more and broke my own rule by going to stand on the landing while Dad went downstairs, soon to reappear with a pint glass and the back cover he'd torn off the *Thompson Local Directory*.

'Make sure you get it!' I squeaked. 'Don't lose it.'

'I won't lose it,' he said and stepped into the bedroom, a paternal David against the eight-legged Goliath. A few moments later and he reappeared holding an empty glass.

'Where is it?' I said. 'Is it dead?'

'Threw him out of the window,' he said. 'Now back to bed, school tomorrow.'

I gingerly peered round the door, and sure enough my foe had been vanquished. I didn't want to pull back the curtain and check the window in case it was clinging on to the glass, staring in and scratching its spidery nails on the pane, like the vampire boy in *Salem's Lot*. I lifted up the duvet to make sure there wasn't another one in my bed and climbed in. Mum and Dad went downstairs and I lay and contemplated both my narrow escape and my own mortality. And then, not five minutes after I had turned the light off, I heard it again. The scratching. The scritching. The crinkly rustle of paper. I was as Edgar Allen Poe's unnamed narrator, except I was hearing the tell-tale heart beating within the walls, rather than under the floorboards.

Except in *my* heart, I knew that what was beside me in the blackness was far worse than Poe's dismembered corpse's still-beating one. I switched the light back on in a flash, saw the lump under the poster and smashed it with the shoe. Then I went straight downstairs to where Mum and Dad were watching a repeat of *Shoestring*.[5]

'You lied! You didn't throw the spider out of the window! Why did you tell me that you'd thrown the spider out of the window?'

'When I went in, it'd disappeared.' said Dad.

Dammit. I knew when I broke Spider Rule Number One there would be terrible consequences.

'Why didn't you tell me?' I demanded. 'It was still in there!'

'Because if I told you it was still in there you'd have never gone to bed.'

You couldn't fault his logic.

'Dad! You shouldn't have told me you'd thrown it out the window.' I said, 'I hate spiders.'

Mum looked up from where Eddie Shoestring was talking to Sonia, Radio West's receptionist, about a murder. 'I don't like cows,' she said, 'You should do what I do and ignore them.'

Years later, on a travel assignment for the *Sunday Times* in Brazil I was staying in a lodge deep into the wetlands of

---

5 Curious TV drama series about Eddie Shoestring, a private eye who worked for a radio station. Of course, this was back when all radio stations had their own private investigator on the staff. These days, what with the cutbacks, they've really only got their in-house assassins and morally repugnant kill squads left.

the Pantanal. On the first night, my local guide came to my room, and warned me that a distant forest fire meant that the jungle animals were fleeing ahead of it, so to be wary of snakes and spiders because they would come this way, towards the river.

'Spiders?' I said. I am not naive; I knew staying in the Brazilian wilderness carried a certain risk.

'Brazilian Wandering Spider,' he said. 'Most dangerous in world. They often come into the lodges, especially now they run from fire. If you have one in room, no matter what time tonight, come and find me and I will deal with it. Very dangerous.'

This was terrifying.

'What do you do with them?' I managed to ask, despite having begun to sweat inside my own mouth. '*How* do you deal with them?'

I was imagining some kind of specialist suit and a long pole or a gun or some kind of anti-spider pepper spray, like the stuff that hikers in Alaska carry with them as protection against bears.

'I put him out of window.' he said.

I didn't sleep that night. I sat cross-legged on my bed, my camera tripod clutched in my hand as a weapon.[6] I didn't see any spiders, but it was the longest night of my life.

I had a brush with weapons – specifically guns – a long time before I bought one to save me from spiders. Famously,

---

6 Later during my tenure in the jungle I saw two of these spiders. One was on the wall of the neighbouring lodge and the other on the floor near the mess hall. It was a very uncomfortable two weeks.

utilising every ounce of their all-American brand of back-combed bombast, Bon Jovi once sang of being 'shot through the heart, and you're to blame'[7] but when I was shot through the eye, far from being the fault of Bon Jovi, it was the fault of a man called Bob who lived three doors away.

Bob was the father of Alison, who was my age, and we were regular playmates as we grew up. We were probably about nine or ten and I was happy to hang out with Alison because sometimes we would go over the fields behind our houses to play Doctors and Nurses and she would show me her bottom. This had come about thanks to my sister, Kelda, who had joined the Holmes family five and a half years previously[8] and, despite being six, had declared her boyfriend to be Andrew, Alison's younger brother. Kelda and I had ridden my bike (a sort of blue and red non-specific model that my dad had found in a skip and 'fixed up') in tandem down the road. I was pedalling, and giving my sister what was, and probably still is, known in the childhood bicycling community as 'a backie'; a technique most notable for being incredibly dangerous and abhorrent to parents, featuring as it does one clumsy child riding pillion behind another, slightly older one – the former clinging on to the latter's Spiderman T-shirt. Two children, looking sweet, on the seat, of a bicycle made for one, and then weaving it unevenly at high speed across the driveways and between the parked cars of their neighbours. It was a practice thrown into sharp

7 'You Give Love A Bad Name' on Bon Jovi's *Slippery When Wet* album, from a time when hairspray was more important than lyrics.
8 Kelda, like me, is adopted. See Chapter Eleven for details of not only how that came about, but also why the hell she ended up being called 'Kelda'.

relief and immediately banned when I failed to brake and, not for the first time, crashed into the stone with 'Mycroft' written on it that was outside our house.[9] On this occasion it was Kelda's face that broke our fall, resulting in the type of injury that my mum still, to this day, refers to as 'an egg' coming up on her forehead. We ignored the ban, and consequently there were a lot of head-eggs that summer, not least when we cycled round to Alison and Andrew's house and I got shot in the face.

We were in the garden and it must have been a hot day because Kelda and Andrew were squirting a garden hose at each other and Alison, rather than her bottom, was showing me her impressive paddling pool.[10]

 And then her dad came into the garden with a gun.

It wasn't a real gun. Well, it was, but a starting one – a starting pistol with which Alison's dad would start basketball matches. He was a coach for a local team and for some reason this was the day that he had decided that it would be amusing to point his starting pistol at me – a ten-year-old child – and fire it. To be fair to him, this was the seventies, so perhaps the health and safety guidelines that today are quite clear regarding the do's and don'ts of pointing a gun at a small boy were not yet in force. To this day, I don't know whether Bob was showing off or genuinely trying to kill me because his daughter had showed me her bottom in the woods, but it's fair to say that the only bottom I was particularly concerned with at that particular moment was the bottom

---

9 See Chapter Three.
10 Not a euphemism.

line, which was that a man had a gun and was pointing it at my face.

'You may well be ten, and experimenting with bottom-showing during a play game of "doctors and nurses",' he said. 'And that may well be a perfectly normal part of growing up, but that's my daughter and you are a fucking dead man.'

'But—' I began. He interrupted me.

'I know what you're thinking,' he said. 'Did he fire six shots or only five? Well, to tell you the truth, in all this excitement I've kinda lost track myself.'

I'd lost track too. And also control of my bowels. I was still in short trousers and I was staring down the BARREL OF A GUN.

'But this is a starting pistol,' he continued, 'the most powerful handgun in the sporting community, and would blow your head clean off. You've got to ask yourself one question.'

I *was* asking myself a question. And the question I was asking was 'Will he dispose of my body in the paddling pool? Leave me floating face down between the inflatable seal and the pile of armbands thrown there by Alison's younger brother.'

'Do you feel lucky? Well, do ya, punk?' said Bob, and pulled the trigger.

He didn't say any of this, or he said all of it. To be honest, when someone points a gun at you there's every chance you may misremember the exact sequence of events. But he did pull the trigger, because I certainly remember the blast. Starting pistols are very, very loud, not least because they have to be heard by athletes who are about to start running, jumping, or in Rob's case, playing basketball. It was deafening and I was shot right in the eye.

Granted, starting pistols are not capable of firing live rounds, but what does come out of them is a bang, a flash and microscopic fragments of whatever it is that you put in starting pistols to make them flash and go bang. In short, they're still dangerous. During the 2012 London Olympics, I met with the official race starter as part of a recorded piece I was doing for the BBC Radio 4 comedy *The Now Show*, and after taking it out of a locked metal box, he let me fire his gun into the air, but not before I'd had a strict lecture on the danger of it and had it explained to me that the rules surrounding their handling and use are more or less the same rules that are in place for handling proper firearms; rules that Bob would have laughed in the face of, if he hadn't been so busy shooting me in mine.

I screeched, clutched my eye and bolted for home. Out of the side gate, along the road and back in the sanctuary of my own garden, Mum was hanging out the washing. I screeched again.

'What is it? What's wrong?' she said.

'Bob from up the road shot me in the eye!'

'Let me see . . .'

Somehow the fact that her son had been shot hadn't really prompted the reaction I was expecting. She just took it in her stride, like this kind of thing happened every day, like we were all straight outta Compton, rather than hanging in the hood of Magyar Crescent in Nuneaton.

'I can see some bits,' she said. 'We'll get them out with

a hanky.' She took one of my dad's hankies off the line, twisted the corner into a point and licked it to keep it in place.

'Hold still,' she said.

I did and she fished a couple of bits of starting pistol detritus out of my eye.

'He deliberately shot me in the eye!' I said.

'Don't be silly, I'm sure it was an accident.'

She may well have been right, my memory is sketchy. He could well have just been showing his gun off but, whatever the circumstances, the fact remained that I had been SHOT IN THE FACE and my mum was shrugging it off. If this had happened today, a dozen armed police would've turned up and Bob would be IN PRISON. But this was 1979 and *The Paul Daniels Magic Show* had just made its television debut, so clearly we were living in a more tolerant time.

'No harm done,' she said and pegged the hanky back on the line.

Two years later, Alison's younger brother Andrew (he was now eight) took some matches that Bob had left lying around and, in the middle of the night, accidentally burned their house down. I watched the fire brigade battle the flames from my bedroom window as Bob and his rescued family watched it from their front garden.

'And that's what happens when you display a blatant disregard for basic health and safety,' I thought. Or I would've done, if I hadn't just been concentrating on trying to see Alison's bottom through her nightie. I was entering my teens, and it wasn't just our neighbour's house that was hotting up.

SIX

. . . in which I sit in a bin with an erection.

I once sat in a bin with an erection. I remember it because it was one full year before Channel 4 television came along with its promise of full-frontal nudity, when the all-you-can-wank-over buffet that is the modern Internet was but a distant dream. You'll have heard stand-up comedians of a certain age (mine, usually) bleat on about how the kids have it much easier these days when it comes to access to porn. You've seen them on *Mock the Week* and *Michael MacIntyre's Comedy Roadshow*. 'Remember when porn mags were all in the hedges?' they go. 'That was our Internet, back then. Porn mags in hedges, do you remember?', but you don't need to because they remember it for you and then there's a joke about a bush and everyone goes home happy, having had their fill of humorous stand-up comedy observations.[1]

---

1 'Garlic Bread? Garlic? Bread? Garlic Bread? Remember that? What's all that about?' Well, it's about just some bread, commonly a baguette, topped with garlic butter and then partially slicing it and letting the condiments soak into the loaf while keeping it in one piece. It's been around since the forties, and we don't have to remember it because it's still here. It's not fucking difficult. Stop just remembering things and write a fucking joke. There's probably one in your man drawer. (And yes, I know the man drawer thing is Michael McIntyre, rather than Peter Kay, but my point stands.)

To be fair, it is a universal, if clichéd, truth that pornography did used to be found in the hedgerows and grass verges of Britain, handily put there overnight by the Porn Fairy so we'd find it on the way to school all fresh and shiny with what we hoped to God was just dew. Quite how and why these jazz pages ended up buried in the foliage of Britain remains a mystery of course, but it was a distribution network of which newsprint today can only dream, reaching millions of schoolboy consumers through the late seventies and early eighties.

Paul Harvey went one better. He was fat, with absurd hair, and as such was bullied and the butt of many jokes. I was small and weak and had been adopted, so neither of us stood a chance. Yet Paul was a boy who learned to use skill and ingenuity to overcome his shortcomings. Skill, ingenuity, and the contents of the box in his dad's wardrobe. Over time, Paul Harvey's dad's wardrobe became the stuff of legend. Inside it was a fabled vessel, an old shoebox containing such treasures, such wonders, that we spoke of it only in hushed tones. None of us had ever seen it, but, according to Paul Harvey, it was real, tangible, magical, and it held The Key To All Knowledge. It was like the Ark of the Covenant, except thanks to Paul's exhaustive and detailed research and discovery, everyone at Chetwynd Middle School knew its resting place, which was behind some ties and under an old gardening jumper. Inside the box, which wasn't adorned with cherubim and gold leaf but rather the word 'Adidas', were not the Ten Commandments carved into stone, but rather up to twenty 'Gentleman's Leisure Pamphlets', printed on glossy paper. Golden winged angels it may not have had, but golden showers were there plenty.

Paul's dad's box was *our* Internet. We'd all seen the scrappy bits of porn fluttering among the brambles like witches' knickers, just waiting for the comedians of the future to both observe and remember them, but this was something else. We'd stumbled on a hoard; a game changer, an area of outstanding interest and significance; it was a dirty Sutton Hoo, just waiting to be uncovered bit by bit. And Paul was the Gatekeeper.

In Ethiopia, a remote monastery claims to have the Ark of the Covenant under lock and key. It is guarded by warrior monks, with just one Holy Man granted access to see the wonderful object, and thus its existence cannot truly be verified either way. Paul was the Holy Man of the Adidas Box of Porn, and we certainly knew it existed because what Paul would do was tear pages out of the magazines and smuggle them into school rolled up inside empty Smarties' tubes. And then he'd sell them to us for fifty pence. Paul was a business-genius.

'No. Don't put me in a bin, because I've got some special tubes of Smarties,' said Paul one Monday morning, in the playground, to two of his regular detractors. 'Put Jon Holmes in the bin instead.'

Skill, ingenuity – and all the loyalty of a wolf spider eating its own young, that was Paul.

'How about we put you both in the bin, because you're two gay bummers?' said Thug Number One who was called Ronan and was to be avoided at all costs, not only because his wit was positively Wildean, but because he was a violent bully.

'Yes, but if you don't put *me* in the bin,' countered Paul, his stupid hair blowing in the wind that was also rattling both his anorak and my cagoule, 'I will let you see some pictures of naked ladies.'

'This is the kid what brings in his dad's porn mags,' said Thug Number Two, who had clearly heard the rumours.

'It's not the whole magazine,' said Paul, 'just pages I tear out. Rolled up. In here.' He handed Thug Number One a Smarties' tube. It was the perfect cover. Quite, quite beautiful in its simplicity, the outside illustration promising small, round milk chocolates in a crisp sugar shell quite belying the actual contents. It would fool even the most inquisitive teacher. Even if confiscated under the school 'no sweets' rule, the contents would make no sound when shaken, the telltale Smarties' rattle leading any teacher who had seized it to assume that it was empty (and thus not worth plundering in the staff room) so it would be thrown away and the chances were that its true purpose would never be discovered. It was so clever, that we may as well have had three tubes and called them Tom, Dick and Harry.

'Give it,' said Ronan, the Barbarian.

Paul handed it over. Looking round for teachers, Ronan flipped the lid. It was green, and had a P on the underside. Back then, Smarties' lids came with seemingly random letters stamped on them.[2] To this day I have no idea why.

---

2 Nestle Rowntree replaced the much loved sixty-eight-year-old cylindrical design with a hexagonal pack in 2005. They issued a press release that read: 'Although the empty tubes have been used by creative children to make everything from space rockets to castles, the revamp is needed to ensure the brand remains fresh and interesting to youngsters.' Surprisingly, there was little or no mention of porn smuggling, but Paul Harvey had definitely ensured that the brand remained 'fresh and interesting.'

I can only assume it was some sort of pre-*Coundown* game of *Countdown*. In fact, maybe that's where the creators of *Countdown* (which would make its television debut just a year or so after this exchange) got the idea. Perhaps it was simply there to help kids maintain an interest in the alphabet while stuffing themselves full of chocolate? Or, heaven forfend, maybe it was a cynical way of making them collectible, thereby ensuring more and more Smarties' purchases. It almost worked on me. At one point I remember I had some on my windowsill waiting to see if I could ever get them to spell out anything useful. I think I managed 'PPPFRT-VAUKG' before I gave up.

Back in the playground, Paul wasn't interested in the lettered lid and threw it in the bin. He peered into the tube, and fished out the rolled-up paper inside. Thug Number Two leaned in for a closer look, as did I.

'Fuck off, Holmes,' he said. 'This isn't for bummers.'

It was the first time I had seen lesbian sex. It was a fleeting glimpse, but it was enough to see a tangle of limbs and the intersection of mouthparts on other, hairier, parts.[3] My jaw, like the one of the nice lady in the picture, was open. Thug Number One stared at it. Thug Number Two shifted his stance. So did I. So did Paul. Boys have to do that, when nature strikes, or it gets tangled. Thug Number One quickly regained his composure.

---

3 Remember, this was the seventies, and the cultivating of a ladies' front garden in the way that would eventually go on to annoy the lovely Caitlin Moran so much in her memoir hadn't been invented yet.

'This is shit,' he said, indicating the nice lady on the receiving end. 'She looks like your mum, Holmesy.' I thought about telling him that I was adopted and, to be honest, it could well *be* her for all I knew (assuming the whole 'lesbian' thing was faux, for the purposes of adult entertainment) but I thought better of it. It didn't look like my new mum either. She was, at this point in time, around thirty-eight and while attractive (I guess?)[4] in a mum sort of a way, she wasn't blonde, and I'm fairly sure she wouldn't have contemplated posing for the tableau that we were standing in the drizzle looking at next to the outdoor games cupboard.

'Got anything else?' said Thug Number One to Paul, chucking the picture, Smarties' tube and all, into the bin. If nothing else, and despite the rest of his shortcomings, I have to report that Thug Number One was not a litterbug.

'No', said Paul, meekly, because he knew that his Get-Out-Of-Jail-Free card had just been literally screwed up and he, like Amber (19) and Cyndy (22) was now screwed. Except for real and not in a schoolgirl outfit.

'Bring a better one in tomorrow, or I'll kick your head in,' said Thug Number One.

I felt for Paul, then. Even in the quick glance I'd managed to get in, I found it difficult to see how this nudity could be improved upon. That picture had everything a twelve-year-old boy on the cusp of his sexual awakening could ever need. Plus, as we all know, pornography is in the eye of the

---

4 Is this weird? Speculating on whether your own mother is attractive in the context of whether or not she could be a (faux) lesbian porn star? *Note to Editor – can we check if this is weird or not, before we put it in the finished book? I don't want to come across as some kind of Oedipal freak. Thanks.*

beholder. As they say, one man's turn-on is another man's penis, while another, different man's turn-on might well be a lady's hoo-ha. And in turn a lady's hoo-ha could well be turned on by the aforementioned man's penis or it may well be turned on by another proud hoo-ha owner bringing round wine and a DVD of *Blue is the Warmest Colour*. And elsewhere,[5] someone else's turn-on will be dressing as a baby and paying someone to put apples put into their bottom. Sex is complex. I have a friend who masturbates to pictures of Jessica Rabbit from *Who Framed Roger Rabbit* and she's a cartoon – and not just a cartoon either, but the cartoon wife of a rabbit.[6] He's weird. But that's the point, and while this book that you're holding is no sociological tome offering an illuminating insight into the vagaries of human nature, and while I'm no Desmond Morris, I think one thing we can all agree on is that we are all different. Which is why, without any real prior knowledge or insight into exactly what was going to float Thug Number One's boat, Paul was fucked.

As he was contemplating his evening ahead, sneaking into his parents' room and actually having to be selective about tearing out pages of porn in order to not have his head kicked in, Thugs Number One and Two bade us farewell, but not before dumping me in the bin as promised, where I was able to retrieve the porn page and which is why I found myself, as the bell went and the bellends left, sitting amongst the Fanta and crisp packet debris of a hundred

---

5 I'm thinking Conservative Party Conference.
6 For that reason alone, I'd like to tell you that my friend is called 'Warren', but he isn't.

schoolkids, with an erection.[7] Still, on the bright side, Paul let me have the rescued picture at half price (25p), as a gesture of goodwill.

Paul had basically played whistleblower to his own dad. He was the Edward Snowden of his day, bringing secrets out into the open. It wasn't just his dad, either. Once he brought in a vibrator but no one back then, including him, knew what it was. He said he'd found it in a bag under his mum's side of the bed, and it's only with some hindsight, and no little horror, that I now know exactly what we used that day to comically make our playtime milk froth up. But after Paul's foray into his father's wardrobe, I too began to wonder whether my own parents' bedroom cupboard held Narnia-like wonders, where the people inside were enjoying a lot more than Turkish Delight, but my subsequent searches proved fruitless.

Either my dad wasn't bothered, or he hid his stash very, very well. In our house, the most visual titillation I could find growing up were the illustrations in my mum's collection of medical textbooks,[8] which meant that any photographs of breasts and/or vaginas on show either a) had something visually wrong with them or, b) were drawings, so that while the details might have been right and anatomically correct, I had to squint or look slightly off-centre to avoid ejaculating at the wrong time, such as when looking at a diseased

---

7 Hey 'modern youth', try doing that with the Internet. I'm yet to see a teenager sitting in a skip wanking onto a Kindle Fire. Although it's probably only a matter of time.
8 You may recall that she was a nurse, rather than a weirdo.

anus, or a plate diagram of a cutaway of a fallopian tube. It was like wanking in an illustrated minefield. I look back now, wondering what the hell I was thinking. If anyone had caught me they'd have assumed I was going to grow up to become a serial killer. It wasn't just medical textbooks that contained such riches either, because as any schoolboy growing up in the eighties will tell you, clothing retail catalogues could work, too. Certainly both Grattan and Universal had capricious underwear sections which could be relied upon in an emergency, although while a bit sexy, the important bits were covered. No, if you wanted full frontal nude action then Quinn's *Principle and Practice of Nurse Education* was your only friend. Back then, I knew exactly where the most blemish- or lump-free genital photographs were, and I was not afraid to use them.

Boys will do this kind of thing. A woman, we are told,[9] should she wish to indulge in a little me-time, will perhaps have a bath, light up some scented candles, and perhaps enjoy a little massage oil, post-bathe. I'm not for one moment suggesting a quickie with the handle of a hairbrush or a shower head turned up to max pressure isn't equally fun if the time is right, but at no time in history has a man enjoyed a slow, leisurely bout of anything like this whatsoever – unless you count a poo, while we're sat reading a book, or *Viz* magazine. All we need is a picture, approximately two minutes, and a sock to catch it in. For wanking, I mean, not pooing. We are nothing if not simple creatures, and anyone who says otherwise is lying. We can also do it anywhere at any time, which

9 By *Cosmo* or something, probably.

is why sometimes speed is of the essence. Don't blame us, we have evolved in this way thanks to Nature, which has rightly given up on men and begrudgingly acknowledged that the male's need to masturbate can both arise[10] fairly regularly and when they least expect it, so it had to adapt. The urge can strike at any time, and you just have to deal with it, and fast. There are times, for instance, when you've realistically only got two minutes before your boss will notice that you're not at your desk, or that, in a moment, you're about to land on enemy soil and are going to need to open the parachute, so you'd better be quick. We're men, we do this, and I can only apologise on behalf of an entire gender. Serious bit: writing in *Psychology Today*, in 2010, Professor Roy F Baumeister undertook some research:[11]

'After months of reading and compiling results, the answer was clear [. . .] Men masturbate more than women – much more. Masturbation is considered by sex researchers to be one of the purest measures of sex drive, because it is not much constrained by external factors (such as the need to find a partner, or the risk of <u>pregnancy</u> or disease). Some people say that women feel <u>guilty</u> about masturbation, but that's not what the data say, at least not any more. In fact, it's mainly the (few) non-masturbating men who associated masturbation with guilt. Non-masturbating women generally say they just don't feel any inclination to do it.

---

10 No pun intende . . . Oh, who am I kidding? Of course it was.
11 *Psychology Today*, December 8, 2010 'The Reality of the Male Sex Drive' by Roy F Baumeister, Eppes Eminent Scholar and Professor of Psychology at Florida State University.

They don't need guilt to resist the impulse, because they aren't resisting – because they don't have the impulse.'

Basically, if Roy says men are fucking obsessed with it, then who are we to argue? We're men, ergo, we fiddle with ourselves. That's proper psychological research, that is. Gentlemen, it's not our fault. Our actual genetic brains make us do it, just like women's brains make them enjoy talking about 'feelings' and liking films such as *Marley & Me*.

Looking back, I think we all knew this as we were growing up. We knew where our masturbatory destiny lay: we couldn't not, given that Paul Harvey's dad had a stash of porn mags and was obviously still doing it well into his forties. It also made going round Paul's house for tea[12] especially awkward, knowing that in the room above us, a succession of pictured ladies were bending over and waiting for him. 'All right boys,' he'd say, on arriving home from work, 'I'm just going upstairs to change out of this suit' and both Paul and I would exchange a glance and shudder through our spaghetti hoops on toast.

It has to be said that there must have come a point when Mr Harvey began to notice that various pages had been mysteriously torn out of his collection but, of course, even

---

12 This was a thing. You don't do it as an adult. You don't say to your colleague at work 'Hey, tonight, do you want to come round after work for tea?' And that is a shame. Imagine how much nicer the world would be if, after a hard day working on a core strategy for client integration into brand synergy you invited Neil from HR round and you had some spaghetti hoops on toast and then went and played war outside until it got dark.

though he must have also been aware as to exactly who the perpetrator was, it was something that remained entirely unspoken between father and son. Yes, there are things father and son *can* talk about, sometimes quite moving things, but that certainly isn't going to be one of them. I notice that in Cat Stevens' song 'Father and Son', the whole thorny subject of a Father to Son wanking chat is notorious by its absence. It begins with 'Father' talking to 'Son', imparting advice about 'change', 'relaxing' and 'taking it easy'. And Son is probably sitting there thinking 'Oh, shit. Dad's about to start talking to me about wanking.' But no, of course he isn't. Cat Stevens knows full well that that would never happen, which is why he goes on to suggest 'take your time to think a lot' rather than 'take your time to wank a lot'. Cat Stevens isn't stupid, he knows the score. I haven't got sons, I have two young daughters, but I would be just as comfortable talking them through correctly inserting their own tampons when they eventually need them, as my dad would have been if he'd had to detail onanism to his boy. The other reason I wouldn't do this is that I have no idea how to correctly insert tampons, but it doesn't matter that I can't pass this information on because there are leaflets for that sort of thing in Lil-Lets packets.

Twice in the song, Father goes on to implore Son 'Look at me, I am old, but I'm happy.' Yes, of course you're happy, because you know that straight after you've finished warbling suspect advice at your Son, you're going straight upstairs, rummaging through your wardrobe and heading to the bathroom with a shoebox full of *Razzle*.

*

We never talked about that stuff. Over the years I've shared walks with my dad, I've had a pint with my dad, he's picked me up when I've fallen off my bike and been there to wipe my tears with his ever-present hanky, he helped me to mend my first car (to be fair, he mended it, I stood nearby and held a spanner that he didn't need), we even once went to a Motörhead concert together where he wore bright orange builder's industrial earplugs throughout the whole thing, but there was never a time when *that* kind of conversation came close to happening. In real terms I'd say that, over the years, there's been more chance of Israel asking Palestine round for a mince pie and a glass of wine at Christmas than there is of my dad saying 'So, Son. Is there anything you'd like to know about your penis?' In fact, there's more chance of Israel asking Palestine to accompany it to a Motörhead concert than there is of me and my dad musing on masturbation. Although there was one time when it was almost forced upon us, mainly thanks to my lackadaisical attitude towards discretion.

SEVEN

. . . in which my dad thinks I am a transvestite.

What happened was this: sometime in the summer of 1985 I went on a youth club weekend to London. The youth club in question was a church one, and it belonged to the Methodist Association of Youth Clubs who organised an annual shindig for impressionable youngsters who had been forced to do something worthwhile like this by their parents. Going to the church youth club was clearly something that my mum thought I should be doing on Friday nights and so I spent them in a cold hall at St John's Methodist Church, Nuncaton. I enjoyed it tremendously, but the reason wasn't that it put me in touch with God, far from it. It was mostly because everyone there was the same age; we were all teenagers, we were all growing up and our minds and bodies were a riot of dirty thoughts and hormones which is probably why, even though our parents were oblivious, church youth club was a hotbed of the kind of sleaze and debauchery that would have made Jesus, had he been able to see into the future, think twice about coming on board with. As it is written in the Bible:

Then Jesus was led by the Spirit into the wilderness to be tempted there by the Devil. For forty days and forty nights he jested and became very hungry.

During that time the Devil came and said to him, 'If you are the Son of God, tell these stones to become loaves of bread.'

But Jesus told him, 'No! The Scriptures say people should not live by bread alone but by every word that comes from the mouth of God.'

And the Tempter replied, 'You do realise that in the future, probably just under 2000 years from now, a number of horny teenagers will be gathered together in your name and the name of your Father on a Friday night in Nuneaton and lo, they will be getting off with each other like there's no tomorrow? Quite frankly, mate, it's not the mouth of God you need to be worried about, but the mouth of Jennifer Collins.'

And Jesus said, 'Well, if that's the worst that can happen in God's name, then fine. It's not like anyone's ever going to be killing anyone because of religion or going to war or violently disputing territories or torturing people for their beliefs or anything.' *(Matthew, 4:1–11)*

A tradition at one of these Methodist Association of Youth Clubs' weekends away – in the heady days before email or mobile phones – was to make a small pom-pom, attach your name and address to it and, at a gathering of two thousand teenagers in central London, throw it into the air and then become pen pals with whoever caught yours. It was the church's way of reaching out, of connecting. And so it was that my furry missive was captured by a girl who lived near Croydon, and to cut a long story short, after a few weeks of letter writing back and forth, she sent me a pair of her knickers in the post. As a man, and as discussed previously, I have little insight into the workings of the female mind and, alas, I no longer have the letters[1] so the exact chain of events that led to this seminal moment are lost in the mists of time, but I do recall opening the package (fortuitously on my own, rather than at the breakfast table in front of my parents and my sister) and being both surprised and confused by the contents. Let us remember that this was a girl that I had never met, and our paths had only crossed via pom-pom at a church weekend, but what it taught me was:

a) Girls are weird, yet exciting and,
b) clearly, St John's Methodist wasn't the only church in the country that harboured a youth group that was hell bent on heavy petting.

I was turned on by the mystery black lacy pants, so naturally I did what any red-blooded teenager would do and hid them under my mattress. To understand what happened next, you should know about the design of my teenage bedroom, circa aged thirteen to nineteen. It was tiny, for a start. When we'd moved from our home in Magyar Crescent, it had been to a much smaller house that hadn't been lived in for over seventeen years and, in my memory, was more or less

---

[1] Or the knickers. Come on, what do you take me for?

falling down and full of soot. Still in Nuneaton, yet down an obscure lane, it was a two-up, two-down with a bathroom tagged on the side and a small front garden that my dad had to scythe away in order for us even get a viewing. We'd been forced to move there by the collapse of dad's building business sometime in 1977,[2] yet over this terrible time Dad worked tirelessly to turn the shell of this building into a home for his family, which involved splitting one of the two bedrooms in half to make three and, as a result, the floor space was minimal. This particular problem was solved by my grandad, a skilled carpenter, building me a sort of 'captain's bed' high up on the bedroom wall with a wardrobe and desk space beneath. I mention this because, as the bed was fixed to the wall it was, unbeknownst to me, occasionally checked for safety by my ever-vigilant dad.[3] This involved him lifting the mattress to check the fittings. And on one occasion, rather than just dust and Rawlplugs, he found something he wasn't expecting, which was a pair of black lacy pants.

Now, there was no way he was going to take me aside and ask me exactly why there were girl's pants in my bed, so he did what any man would do, and indeed what I would, as a

---

2 See Chapter Eleven. Incidentally, our family upheaval happened just after we'd celebrated Her Majesty the Queen's Silver Jubilee. We'd spent time and street parties on commemorating her time on the throne in Buckingham Palace, one of her many homes. Yet when it came to us losing our house, where was she? Eh? Thanks for nothing, Liz.

3 You may remember that our previous house had always tried to kill us, but in this new one, Dad had seemingly become more safety conscious.

father, now do myself[4] – he asked my mum to deal with it. Consequently, I arrived home from school that evening expecting egg and chips and instead, there on the table, were some pants.

'Can I ask you about these?' said my mum, before I'd barely had time to put my bag down. She waved her hand towards the knickers. I followed her gesture and, next to that afternoon's copy of the *Coventry Evening Telegraph* and a placemat, I saw the pants. The pants from under my mattress. The pants that had been sent to me in the post by a complete stranger. And now the pants were on the kitchen table.

My first thought was that I would've thought that my mum, being a nurse, would have had a better grasp of basic hygiene. I haven't checked, but on this evidence, the subsequent outbreak of MRSA in hospital wards could well be down to her and her poor standards. OK, that wasn't my first thought. It wasn't even my second thought. My first thought was one of abject horror while, almost simultaneously, my second one was panic coupled with an overwhelming desire to run away from home. As I stood there in distress, a thousand implausible explanations running through my head at high speed, another part of me was mentally packing some essentials (toothbrush, clean shirt, the black lacy pants)

---

4 As the father of two girls, if I found a pair of girl's knickers in either of their beds of course I wouldn't bat an eyelid, because they would probably be theirs. I am obviously speaking hypothetically. My daughters are currently five and three. To be honest if I *didn't* find items of their clothing in odd places I'd think something was up. Not so long ago I fished a mitten out of the fish tank and found a pair of Miffy earmuffs in the fridge.

and getting out of there, possibly never to return. I would become an urchin, living by my wits on the street, with a sad life story that went 'I was forced into homelessness because my birth parents abandoned me and then the other ones found some pants'. It would be a tale of woe I would tell time and time again, bleating it at passers-by as I glugged strong, continental lager from a can in the doorway of Victoria's Secret.

Dismissing this option, instead I did what any man would do in the circumstances. I denied it.

'I've never seen them before,' I tried.

'Well, that's funny because your dad found them under your mattress.'

Trapped, I decided that teenage indignation was only the way forward.

'What the hell was he doing under my mattress? Under my mattress is my mattress and he shouldn't be looking under my mattress!'

'He's not cross. I'm not cross. *We're* not cross. We just wondered why you had some girl's knickers under your mattress?'

Mum had clearly failed to grasp what it was like to be a teenage boy. But then, seemingly, so had Dad. Which was weird. He must have been one at some point but, then again, my investigations into his wardrobe for porn had been fruitless, so I guess he just wasn't into this stuff.

'I don't know, I just got sent them in the post.'

'You got sent them in the post?' My mum's face was slightly confused, and not surprisingly, because here, in the eighties, the only things you sent off for in the post was membership of the Dennis the Menace Fan Club or Frisbees that you would find tokens for on the side of cereal packets. But Rice Krispies or Frosties were yet to have an offer where you could send off for girls' knickers.[5]

'Yes.'

She remained confused.

'Why?'

Good question.

'I mean, who sent them?' she said.

The honest answer was someone who I'd never met, at an event she'd insisted I attend because 'church youth club is a good thing'. However, I wasn't quite at the point in my life where I would be comfortable saying this so instead I fell back on the standard emergency teenage response in interrogations of this nature.

'Dunno.'

'You don't know? What do you mean, you don't know? You must know. People don't just go round sending their pants to random addresses they've just picked out of the phone book.'[6]

'I want to know what you were doing in my room!'

Diversion tactic. Nice.

'I wasn't in your room, your dad was. Your dad was checking your bed wasn't going to fall off the wall.'

---

5 Although in Japan, they probably do.
6 Do you know what, I fucking bet they do. I bet loads of them are churchgoers too. Weirdos.

I had one shot here. One shot at getting out of this nightmare.

'Well, why have I even GOT a bed that could fall off the wall?! You must HATE ME AND WANT ME DEAD.'

I'd done a sharp handbrake turn and gone off piste. It was a bold move, but I was desperate. The last thing I wanted my mum to be privy to was my wanking habits. I was attempting to turn hideous embarrassment into righteous anger. I was angry with my dad. Not for allowing his dad, my grandad, to construct rickety sleeping arrangements, but for finding some girl's pants under his son's mattress and not following Man's strict code of Omerta. He should've taken one look at the pants and left them where they were, thinking, 'That's my boy. He's wanking with the added visual stimulus of female underwear. Nice work.' But no, instead he'd been too uncomfortable to mention it himself or GOD FORBID leave them there and not say ANYTHING, so instead he'd asked my mum to speak to me about it and here I was angry at him, angry at him for violating The Code of Man. Why? Why had he done this? What kind of man breaks The Code? Is he even a man anymore? He had let us all down and allowed a woman to know our secrets. He had revealed man's Great Secret to Womankind. He was dead to me.

'Your dad only mentioned it because he thought you might be becoming a transvestite.'

'What?'

'He was worried.[7] Are you becoming a transvestite?'

'No,' I mumbled.

'I told him you weren't. I just said you were a teenage boy with a teenage boy's needs,' she said, and passed me the pants.

I think I speak from experience when I say that when your own mother has handed your own masturbatory aid back to you with the same hand that she raised you, you know you have hit auto-erotic rock bottom.

Yet it turned out I hadn't. Auto-erotic rock bottom was to came later, in 1986.

---

7 I don't know why he was necessarily worried about this, but he's of a different generation and I'm looking at it through the prism of the modern age. It's 2015 at time of writing and the world has moved on, which is why I think I can call him and ask what he was really so concerned about, given that it's no big deal. Wait there. I'm going to call him now. I'll report back momentarily. Talk amongst yourselves.

[. . .]

Right. I'm off the phone. We had a brief conservation about how he is. I bottled it and didn't ask him about the pants.

EIGHT

. . . In which I eat a packed lunch in the face of adversity.

Mums are different to dads. Mums have no fear of confronting things head on, no matter how sensitive or difficult. Mine will, anyway. She wades into anything, no matter how deep, like a particularly fearless Range Rover. If she was a police negotiator trying to talk a suicide jumper off a ledge she wouldn't pussyfoot around with him, she'd get out there like Mel Gibson in *Lethal Weapon* and chuck him off herself, but not before she'd spat on a tissue and wiped his face so that he looked tidy for the watching media.

Mums rush in where fathers fear to tread. They do not flinch in the face of very much at all, and it can be excruciating. I think that I can illustrate this in two ways. First, aged about fifteen, I was in the habit, with three friends, Matthew, Woody and Dave, of going to eat our lunchtime sandwiches at one of their houses. Dave and I both lived too far away from school for it to be viable, but both Woody and Matthew's homes were close so we would alternate between abodes. At Woody's house we sat in the front room and were bothered by his parents' Doberman Pinscher, at Matthew's we sat at the kitchen table and bantered over a packed lunch.

*

School packed lunches were a thing of beauty. At primary school (aged 4-8) I'd gone home for lunch, because our house in Magyar Crescent was directly opposite the school gates. At middle school[1] I'd had school dinners,[2] which came with their own set of problems, not least the Rhetorical Rule of Pudding[3] that was so eloquently encapsulated in 1979 by Roger Waters on Pink Floyd's *The Wall* album:

'If you don't eat your meat, you can't have any pudding! How can you have any pudding if you don't eat your meat!?'

What a stupid question. Yet it didn't stop it being bellowed at you by a hot-faced dining witch, hence the frustration shared first by Roger Waters and then me. The correct response to any dinner lady shouting this question is, of course, 'My good lady, I think you'll find that whether or not I eat my meat (and I use the term loosely, given the gristly grey substance on my plate) *ipso facto* in no way has any reflection on, or bears any relation to, my ability, or not,

---

1 In modern parlance this is Year 3. Back then it went First School, Middle School then Secondary or 'Big' School.
2 Dinner. Yes, dinner. In the Midlands we had dinner at lunchtime and tea at teatime. That's why the ladies in charge of dinner at school were called dinner ladies. They were not called 'lunch ladies' were they? Wherever you went in the country dinner ladies were called dinner ladies, proof, if proof were needed, that the correct time to eat dinner is at lunchtime. I don't suppose they're called dinner ladies any more. There's probably some kind of rule that they now have to be called something politically correct like 'Non-Specific Gender Nourishment Coordinators' or 'Food People' and they all have to be Fairtrade. But when I was at school they were called dinner ladies because dinner was at lunchtime and tea was at teatime. This rule meant that in actual fact I didn't even have a meal called 'dinner' until I moved south to go to university and went all poncey and middle class.
3 Pudding. Not dessert; 'pudding'. See footnote 2, (above)

to consume pudding. In fact, I would go so far as to say that the less meat I consume, then the more room in my tummy I will have left for pudding, thus rendering your question moot.'

I could have said this, but instead, when she turned her back to harangue some other child for avoiding what was being passed off as pork, I stuck my tongue out at her. Unluckily for me, I was seen to do this by a teacher, Mrs Cooper, who strode over, plucked me from my chair and made me stand in the corridor. Thus I lost out on pudding entirely, and it was marble sponge and custard, so I was not best pleased.

But when I went to 'big school', it was packed lunches all the way. Sandwiches ranged from jam to ham to sandwich spread, by way of Shippam's meat paste. It was a daily gastronomic adventure and you didn't know which gourmet path you would be set upon until you opened your box to see what your mum had made. In truth, while I liked ham, or paste, I was always disappointed on jam days and I positively dreaded sandwich spread because eating sandwich spread was – and still is – like eating some white sick. To prove my point, it even had bits of carrot in it.

The rules of the Eighties packed lunch were simple: sandwiches, crisps, chocolate bar. It was three of your 5 A Day, with the fourth being a carton of Ribena or orange juice and the fifth being another chocolate bar. The crisps were interchangeable – anything from Outer Spacers to Frazzles to Chipsticks to Monster Munch – but what united them was that they were all equally bad for your health, ditto the chocolate choice of Penguin Bar, Club Biscuit or Blue

Riband. We would sit, my friends and I, and we would almost ritualistically open our boxes together and – just as everyone does in restaurants nowadays when your main course arrives and you look at your dining companion's food and wish you'd had what they're having – we expressed food envy. Trades were made: Salt & Shake crisps were a straight swap for Horror Bags Fangs ('Snacks that go crunch in the night!') and, chocolate-wise, two Bandits were worth one Breakaway on the unofficial brown market.

And it was at this point, as we were dining at Matthew's house, monster-munching our way through our crisps, that Matthew's mum came into the kitchen with an armful of washing. We mumbled a sort of 'hello' in that clumsy, yet polite way that fifteen-year-olds have, and then she dropped the M-bomb.

'Matthew,' she said in front of us all, 'if you must masturbate, could you do it into tissue paper, because I'm the one that has to wash all these towels.'

The depth of the silence that fell was one to rival a sponsored one, organised by a group of elective mutes, in a library. Not one of us knew where to look, so we all stared into our sandwich boxes. Mine had some sandwich spread smeared on the inside, which didn't help the mood. For his part, Matthew went the colour of the red wrapper on his Penguin biscuit. Suddenly, in this kitchen, it was like the film *Stand By Me* but, instead of us, a group of kids flung together by fate and friendship in a coming-of-age drama, being sickened and horrified at finding the body of a dead boy in the woods, we were faced with Matthew's mum holding an armful of washing and talking about sperm. I didn't conduct a straw poll but, if I had, I think I can say with some certainty that each and every one of us would have taken that dead body and kissed it, rather than have to deal with this.

No one dared to breathe, but I knew that we were all thinking the same thing: 'There but for the Grace of God, go I.' Not only had Matthew's mum SPOKEN ABOUT HIM WANKING but SHE HAD DONE IT IN FRONT OF HIS FRIENDS. To add insult to injury, she then breezed about the kitchen as though nothing had happened. She deposited the load with the deposited load on it into the washing machine, filled the kettle up and sat down at the table with us.

'How's school?' she said.

For my part, I was now finding Tupperware so fascinating that I couldn't look up.

'Darren?' That was Woody's real and given name.

He said nothing.

'Darren?' she repeated.

'It's fine,' he squeaked. He put his Shippam's paste-roll down, uneaten. It was my turn.

'Jonathan?'

'S'fine.'

'How's revision?'

Some exams were looming.

'Fine, thanks.'

'Matthew's a bit worried about physics.' Matthew didn't look worried about physics. He currently looked worried about something else entirely. Like the story of what had just happened being repeated at school.

On the way back we tried to make light of it, reassuring him that while his mum's indiscretion had been inappropriate, it was hardly anything to worry about, given that every single boy in the school had probably done the same thing, admittedly with the difference that their mums weren't blasé enough to introduce it as a topic of conversation over a lunch of Wagon Wheels and processed cheese. He was suitably reassured, but it was short-lived because the moment we got back to the playground we told everyone we knew. Life can be so cruel.

(Despite Matthew's misfortunes, we still haven't got to the bit where I hit Auto-erotic Rock Bottom. Keep reading.)

The school we were at was Higham Lane Secondary School, Nuneaton. A bus or a bike ride away from where I lived, it was on the other side of town and was particularly noted nationally for having a school farm run by teacher Mr Terry, who walked with a severe limp and a slightly hunched back due to contracting polio as a child.[4] It was an incredibly successful venture and enthusiastic pupils with a passing interest in sheep, chickens or skiving off from real, proper lessons could take time out of their day to enjoy 'Rural Studies',

---

4 During our time at Higham Lane, there was a poster advertising Polo Mints at the Tuck Shop telling us (for it was their advertising slogan at the time) that 'People Like Polo'. Because teenage boys are heartless little fuckers, a cut-out picture of Mr Terry was often stuck on the top of the tube of mints and the slogan amended to read 'People Like Polio'. It all came to a bit of a head when my friend handed it in as his official entry for a *Blue Peter* competition to design a logo for the International Year of Disabled.

which seemed to the rest of us to mostly involve collecting eggs and drawing pictures of goats on the blackboard, which are banned now.[5] Naturally anyone who 'studied' this was roundly mocked and accused of varying degrees of animal loving that, as a subject, would almost certainly not crop up in any exam on agricultural husbandry. During his tenure, Mr Terry even achieved a certain level of local, if not national, fame, writing three books of his adventures on a school farm.[6] When I left school in 1985 both Mr Terry and his farm were still going strong. When he retired in 1998 the farm fell into disrepair and was converted into workshops because not one of the other teachers gave a shit.

I mention this only because, on an almost constant basis, Mr Terry's achievements were celebrated on the school notice board outside the Headmaster's office. His name was Mr Breed and he had a notable nose and lived at home with his mother. He was very proud of his notice board because

---

5 Of course they aren't. No one's ever banned blackboards. They were done for by technology, rather than political correctness gone mad. Despite countless *Daily Mail* or *Sunday Express* headlines that say 'Headteacher Bans Christmas Because It Offends Muslims' or 'Primary School Nativity Play Replaced With Multi-Ethnic Pig and Cow Free Halal Celebration of Diversity Which Is Also Suitable For Jews', no one has ever stopped anyone from dressing up with a tea towel on their head for an end-of-year play. Oh, apart from when I suggested that my daughter's primary school should mount an amateur production of *Zero Dark Thirty*. And that was the last PTA meeting I was ever allowed to attend. (Actually, can you still say 'political correctness gone mad'? I have a feeling that the correct term is now 'political correctness consistent with diagnostic criteria specified by DSM-V'.)
6 *Pigs in the Playground* (1986), *Calves in the Classroom* (1987) and *Ducks in Detention* (1990). He was nothing if not a fan of animal/school-based alliteration.

on it he would enthusiastically display any cuttings from local and national press that detailed the accomplishments of pupils past and present. If someone did well at County level in a sport, they were up there. If someone musical had joined an orchestra and subsequently travelled with that orchestra to play in London or Birmingham, then it was exhibited. If someone who'd taken Rural Studies to O level had ever gone to work anywhere other than an abattoir, or somehow avoided being arrested on suspicion of bestiality, then the Headmaster had it covered, painstakingly going over the names of Breed's brood with a highlighter pen. This shrine to education stood right by the main entrance and was as a beacon of hope for everyone still at the school, and a proud symbol of what could be achieved under his stewardship.

I will make the confession here and now that it was myself, Nick Roser and Graham Bosworth who took to ripping pages out of porn mags, highlighting the names under the highly detailed and explicit open-crotch grot shots and pinning them to Mr Breed's Wall of Triumph. At one point it would have seemed to even the most casual observer that Higham Lane Secondary School, Nuneaton, was churning out the majority of the country's adult models. And as fast as they were taken down, the more ridiculous it got. Soon, once we got into our stride, ex-Higham Lane pupils were seemingly responsible for the assassination of John F. Kennedy, the Moon landings, the Yorkshire Ripper murders, cold fusion, scramjet technology, the kidnapping of the racehorse Shergar, the Birmingham pub bombings and the shooting, outside the Libyan Embassy in London, of WPC Yvonne

Fletcher. And we were all so *very* proud of school alumni, The Herreys, when they won the 1984 Eurovision Song Contest for Sweden with their song *Diggi-Loo, Diggi-Ley*.

At least we were being harmlessly creative; clearly an early attempt at the kind of childish comedy that appeals to mostly just me regardless of what anyone else thinks – something which various radio bosses over the years have not been backwards in coming forward to point out. Mr Breed was of much the same opinion, or would have been, if we'd ever been caught. Of the three of us, only Graham Bosworth was punished, but that was because he later moved on to experimenting with ballistics by launching a firework at Mr Saunders, the Stand-in Deputy Head, from across the playground. He was given the cane, because back then, in the good old days, you could still be physically beaten by those with a duty of care towards you.[7] Happy days.

Speaking of porn, one of my earliest memories is having the end of my penis cut off. I don't mean that I was involved in some kind of bizarre farming accident or that I was mutilated in a John Bobbit[8] or *Fatal Attraction*-style revenge act; I wasn't one of those people who you hear about occasionally

---

7 Not any more though. I tell you, it's political correctness consistent with diagnostic criteria specified by DSM-V. The beating worked on Graham Bosworth, though, because to the best of my knowledge he never fired anything across a playground at a teacher ever again and instead eventually took his fascination with rockets to RAF Halton where he trained to become an officer in the Royal Air Force.

8 John Bobbit was a man whose spouse famously cut his penis off while he was sleeping, drove off with it and threw it into a field. Ironically, considering the details of the case, the case filled quite a few column inches.

having a bit of themselves severed in a threshing machine and then picking it up and walking miles with it to seek help. I've never picked up my penis from the gears of a hay baler, or had it lobbed out of a car window by a cross wife. The fact of the matter is that the end of mine was cut off when I was eleven months old.

I was circumcised. By which I mean I *am* circumcised, because my foreskin hasn't miraculously grown back like a salamander's leg. My memory of this significant event is limited, and chiefly consists of standing up in a cot in hospital and, post-procedure, being given a digestive biscuit. This is a firm memory in my mind, except for just one problem: I was under a year old, and surely that is too young to a) stand up in a cot and b) eat a digestive biscuit. And yet, other than on Severed Penis Day, I have never otherwise been hospitalised, so the memory can't have come from anywhere else. The obvious other solution is that I have dreamt this scenario at some point, but that's a weird dream to have: standing up in a cot eating an oaty biscuit. When Carl Jung studied dreams and wrote of them being 'an indicator of those changes that sometimes point to the development of the individuation process', and how they 'suggest a more balanced relationship between the ego and the Self', as far as I'm aware, nowhere in his work (widely considered to be the definitive study on the subject) was an interpretation of a dream involving a boy's cock and a McVities' favourite. Yet false memory or not, the end result is that I am circumcised, and that brings with it its own set of problems.

Well, not problems exactly. Not in the sense that it makes sex any more complicated or changes the way you wee, it just makes you more aware of your surroundings. School showers were the worst. I was at school in the seventies and eighties and I reached puberty roundabout 1980/81 when I was eleven or twelve and, because schools are sadistic, this is, of course, also round about the time that they make you have communal showers after PE. Who invented the idea of communal school showers? Who decided that the best thing to have in secondary schools, just when boys and girls are entering a confusing stage of life, their bodies and physicality changing on an almost daily basis, hormones raging, budding breasts here, thickening penises there and pubic hair everywhere – who decided that this would be the ideal time to force everyone of a certain age to strip naked in front of each other and get all soapy? What the hell were they thinking? Unfortunately the answer to that question is probably, 'I am a paedophile, and have happily secured employment as a teacher. My first act will introduce communal showers so I can look at some pubescent cocks.' And then the idea stuck. Just because some weird PE perv once had an idea, suddenly this made it acceptable to stand in a naked line with your peers under a spray of tepid water. No one questioned it, we just did it and thus, if you were circumcised, you were subject to all manner of stimulating grown-up debate.

'Oy, Holmesy. You've got a gay knob.'

This intellectual discourse came from Paul Bolton, who we first met back in Chapter Two, and who was the school twat. Not only would he call people 'gay' and then go and draw cocks on school walls, the irony of him peering at my knob yet accusing *me* of being gay was also completely lost on him.

'Who are you?' he would say, 'Jeremy Thorpe?'

Though I was unaware of it at the time, Jeremy Thorpe was the leader of the Liberal Party from 1967–1976, and was so liberal that he had an alleged homosexual affair with a man called Norman Scott (when such acts were still illegal) and then resigned. He was subsequently named in a plot to kill Scott and went on trial at the Old Bailey. In 1979 he was acquitted of charges of homosexuality and conspiring to murder and was all over the news. I didn't know the details, but I'd certainly heard the name,[9] my lack of political insight exposed on a daily basis by Paul Bolton who, despite him being a maniac, was seemingly up there with Sir Robin Day.

'Are you Jeremy Thorpe?' he would repeat whenever I saw him in a corridor or the playground, and then he would threaten to punch me unless I said yes. For about three months, during the tribulations of the then-MP for North Devon, I was forced to admit that yes, I was him, for fear of being hit in the face. And all because I was circumcised, a medical necessity that Paul Bolton had somehow, in his own head, linked to homosexuality.

'Yes. I am Jeremy Thorpe,' I would say, and he would be satisfied with that. 'That's what I thought, Thorpey,' he'd reply and then point at me and say 'He's Jeremy Thorpe' to anyone in listening distance, not one of whom really knew who Jeremy Thorpe was either, on the grounds of also being eleven. When I look back on it now, it was a curious

---

9 Probably on John Craven's *Newsround*, the seventies' daily children's teatime news bulletin on BBC1, which one would politely tolerate while waiting for *Crackerjack* to start.

bullying technique; having to admit to a thug, under threat of violence, that you were an Eton- and Oxford-educated politician and a key figure in the campaign for Britain to join the Common Market. In truth, of course, Paul Bolton had just heard the words 'gay' and 'Jeremy Thorpe' somewhere and carved himself a home-made insult. A long-since vindicated Jeremy Thorpe lived out his final days in Devon and died in December 2014. I've no idea of the whereabouts of Paul Bolton. He's probably the Political Correspondent for *Attitude* magazine.

The rite of circumcision is a tradition that cuts back through the centuries. Its actual origins are uncertain; some say it was an act of religious sacrifice, others that it simply marked the transition of boy to man. Others say that it was originally practised to discourage masturbation (yeah, like that worked).[10] The oldest documentary evidence of it comes from Ancient Egypt; there are even hieroglyphics at Luxor depicting the procedure in quite some detail, like the world's oldest fetish porn. Naturally, it also crops up in the Bible, with God telling Abraham to circumcise himself, otherwise he'd 'cut off' Abraham from his people, which to my mind makes God a bigger bully than even Paul Bolton. By the second century it had all fallen a bit out of favour, except for within the Jewish community, after the Jewish writer Philio Judaeus (20 BC–50 AD) posited that hacking a bit of cock off was clean, healthy and would increase fertility. Meanwhile, back in the Bible, Jesus was going round telling anyone who'd listen that circumcision wasn't much use. In

---

10 See various other chapters in the book.

the Gospel according to Thomas, when his disciples pipe up with a definitive, 'Hey, Jeezy-boy, yes or no, is circumcision useful or not?' he replies, sagely, 'If it were useful, their father would produce children already circumcised from their mother.' And it was thus that Jesus did seem to admit that there *is* such a thing as evolution, which rather pisses on his own legacy.

I'm not Jewish. Mine was whipped off simply because it wouldn't pull back properly. Without going into too much detail, it was technically a bit too connected at the front end and so, for medical reasons, rather than anything to do with religion or vanity, it had to go.[11] A question I'm almost never asked by anyone at all isn't 'what's it like being circumcised?' And the answer to that is 'I don't know' because I don't know what it's like *not* to be circumcised. I am told that 'Little Jonathan' is probably more sensitive down there, given that there is now nothing to protect whatever it is that the foreskin protects,[12] but if you haven't had one since you were a baby, then it's hard to know what living with a foreskin on your penis is actually like.

It's never been an issue. Not to anyone other than Paul Bolton anyway. To my knowledge, it's never put anyone off, but equally I don't think I've ever been busy enjoying some sexy-time during which my partner has gone down there and popped up again, all cock-a-hoop with praise, if you'll pardon the expression. No one's had a quick look, checked out the action, and then said 'Well. That. Is. Excellent. Nice

---

11 Actually, that *is* too much detail. Sorry.
12 I am not a doctor.

job. You can't even see the join. What knife did they use? P'robly one of those expensive Japanese steel ones you get for boning fish, yeah?' So while I'm prepared to believe that anyone who has ever been on the receiving end of both kinds of penis (skin on and skin off)[13] may well have a preference, no one's ever mentioned it to me. Then again, it would be incredibly impolite to visibly recoil, wouldn't it? That said, many years ago, a girlfriend suggested drawing a face on it, so that it looked like 'a cute mouse',[14] but I declined. She was weird.

I'm not sure why, but girls do tend to be sympathetic towards an injury. Maybe it brings out their maternal instinct; when presented with evidence of wounding they will often exhibit caring tendencies which is something that, with a little planning, can be exploited by any horny teenager whose head has recently come into contact with a big bit of rock in a disused quarry.

Sometime in the early to mid-eighties the word 'slaphead' became a staple playground insult. It was later generally reserved for any balding teachers, but the first time I ever heard it, it was being directed at me. In fact, prior to this I am fairly sure that it had never been said anywhere before, and that I was unwittingly responsible for bringing this word into the lexicon of the English language[15] and it was all thanks to a lump of concrete.

---

13 I am aware that I am now making penises sound like grilled chicken.
14 A big mouse, obviously. A *massive* mouse.
15 I realise that this is probably bollocks, but in our school at least, this was definitely its first outing.

Prior to this, the preferred insult of choice amongst the playground cognoscenti was, simply, 'Joey'. Famously, this was because the children's TV show, *Blue Peter*, regularly reported on the life of Joey Deacon, an elderly man with cerebral palsy whose moving story was immediately inappropriately appropriated by schoolchildren everywhere and used as a term of abuse. Joey made the involuntary noises and spasmodic movements of the cerebral palsy sufferer; henceforth, if you did anything at school that singled you out in any given moment (say, dropping a pencil) then these sounds and actions would be imitated by those around you and the word 'Joey' said at you in what, back then, it seemed to us to be perfectly reasonable to call a 'spaz voice'. I don't suppose for one moment that this was the effect that *Blue Peter* wanted their short, emotional films to have on the nation's young, but so it was that presenters Simon Groom and Sarah Greene single-handedly gave a generation its best and most versatile insult. In 1994 The Spastics Society, a charity dedicated to working with disabled people and their families, realised that their name had been seized by the nation's evil schoolchildren and attempted to head it off at the pass.[16] The word 'spastic' was continually being used as an insult, and much time and effort was put into rebranding The Spastics Society with a new name. On the twentieth anniversary of its name change, a former member of The Spastics Society's executive council, a seemingly pleasant

---

16 They were a bit late to catch on. This was *twenty-three* years later. The insult had long since passed the point where it could be headed off at the pass and had long-since disappeared over the cultural horizon.

lady called Valerie Lang, told *BBC News* that, as a sufferer of cerebral palsy herself, she was passionate about a name change: 'I felt we could not afford to stay with the name we had,' she told them in March 2014. 'The name "spastic" was a playground term of abuse. Children would shout to each other "You big spastic" every time someone was clumsy, or even if they just disagreed with them.' She was right, too, and what the Society needed was something neutral, something impersonal and middle of the road that would not be hijacked by little shits like us. So they thought long and hard and eventually came up with the name 'Scope'. It had no obvious links to disability, nothing that had a personal connotation, and thus could not be turned into a form of abuse. Except they forgot one vital thing: never underestimate a child. Within a month, the new playground insult of choice countrywide was 'Scopey'.

But I was, I think, the first 'slaphead', certainly in our school. The lobbed lump of concrete that gave rise to what was to become a national insult was hurled from atop a high railway embankment by a girl from the council estate that was, quite literally, on the wrong side of the tracks. Quarry Lane, where we lived at this time, led down to woodland, (in actual fact, an overgrown disused quarry) and its boundary was the mainline railway from London to Birmingham and beyond. It passed through Nuneaton and as thirteen- or fourteen-year-olds we would often play in the woods as the trains hurtled by, yards from where we were dicking about. And quite often, a couple of kids from the council estate would cross the tracks and join in by throwing rocks at us from on high. I didn't see mine coming. I was aware of a rushing sound as something that was possibly part of the support for an old railway sleeper came hurtling through the canopy of leaves above us but didn't really notice that anything was amiss until it hit me straight on the top of my head. It was so sudden that it didn't really hurt, but as I felt some warm stuff running down my face and watched my clothes begin to turn red, I decided that this, coupled with the look of abject horror on the faces of my friends, was a good time to head for home. It was about five minutes away so, with hand clamped firmly to skull, and spraying blood all over the path, I made a run for it.

It was a summer's evening, and my dad was tending the garden. As I rounded the corner and appeared on the drive he saw me and dropped his trowel. My mum wasn't in, because she'd just left to go to a church meeting so naturally, my dad, left alone in charge of a broken head, hadn't got a clue what to do.

'Wha . . .?' he sort of said, which was midway between a noise and an actual word.

'I think I might have cut my head,' I said, which was kind of an understatement, given the Tarantino-esque levels of blood all over my clothes, hands and face. His eyes were saying, 'Shit. His mum is out. Our child looks like he's just staggered up the beach in *Saving Private Ryan*[17] and I have no idea what to do.'

'Wha . . .?' he said again.

---

[17] Despite *Saving Private Ryan* not making it to the big screen for another fourteen years. My dad was, and is, a visionary.

As luck would have it, Mum chose this exact moment to drive past the house. We lived on a small lane, and she'd been along it to pick up our equally church-minded neighbour to give her a lift, and was now driving back the other way. From the car, she caught sight of the *Kill Bill*-style bloodbath in the garden and screeched to a halt. One garbled explanation later and I was on the way to casualty with a towel my dad had swapped for his trowel wrapped round my head like a battle-scarred turban.

'Wha . . .?' said my dad, still standing in the garden as we drove off.

I had thirteen stitches and the top of my head was shaved into a big round bald circle like a monk. Yet after a few days off school I was back, feeling quite smug that I was wounded and thus confident that girls would take pity on me.

'Slaphead,' said Paul Bolton in the corridor, even before registration.

I had genuinely never heard the word before. It had never been said. I can only reiterate that no one at our school had ever uttered it before, and I'm pretty sure no one else in the world had either. I am making no claim as to the two words 'slap' and 'head' as separate entities but, ironically, given his general level of ignorance, I genuinely think Paul Bolton was the first (sub) human to put them together, and a whole new word was born. It was a word alloy, forged in the tepid fires that sputtered behind the dead, fishlike eyes of Paul's pointy face. Of course, there's every chance that Paul had heard it somewhere and had been keeping it back for an occasion such as this, but it was new to Higham Lane School and it spread as rapidly as the blood through one of my mum's best bath towels. By break time, everyone was on the case. I wore my stiches proudly as they peeked up through my new monk's haircut, and did what every fifteen-year-old would do in this situation, which was continue to embellish the story to girls, in the vain hope that they would get off with me.

'Fell down a cliff,' I probably said at some point, 'while I was trying to rescue a trapped kitten.'

'Foiled a bank robbery' may have been another. 'Saw three armed robbers come out of a bank, while I was trying to rescue a trapped kitten.'

'Can't talk about it. Covert intelligence'; I genuinely said this to Jennifer Bazeley, who I really, really fancied. She just looked at me as though I were mentally ill, rather than physically.

By lunchtime, my injury was a 'bullet graze' to which I added no further details in a bid to appear enigmatic, or as enigmatic as anyone can while they're queuing up for chips as their stitches begin to leak. By home time I'd ascertained that the 'kitten rescue' angle was by far the most successful one to run with, given its popularity with girls, so I cleverly hatched a plan to work on this moving and emotional story overnight, in order to build upon my newfound admiration the next day. My strategy completely failed, however, because when I got home I was sick and thus was kept off school for a week with concussion. By the time I got back, my fictional cat-saving exploits had been long forgotten, the girls having moved on to Andrew Strong who'd fractured his elbow playing rugby. I later learned he'd apparently been telling everyone that he'd done it when he temporarily left the field of play to rescue a trapped kitten. It was an amazing coincidence.

With girls, I wasn't quite so forward with the circumcision story. For a start, circumcision isn't technically an injury, and coming up with a story that a kitten could somehow have been involved in it was never going to be advisable. What *was* in my favour, I reasoned, was the school of thought that says that if you're circumcised then it's easier to delay ejaculation because there's one less thing rubbing against the sensitive underneath bit of your penis than there is for those that still have a full compliment of prepuce. In fact, I was full of misplaced confidence in this regard, believing that when it came to making sweet, sweet love with a lady, I could consistently out perform my peers. But you try telling that to Lisa Hardy.

NINE

... in which I come too quickly.

Lisa Hardy was way out of my league. She was gorgeous and had bright, sparkling eyes and long dark hair and lived on the housing estate about half a mile away. She wasn't my first girlfriend but we'd been seeing each other for a bit during our teenage years and, once again, we found ourselves upstairs in my bedroom snogging on a beanbag. It was mid-afternoon at some point in the school holidays, we were probably about sixteen, and things were getting interesting. There had certainly been kissing and more beneath my posters for *The Evil Dead* and the little-watched and long-forgotten straight-to-video Sci-Fi horror *Titan Find*, and on this occasion, if memory serves, I was mid-breast grope (over clothes) when she slid her hand down to my crotch where it would be accurate to say that I was harbouring an erection. Taking her move as a cue to progress things further, I slipped my hand under her top and went for the bra,[1] and it was at this point, way too early, that I ejaculated. And now we had a problem. Any further and she'd pretty soon find out what

---

1 I'm hoping this description of my teenage fumblings gets me at least *nominated* for the literary Bad Sex Award.

had happened and, given my subsiding gentleman's area, it was going to be sooner rather than later.

If you are, or ever have been, a man, then this is a scenario that you may well recognise. To men, the fear of premature ejaculation is generally up there with that of drowning, being buried alive, or being killed in a fire. In fact, the only thing worse than drowning, being buried alive or being killed in a fire is ejaculating prematurely while each or any of these things are happening to you. And when it does happen it is mortifying because a) you've rather killed the mood and, b) the person you're with thinks you're shit in bed. Or, as in this case, thinks you're shit on a beanbag. It's something that can, apparently, be caused by any number of factors including stress, diabetes, depression, anxiety, or, as in my case, being really horny because you are sixteen and getting off with Lisa Hardy.[2] Men live in perpetual fear of it, and that's why sometimes, when we're having sex, I'm afraid the answer to your question 'when we make love, do you ever think of anyone else?' is 'yes', but, more often than not, rather than be picturing oneself enjoying ingress to the nethers of a supermodel or that girl who works in Sales, what we're actually thinking of is anyone – *anything* – that will stave off the point of no return; Anne Widdecombe, the comedian Josh Widdicombe, Optimus Prime – quite literally, *anything* that you think will help. If you are a woman, I appreciate that it may well seem a bit strange for you to know that while your current beau is inside you, he is more than likely picturing a former MP, a cheerful, curly haired, boyish comedian and

---

2 I admit I self-diagnosed that last one.

the leader of the Autobots having a threesome, but I'm sorry to have to tell you that that's probably what's going on.

The older you get, the less you need this technique, as quite the opposite can be true. For example, after a few glasses of wine, for much of the time you'll be trying your damndest to get,[3] rather than maintain, an erection and for this you'll need access to your Wank Library.[4] Think of it like this: you could well be reading the best novel ever written, its prose beautiful, its wordplay exquisite, the curve of its spine just gorgeous to behold and trace delicately with your fingers but, try as you might, even though it's in front of you begging you to plunge in, you just can't. Instead you find yourself reading the same sentence over and over

---

3 Or 'achieve' one, as is the usual term. You might be wondering why the word 'achieve' is used when describing the arrival of an erection, given it's not used for anything else in or around our physiology. We don't 'achieve' a headache, for example, or a bowel movement, do we, so why do we 'achieve' an erection? It makes it sound like getting one is akin to climbing Everest. Although after a few too many glasses of sémillion, it could well be.

4 An oft-visited vast resource — a private collection, really – with which every man is familiar, the Wank Library (aka Wank Bank), is where one holds both an enormous catalogue of stills and moving images both from films and real life, from any sexual experiences that we may have ever had. If, ladies, you've ever wondered why a man is often quite keen that a light is left on somewhere during what an instruction leaflet for Durex would term 'love play', well, that's because of the library. It can be a bedside light, the flicker of a TV screen, or even the light from a hallway or bathroom playing delicately over the scene; we don't mind, as long as we can see stuff. And later, in quiet moments alone (or even in emergency situations of togetherness) we can draw upon any of these scenes. For balance, I should point out that I've asked around and women, it seems, on occasion, tend to do much the same, so happily the Wank Library doesn't have any kind of limited membership policy.

again. Instead you find yourself reading the same sentence over and over again. Instead you find yourself reading the same sentence over and over again. Instead you find yourself reading the same sentence over and over again, unable to proceed. Rather than enjoying this magnificent work, mentally you somehow find yourself drawn to Dan Brown or John Grisham, something easy to read and fun while it lasts, able to satisfy in one, quick forgettable hit. Once, on a summer holiday away from university, my reading list included an Ibsen, a couple of Dickens, an Austen or two and a Charlotte Brontë. I could see the appeal of Charlotte Brontë – she almost had me at 'Reader, I married him' – but try as I might I failed to be completely aroused by her words, and instead kept remembering bits of *Pet Sematary* by Stephen King. Sometimes I would almost be there with Charlotte and especially her sister Emily, because she'd had the nous to at least put a ghost into *Wuthering Heights* to liven it up, but still my mind would wander, I'd lose the thread of where I was up to, and instead find myself picturing the gruesome return of a dead cat.

(I've just read that paragraph back, and I realise that I have just written the worst analogy for 'trying to have sex' in the history of writing, ever. For the record, I have never had sexual intercourse while thinking of a dead cat. Although now I've written this, next time it'll probably be all I think of. If you're a man reading this, feel free to borrow the mental image for your own use. Throw it in there with Widdecombe and Widdicombe and Optimus Prime. You're welcome.)

Back to the beanbag where I have an issue, in both senses of the word. Lisa is expectant and I have just come in my pants. Do I also come clean, or do I take drastic action? There are two ways of dealing with this.[5] Option one is to physically move downwards, towards the area usually reserved for 'oral sex'. That way your rapidly becoming-flaccid penis moves out of reach, thus buying you some time, preferably long enough to coax yourself back to life. This also has the advantage that your partner thinks you are very keen on – and happy to take quite a long time over – orally pleasuring them. Ladies, if you're reading, I realise that, again, if you'll pardon the expression, I am somewhat 'lifting the curtain' on something that you always assumed to be the actions of a gentle and considerate lover. Don't get me wrong, most times it is, but I promise you, there's been more than one occasion when he's moved out of your reach for fear of going off too early. Yet in this particular situation, we were both still pretty much fully dressed and hadn't even progressed as far as bra undoing, so I didn't think option one was an option. Which is why I plumped for option two.

'I just need the toilet,' I said.

'OK,' said Lisa.

I left the bedroom and walked the length of the landing. Safely in the upstairs toilet, I checked the damage. I was wearing bleached jeans, quite tight, because at this time in my life I wanted to be Jon Bon Jovi. The problem was that there was a wet patch on the front of them and it was blindingly obvious what it was. Toilet paper or a hand towel would be useless as neither would dry the area quickly nor

---

5 Three, actually, if you count owning up, but who the hell is going to take that as an option?

effectively in the time I had, so there was only one thing for it; I was going to have to make everything wetter. And that's why I turned on the tap and deliberately and quite methodically splashed my groin area with handfuls of water. Now I just looked like I'd pissed myself, which I genuinely considered to be less embarrassing than the alternative. I checked myself in the mirror and went back to the bedroom.

'Bloody taps,' I said. 'I turned them on and the water came out really fast and splashed all over my trousers, look . . .' I indicated the spreading crotch stain. Lisa looked at the trousers, reached under her top to pop herself back into her bra and adjusted her skirt.

'I'd better be going,' she said. She'd known all along what had happened, and me trying to get out of it with the lamest, most obvious excuse in the world had now brought my hopes and dreams of ever being with Lisa Hardy crashing down. The only thing getting blown in this fledgling relationship anytime soon was my chances of being Lisa Hardy's proper boyfriend, and all I was left with was the memory of a maroon-coloured bra[6] and anger at my own loins.

---

6 Don't for one moment think that that bra isn't in the Wank Library, because it certainly is.

TEN

...in which I get my first proper girlfriend.

If the concept of a Sex Tape had been invented in the early eighties and Lisa and I had been making one, it's fair to say that I didn't even last long enough for it to have made a decent Vine. Yet this formative, humiliating, early sexual experience still wasn't the most embarrassing that I was to have; that was to come later in 1986,[1] thanks to the fledgling TV network, Channel 4, designating that year to be that of the Red Triangle.

Four years previously, UK television had got its fourth button and with it came the promise of edgier comedy, edgier music programmes, edgier soap operas and edgier everything, and it spoke straight to us because we were teenagers and thought it was all cool. Before long the late, great Rik Mayall and Ade Edmondson were a brilliant, hilarious, dangerous thing, Jools Holland popped up to say 'Groovy Fucker' on live TV, *Brookside* had shoved someone under a patio and had a pre-watershed lesbian kiss and Richard Whiteley's word game *Countdown* had Carol Vorderman picking letters which, in one memorable episode had inadvertently spelt

---

1 Auto-erotic Rock Bottom. It's finally here.

out the whole paragraph of *American Psycho* where Patrick Bateman does something unspeakable with a rat.[2] But then, finally, after all those years of smut-smuggled Smarties' tubes and scrabbling round for scraps of porn mags gathered like nuts in May from hedges, suddenly, in 1986, Channel 4 properly opened the doors to my adolescence. And those doors were in the shape of a red triangle.

For the uninitiated, the 'Red Triangle' was a cheap gimmick which took the form of a geometric warning in the top right-hand corner of the screen to indicate that the programme or film it was superimposed on contained 'explicit adult content'. They'd done it in the guise of a 'Censorship Season', back when Channel 4 was interesting (before they'd cluttered their airwaves with programmes like *Big Brother*, or something with one of the Carrs,[3] or *My 40-Stone Hairy Gypsy Tumour*) and, as sixteen- and seventeen-year-olds, it was music to our horny eyes. The idea was that they'd show films with nudity in late at night, but deploy the triangle in advance, so you knew when to stay up. It was damn handy, like having a wank alarm.

'Red triangle tonight,' we'd say at school. Let me reiterate, there was no Internet back then.

'What is it?'

'Something foreign. Film. Possibly French.'

'Sounds promising.'

---

2 I may have misremembered this. It may simply have been an accidental mild swearword.

3 Alan or Jimmy. Doesn't really matter which. Both much of a muchness. Not Maxine though.

And then we'd go home, those with televisions in their bedrooms all smug, those without relying on a plan to surreptitiously set their parents' video recorders and hope they wouldn't notice. Or, like me, you'd make a bid for staying up.

'Les, have you locked up?'

It was Friday night and my mum was asking Dad if he'd secured the property, thereby signifying bedtime. For them.

'I thought I'd stay up for a bit,' I said. 'There's a film on.'

'OK. Make sure the dog is shut in the kitchen before you come up. Goodnight.' And with that, off they went, leaving me and Channel 4 to get better acquainted.

Often the films weren't fit for purpose. For a start, there was little or no consistency. One week you could be faced with something curious from the Japanese art house circuit, the next a worthy, impenetrable, slow-moving piece based on a letter received from a schizophrenic woman as she writes about her life, but occasionally there was a gem. On this occasion, I don't recall the name of the film, but I do remember that it had subtitles and no small amount of full-frontal female nudity – it seemed my luck was in. It was one o'clock in the morning, and in the Holmes' household, all was quiet. The volume on the TV was low, on the screen a lady was standing naked in the snow, and in my parents' lounge, I had my erect penis in my hand. And that is the point at which I heard the stairs creak.

The stairs were in the hall, the bottom step was right outside the lounge door, and I knew the creaky stair to be the fourth or fifth one from the bottom, which meant I had approximately three more stairs before my mum was on-site. I had three steps to maintain my dignity. I failed. Hurriedly, I tried to put my erection back into my pants while simultaneously trying to pull my trousers up and change channel. Any man will tell you that this is no mean feat, which is why I'd only made it halfway when my mum came into the room. Time stopped. We both froze as she looked first at a half-naked me, and then at the TV. All the horror of the pants-in-the-post incident of the year before came flooding back, and I was struck dumb by the horror of what was happening. My mum looked at my boxer shorts that, like the Grand Old Duke of York, were neither up nor down, and while I may have seen a flicker of gratitude that they weren't girls pants and that I still wasn't a transvestite, it was short-lived. She looked at the TV again. In all honesty, the only successful part of the cover-up operation had been for me to have time to change the channel, so what my mum was now looking at was her only son openly masturbating to Pages From Ceefax. A sort of 'fnnnnr' noise escaped from me and after that it was silent; a nightmarish tableau of hideous humiliation involving a boy, his mum and a pixelated yellow and blue weather map of the UK. There was nothing to say. Nothing I could do. What I'd been doing was obvious. It was, quite literally, out in the open.

But my mum then spoke eight words that have never left me: eight simple words that will haunt me for the rest of my days; eight words that I will never forget, and that are seared into my soul.

'Don't get any on the sofa,' she said.

And, with that, she turned round and went back upstairs. I never found out what she came down for in the first place, but what I do know is that she will have gone back upstairs and told my dad what she'd just witnessed. Needless to say, he never mentioned it.

My first proper girlfriend was from church youth club. In fact, my first few girlfriends were all from the church, rather than school, and I think it helped my adolescent development because the church youth club had various activities and weekends away that leant themselves handily towards youthful sexual experimentation. We weren't Catholic, we were Methodist, so it wasn't like the church leaders were trying it on as well, but I have to say their level of care, while exemplary on one level, left a lot to be desired in the middle of the night when everyone was fingering everyone else in sleeping bags on a dusty church hall floor in Chilvers Coton.

We were all at it. On the surface we were all dutiful teenage churchgoers who would meet on Friday nights at youth club or Sundays at Sunday School and then, later, when some well-intentioned youth leader thought we were all so into the God stuff, rather than just into each other, that he organised Bible Studies on a Sunday evening in his own house. We'd all turn up, look at the story of Joshua for a bit, and then snog each other's faces off when he went to the kitchen to put the kettle on. My friend Wayne undid his first bra[4] in the Bible-study leader's downstairs toilet while

---

4 I don't mean his own. It belonged to someone called Jo. She was wearing it, not him.

he was supposed to be applying an academic application of a set of diverse disciplines to John 13:34–35. Although, to be fair, that's the bit of the Bible that urges you to 'love one another', so in many ways he was just doing his bit.

For my own part, I was 'courting' (my mum's word, not mine) a girl called Jenny. Jenny was a few months younger than me, yet infinitely more experienced. Well, she wasn't at first, but then she suddenly was. One summer, Jenny and family went on holiday for a week. When she left, Jenny and I were in love; innocently virginal, holding hands and kissing in a slow-motion, romantic notion sort of a way like we'd seen on TV. We'd spent the summer together, laughing, living and looking at the world with the eternal naivety of youth. Neither of us had fumbled with anything of each other's at this point, no body parts had been touched, we were unsullied by fluids; just young, innocent and carefree. That all changed when she came back from holiday. The Jenny I'd known seven days previously had disappeared and had been replaced, *Invasion of the Body Snatchers*-style, by some kind of sultry sex goddess. Almost overnight she'd gone from *Pollyanna* meets Anne from *The Famous Five* to *Fifty Shades of Grey* meets the Wife of Bath. And I found this out in a hurry when, going in for the first peck on the cheek upon her return, she took my hand and put it on her breast. For the first time, I had an actual girl's breast in my boy's hand. It was through clothes, granted, but suddenly every vague sexual experience I'd ever had up to that point in my life so far sort of simultaneously tracked back and zoomed in to this one single moment, like my life was a shot being directed by Martin Scorsese. There were the contents of Paul

Harvey's dad's wardrobe, there was me looking at pictures of lesbians in a bin in the rain, there's the damage to my parents' sofa, the pants under the mattress, the horrific picture of a vagina with a lump on it in one of my mum's textbooks that I had to squint not to see when ejaculating – everything. And all because there was an ACTUAL boob present, and I was cupping it.

Of course, I wasn't an idiot; I knew immediately what had happened. Something had occurred during the holiday. And over the next week or so it became quite clear what that something had been. Very quickly, at Jenny's instigation, we'd moved on from over-clothes boob touching to under bra boob touching, something new she decided to introduce while we were in the back of her parents' car on the way to a barn dance. *Dance, then, wherever you may be, I'm touching boob in a car said He.* I won't bore you with the details, but we got away with it due to a strategically placed car blanket, a feigning of sleep (this was in the days before compulsory rear seat belts) and Jenny's sheer balls. Hers were sheer, mine were going into overdrive, and her mum and dad were centimetres away, sitting in the front of their Vauxhall. On the way back from the barn dance, she did it all over again, but this time she took my hand and put it up her skirt. *And lo, the Angels sang that night. She will lead us all, wherever we may be, for I am Hot Girlfriend of the (barn) dance said She.*

Before long we graduated to having actual fumbling teenage sex. To paraphrase Meat Loaf, we were barely seventeen and, throughout that entire summer, we were barely dressed.

We used to do it in our parents' houses; upstairs, downstairs – wherever there was an opportunity to slip into the ladies' chamber, we took it, often under the guise of 'going up to the bedroom to play Yahtzee'.[5] I lost my virginity on a beanbag next to a pair of Yahtzee scorecards which were, appropriately enough, divided into both upper and lower sections with points awarded depending on which of the sections you scored highly in. Jenny and I always had Yahtzee standing by, just in case we heard anyone coming upstairs and we had to fake it to make it look like we were halfway through a game. Once, Jenny came for a sleepover, and I was told in no uncertain terms by my mum that she was going in the spare room.

'Oh, come on, Mum, why's she got to be in the spare room? We're not going to do anything. We'll just play Yahtzee.'

My mum eyed her adolescent son in exactly the same way that a lioness might eye her cub if he'd just promised to play nicely with the gazelle, rather than eat it.

'Spare room. And I'll be keeping my ear out.'

To be fair, I wasn't unduly worried by Mum's security plans. After all, we'd been doing it on a beanbag in my bedroom for weeks and were the very model of discretion. And it was nothing compared to what was, if you'll pardon the expression, to come.

Sleepover night arrived and the sexual tension was high. There was some polite chit-chat with Mum and Dad in the

---

5 Yahtzee was (and still is) a dice game which gave you various combinations of ways to score. Worked for us.

lounge, possibly a bit of telly, and then it was time for bed. There may not have been Yahtzee, but the dice had been rolled, the stakes were high and a game of skill and chance was about to begin. I'll be honest – I had no real plan. Jenny was still very much in control of our sexual revolution and I was more than happy with that arrangement, the ball and my balls, were very much in her court. Her genius idea, such as it was, was to wait until my parents were asleep and then sneak into my room. Admittedly, as plans go it wasn't exactly up there with George Clooney's in *Ocean's Eleven*, but given our track record of 'being quite sneaky', we were confident of success. In my room, I stayed awake, probably read a book,[6] and waited. It goes without saying that I promptly fell asleep, only to be woken, some time later, by the voice of my mother.

'What do you think you're doing?'

It wasn't directed at me, and was coming from the landing, outside my bedroom door.

---

6 Around this time it may well have been something by James Herbert, or the *Fifth Armada Book of Ghost Stories*, which was the one with the skeleton riding a horse on the front. I was very into ghosts and ghost hunting at this age, and the Armada and Pan short story collections were required reading. In the one with the skeletal jockey, there was a story called 'Uncle Jim' by Martin Ricketts about a boy who is helped home in thick fog by a kindly old man, who explains that fog is actually made up of a mass of earthbound ghosts who mean the living no harm. To this day, thanks to the Fifth Armada Ghost Book, I still think of this whenever it's foggy. I also think of James Herbert's *The Fog*, which contains a scene where his own students, driven insane by the dangerous mist, strap a screaming naked PE teacher to the climbing bars in the school hall and cut his erection off with garden shears. Lying in bed waiting for Jenny to make her move, this was not a scene I needed to read.

'Erm, looking for the toilet?' I heard Jenny say.

'I know exactly what you were looking for. Get back into your room at once,' said my mum who, it later transpired, had heard Jenny's room door open and floorboards squeak.

And that was it for that night. Next day, after Jenny had gone home, my mum said:

'I caught Jenny trying to sneak into your room last night.'

'Did you?' I said, mustering as much of an innocent tone as I could, but probably sounding like the caretaker in Scooby Doo being caught red-handed under a sheet making ghost noises.

'Had you arranged that?' she asked.

'No!' I protested, doth too much.

'She wasn't wearing very much,' pondered my mother.

What? What fresh hell was this? What was going on? What game was my mum playing? She'd stopped anything from happening, yet was now toying with me, and my unsatiated love, by giving me mental images of my scantily clad girlfriend.

'Just a tiny nightie.'

I knew what she was doing. Trying to get me to confess by deploying psychological warfare.

'It's just that you need to be sensible.'

Oh shit. I had inadvertently walked into the 'birds and the bees' chat.

'Mum!' I said.

'I'm just saying. If you are thinking about that kind of thing then you both need to be sensible about it.'

Shit, shit, *shit*. Don't say 'protection'. I do NOT want to hear my own mother say 'protection'.

'Protection,' she said, and looked at me, pointedly.

In actual fact, we hadn't been sensible. Not at all. What we had been was lucky, so she had a point. In the ensuing few months Jenny's younger sister caught us partially clothed in the laundry room at her house, and we had a narrow escape at my house when my dad came home unexpectedly and we didn't hear him because we were playing my new vinyl picture disc of Iron Maiden's 'Two Minutes To Midnight' very loudly in my bedroom. And then something happened that made the old previous back-of-the-car-under-a-travel-rug scenario look like the work of amateurs. And thinking about it now, I can scarcely believe it happened.

It was a Sunday lunchtime. I know this, because I'd been to church, my group of friends doing the whole social youth group stuff even on a Sunday morning. There was Fat Kev, currently wooing Caroline,[7] Paul 'Bones' Jones and Dawn, Wayne and Jo (which was also Wayne and Laura, Wayne and Cheryl and Wayne and Heather), Steve and Karen, Leon and Catherine, another Steve and another Dawn, the same Steve and a Sarah and me and everyone had gone to church because it gave us a chance to snog each other in one or two of the anterooms upstairs while all parents and supervisory

---

7 Thanks to her descriptions of his sexual technique, his nickname for a short time was 'Octopus'. During his court case in 2013, it transpired that the disgraced entertainer and artist Rolf Harris was also given this nickname by a number of women who were unfortunate enough to have crossed his path. In both cases, I think – I *hope* – that this shared nickname came about because their 'hands are everywhere' rather than the fact that either of them squirted ink.

adults were downstairs drinking post service coffee and iron-ically discussing the all-seeing nature of God.

It's fair to say that the last time I'd seen Jenny things had become quite amorous and, as luck would have it (or not, as it happened) after church I was due to go over her par-ents' house for Sunday lunch. Upon arrival, we announced that we were going upstairs to play Yahtzee. And so it was that with her mum and dad downstairs busying themselves with roast potatoes and carving chicken respectively, and Jenny's two younger sisters elsewhere, we got to a point where all systems were go. Jenny was wearing a flowing sort of Sunday-best dress, I was in smart trousers and, keeping all of our clothes in place as best we could, she unzipped my trousers, pulled her knickers aside and strad-dled me as I lay back and, to continue the Yahtzee theme, rolled a six.

It was at that point that her mum walked in.[8]

Now. This was awkward. Bear in mind that, while things possibly looked *mildly* intimate from her mum's perspective, we were fortuitous that, as I was lying on my back, Jenny's flowing dress was covering everything from my sternum to my knees and, to all intents and purposes, it looked like she was just sitting on me; two star-crossed lovers who were having a good-natured wrestle and a tussle over a popular dice-based game. What she couldn't see – and certainly wouldn't have guessed in her wildest dreams – was that her

---

8 This was getting to be a habit. First my mum during Channel 4's Red Triangle season and now this.

daughter had suddenly tensed up to the point where I was trapped in her and couldn't have moved even if I'd wanted to. What I found myself in now was the unenviable situation of having to have a difficult conversation about what cut of meat I'd prefer for lunch, while fully engaged in the act of sexual intercourse with the chef's daughter. In all honesty, as situations go, I don't recommend it.

'What are you two up to?' she said, half smiling.

'Nothing!' we both said, a bit too quickly.

'Well, get off him, Jenny, because it's time to sit up for lunch.'

It's fair to say that if Jenny had chosen to get off at this time, revealing the spectacle beneath, all her mother's thoughts of lunch would probably have been forgotten.

'Come on, come downstairs,' she said.

What the hell did we do now? Was she going to stand there and wait for us to come downstairs? There was no possible way to get out of this unnoticed. We were bang to rights. Jenny, as ever, took control.

'Not until he admits that I won,' she said indicating the nearby Yahtzee scorecards and pencils, and began to mock fight with me, retaining her overall position yet having to move around quite a lot in order to back up the story.

If you are a man, you can see how this only served to ex-acerbate the problem. My problem, at any rate. The trouble was that we were young and stupid and despite my mum's earlier advice the morning after SneakyLandingGate, I still wasn't wearing a condom, and we'd been happily practis-ing the withdrawal method up until this point. Like I said, we were stupid.⁹ Stupid, stupid, stupid. But right now, at this point, my girlfriend was writhing on top of me and I couldn't pull out because her mum was standing four feet away talking about breasts and thighs.¹⁰ Moments later, I was at the point of no return and as her mum turned to leave I, with unbelievably lucky timing, quickly removed myself and ejaculated to the sound of the door closing and a middle-aged woman saying 'Let me know if you want gravy.'

On all levels, we got away with it. Years later, Jenny married a vicar. They're still together and I went to the wedding. The Lord, just like me in that bedroom many years before, moves in mysterious ways.

---

9 In our defence, this was just before the notion of safe sex went mainstream to people our age. Sure, we had sex education at school but back then it was all a bit half-hearted and the biology textbooks mainly consisted of line drawings of downy hair. Although, given what we learned earlier regarding my adolescent penchant for academic textbooks, that worked fine for me, obviously. Soon afterwards, because of the mid-eighties Aids' crisis, the Government put leaflets through our doors warning us not to 'die of ignorance', and then Radio 1 (now sadly the late) DJ Mike Smith was on early evening television demonstrating exactly how to put a condom on. I should stress that he used a cucumber. Yes, the Aids crisis arguably made us less prudish as a nation but, like the artists in the schoolbook, you have to draw the line somewhere.
10 Of chicken. But at this stage it didn't matter.

ELEVEN

. . . in which I meet my sister for the first time. And she sees a ghost.

I have a sister who, to the uninitiated, appears to be a typo. We first met Kelda back in Chapter Five and that is genuinely her name, rather than an onomatopoeic word for the sound that someone involuntarily makes when they release a piece of food that they're choking on during the Heimlich manoeuvre. Furthermore, my parents chose the name all on their own, without any help from hallucinatory drugs and/or choking on a meal they were eating while leafing through a baby names' book. Kelda is four years younger than me[1] and isn't, in fact, my real sister by blood, because she, like me, is adopted. She was born in 1972, under similar circumstances to me, and came to live with us in Magyar Crescent where, as soon as she could walk, she did so face first into the brick surround of the fireplace. I was actually involved in the

---

1 Unless, that is, you read Wikipedia, where simple maths says that my younger sister is six years older than me. That's because Wikipedia, at time of writing, says I was born in 1978, which I patently wasn't. I hasten to add that this age lie is not of my doing, but the regular doing of my friend Gary who, each year on 24th April shoves my Wikipedia birthday back a year as a present and then texts me 'Happy 36th Birthday'. Every year. I have been thirty-six for years. Kelda is livid about this.

choosing process this time, in that as part of the adoption process, our family had a visit from a man called Mr Oakley who was a social worker and in charge of the procedure. It was an important visit, and would determine my mum and dad's suitability to adopt a second child, although, given that they had managed to keep me alive for four years so far, the signs that they could cope were all good. And so it was that the house was dusted and hoovered, everyone was in their Sunday best,[2] the biting, yappy dog that we owned that hated human beings was shut in the kitchen and all was well. Mr Oakley began by asking the usual questions beloved of social services:

1. 'Do you routinely beat this child?'
2. 'Do you hate children, generally?'
3. 'Are you aware that if the answer to either or both of the above questions is "yes", then, being social services, we won't take any action until it's too late?'

He liked the answers that he heard, which were, in order:

1. No.
2. No.

---

2 Is 'Sunday best' still a thing? Most Sundays I tend to potter around in my slobbiest stuff and would happily spend the day in my pants. Sunday best is probably something to do with going to church, as, in my experience, vicars tend to frown upon an unshaven man, smelling of last night's beer, scratching his bollocks through his Calvins in the pews.

3. Is that supposed to be a bit of cack-handed satire written by our son in his memoir forty years from now?

And then turned his attention to me.

'Hello,' he said.

'Hello,' I said and hid behind my mum's leg.

'You must be Jonathan?'

I didn't answer him.

'Do you like living with your mummy and daddy?'

For any parent, this must have been an awful moment. What if I'd said, even as a joke, 'No. They routinely beat me and they hate children'?

'Yes,' I said.

'And would you like a little sister?'

'Yes,' I said, again. And I meant it, too. It seemed like a great idea to me.

'Good,' he said, and ticked a box on a form.

My in-depth interview over, he turned his attention back to Mum and Dad and I wandered off into the kitchen. I have absolutely no recollection of what happened next, I can only go on my parents' reminiscence of the whole thing, but the scenario that was about to unfold could, given that a man from the adoption agency was grilling them on their child-care techniques, have been better timed. What happened was that I walked back into the lounge holding a large carving knife.

In his overview of the Holmes' household, this immediately presented Mr Oakley with three potential scenarios.

1) I was allowed by my parents to play with large carving knives.
2) I had somehow got hold of a large carving knife on my own.
3) He was seeing things.

For would-be parents, there's pretty much no worse time for your first adopted child to walk into a room with a large carving knife than when you're being interviewed about taking on a second one by the man from social services. The only other time it could be worse is if, midway through making sweet, sweet love to your spouse, your bedroom door swings open to reveal your four-year-old child called Damien silhouetted in the moonlight holding up the knife and lamenting in a child's whisper 'tonight it is time to die'. Scenarios one and two (above) were not good, and only scenario number three could pull this one back from the brink.

Mr Oakley dismissed scenario three almost instantly, mainly on the grounds that I was tapping the blade of the knife against the wall. That left him with two possible explanations, neither of which I suspect he felt he was going to like. Mum was the first to speak:

'He's never done this before,' she said.

It was, she assures me, the truth. I had never at any point before this moment gone into the kitchen, pushed a stool over to a drawer, opened it, and taken out a carving knife. In fact, it was the first time I had touched a knife of any kind, and neither were carving knives left out, willy-nilly, for children to stumble across and become inquisitive about. But of course, right here, right now, in this awkward situation,

Mum's explanation sounded like the worst kind of absolute bollocks.

'Hmm,' said Mr Oakley.

'It's a one-off,' she said. 'We'll be more careful in future. It's not like our next one is going to walk face first into the brick surround of the fireplace.'

She must have been convincing because with everyone still alive and no real harm done, Mr Oakley ticked another box, and, in October 1972, my sister Melanie arrived, promptly had her name changed to the inexplicable 'Kelda', and thus it was that for the next decade the Holmes family set about getting on with their lives as a four-piece. That is until Mum and Dad sat us down one day because they wanted to 'talk to us about something important'. And when mums and dads say that, it really only means one thing. I was thirteen and Kelda was ten. We nervously glanced at each other, expecting divorce. But we got something else entirely.

The previous time they'd sat us down to tell us 'something important' was when I was eight and Kelda was four and it had been bad news. We were being forced to move out of our house, the house at Magyar Crescent that my dad had built for my mum.

'We have to move,' my mum explained, and her tone was one of urgency. Naturally, I immediately assumed we were being haunted and that overnight, Kelda had seen the glowing eyes of a demon pig in the garden, flies had infested the windows, the walls had begun to bleed and the voice of an unseen entity had whispered 'Get out!' at the priest brought in to cleanse the place.[3] But no. Although it turned out that the clergy was indeed involved.

'Your dad has been building a church in Bedworth but because the cost of materials for the floor – special wood from Canada – has doubled in price since the contracts were signed it means his company is liable, which means that we have had to get an overdraft from the bank, which involves the mortgage on the house, and now the bank want the money back and we don't have the money because the church won't help out financially, so what's happened is that we have no money, and if we don't sell the house to pay the bank back they'll take it anyway and we'll have nothing, and we've been trying but we just can't fix it and now we have to move house,' she said. It all came out in a rush and I could see she'd been crying. Kelda looked mournfully at her cuddly rabbit, not because either of us knew what a contract or a mortgage was, but we could tell that whatever was going on, it wasn't a good thing.

'I've had to sell all the diggers and things,' said my dad. At this time, he had a couple of JCBs and a dumper truck that I especially liked to climb on and play inside its bucket, once more laughing in the face of all known health-and-safety laws. For Mr Oakley, it would've been up there with the carving knife.

'Where will we go?' asked Kelda.

'I don't know,' said Mum, and burst into tears.

It was pretty bad. I didn't understand any of it but I knew that it was serious. In the end we were forced to move in

3 Like out of *The Amityville Horror*.

with Nana Smith, Mum's mum, who had a two-bedroom bungalow. My sister and I approached the whole thing with a childlike sense of acceptance and thought it quite the adventure; besides which we loved Nana Smith and what's more she bought us comics and made the best scrambled egg we'd ever tasted. For three months Kelda and I slept in the same bed in the spare room while Mum and Dad were on makeshift beds in the lounge. And it was somewhere around this time that Kelda started to see things.

I don't believe in ghosts. From an early age I really wanted to; I was fascinated with the whole notion of the supernatural and would devour any and every book on the subject. If I wasn't reading *Ghosts of Wales* that I bought from a teashop on one of our holidays to Snowdonia then I was reading *Ghosts of Norfolk*, that I bought from a teashop on one of our holidays to Cromer. At sixteen, I applied to join the Society for Psychical Research, not because I thought I could help, but I'd read they held an archive of ghost sightings to rival no other.[4] At this stage, I was desperate to see a ghost, so was particularly annoyed when my sister did.

I'd like to say maybe it was something she inherited from my mum, except of course Mum wasn't our real mum, and as far as I know (unless something supernatural *is* at work) you can't inherit physical traits from someone you're not actually properly related to. It's simply a coincidence, rather than genetics, that Kelda and I share both hair colour and

---

4 They wouldn't let me join. I got a polite letter back saying that I had to be eighteen or over, as if seeing ghosts was up there with drinking beer or buying pornography.

a capacity to annoy each other in equal measure. Yet Mum had a history of seeing things too. Her dad (our grandad, of course) had died when she was sixteen, long before we arrived, and she still tells the story of waking, a few days after his death, to see him sitting on the end of the bed looking at her. This bed. The bed that Kelda and I were sharing eighteen years later. Of course, I would now, with hindsight, pass off my mum's childhood experience as the trauma of her father's death manifesting itself as a dream, perceived in her grief as a real event. Yet now the bed was being haunted again.

Kelda was close to Auntie Gladys. We both were. Technically, she was our great-aunt, being Nana's sister, but given that both Mum and Dad hadn't any siblings, we tended to skip a generation and call her our aunt too. She was brilliant. She was all ice cream and cake and antimacassars and had a carefree attitude that said, 'What the hell, I'm babysitting tonight, let's all stay up and watch *Dallas.*' I had no interest whatsoever in *Dallas*, but she allowed us to stay up, secretly, when we should've been in bed, so she was all right by me. And then she died. And then Kelda saw her again a few weeks later.

It wasn't quite a demon pig in the garden, like in *The Amittyville Horror*, but I remember it well. I was asleep and, sometime in the middle of the night, I awoke to the sound of screaming. What happened next was confusing, but I remember Kelda saying she'd woken up because she felt something on the bed. She'd turned over to look and there, sitting on the end, was a figure.

'I knew it was Auntie Gladys,' she said.

'How?' I asked, ever the psychic investigator.

'I just did. It was *her*. She was wearing the sort of clothes Auntie Gladys would wear[5] and a headscarf that was covering her head.'

Auntie Gladys famously, in our family, had often worn a rain hood too. It was really just a flimsy bit of shapeless plastic that came in a packet which had two ties on it that did up under her chin, but she wore it irrespective of whether it was raining, looked like rain, or if someone had said the word 'rain' in polite conversation. It lived in her handbag, and sometimes I used it as a parachute for my action man.

'Was it her rain hood?' I said.

'*NO!*' said Kelda, with some emphatic force. 'It was a headscarf. Auntie Gladys' headscarf. And then she turned to look at me, and she had no face.'

So that's when I shit myself. As I say, I loved ghosts and the notion of them and was longing to see one because, y'know, how cool would *that* be? But this was a step too far. There had been a thing with no face on the bed.

'If it was Auntie Gladys, she loves you,' said Mum, in what she hoped was an encouraging tone after she and Dad had come running in at the sound of the screaming. 'She wouldn't mean you any harm.'

I figured that no one present – apart from me – was considering the possibility that it hadn't been Auntie Gladys. In my head, it had been a demon from the netherworld.

---

5 Old people's clothes, I guess. Something nice yet robust and practical from M&S.

'If it was Auntie Gladys,' I asked, to my mind not unreasonably, 'why didn't she have a face?'

'Are you sure she didn't have a face?' said my mum to Kelda. It was two o'clock in the morning. Even though I was looking round nervously, I was aware that this was a bizarre conversation to be having.

'She had her back to me, and then she turned to look at me except she didn't have a face,' repeated my sister, firmly.

For the next two weeks my dad slept in the room because Kelda refused to. To the best of my knowledge, Auntie Gladys didn't show up again. Not until she came back to stroke my mum's neck, six years later.

TWELVE

. . . in which I buy a belt with the word 'Whitesnake' embossed on it, and another sister arrives.

Though he never got his business back to where it had been prior to the intervention of the Lord's desire to have expensive, price-fluctuating Canadian cedar wood installed in His church in Bedworth, and despite us losing the roof over our heads because of God's floor, my dad soon had us all back on our feet. He'd found a house about two miles away from our old one that was a two-up, two-down old quarryman's cottage that hadn't had anyone living in it for thirty years and, when I was taken to see it, was a soot-filled shithole with a tiny garden so overgrown that Dad had to use the aforementioned scythe to get to the front door. It was our new home.

Still living at Nana's, my builder dad set about Number One Quarry Lane with a vengeance and within a few months we had a clean, warm, smart house with new rooms, open fires and a garden that was no longer coming in through the walls. And it was here that dead Auntie Gladys turned up again.

The reason she popped by a second time was because Kelda and I had been seated for the second time, in front of Mum and Dad to hear 'something important'. But this time it was good news: Mum, at the age of forty-three, was pregnant.

While neither Kelda nor I could claim to be experts in the field of biology, we knew enough to know this was unusual, largely because we were both well aware that we'd been adopted 'because Mummy and Daddy couldn't have children of their own'. We also knew enough to understand the concept of being pregnant and how to become it, which meant that we were now faced with two simultaneous thoughts, 1) We were going to have to share our mum and dad with a child of their own making and, 2) We had to contend with the mental image of them having sex.

'We didn't think we could have children,' said Mum. 'So, when your dad and I make love we don't use contracept—'

I didn't hear the rest because, obviously, my mind was now going 'Ewwwwwwww' at both a frequency and pitch high enough to drown out the sound of her voice until she'd stopped. While one shudders with horror at the thought of hearing your parents actually have sex, believe me when I tell you that having them talk to you about their barrier methods does nothing to sugar that particular pill, if you'll pardon the expression. Essentially, they'd gone for years throwing caution to the sexual wind[1] due to the whole unable-to-conceive issue they'd had back when they'd chosen to go down the adoption route, and now either Dad's sperm or Mum's eggs had decided they had lain dormant long enough, and now

---

[1] This was way before Jenny and I were throwing similar caution to the wind. You'd think that I'd have learned from my parents' similar lackadaisical attitude, and its baby-shaped consequences, but apparently not. Like I said, I'm an idiot.

was the time for them to rise from the depths to wreak havoc on Kelda and I.[2]

'. . . will make no difference to how we feel about you,' she finished. 'We're still a family.' I hadn't heard the middle part of her speech because of the screeching noise in my head.

Yet we were still a family, and closer than ever. Over the next few months Kelda and I became quite excited about the whole thing, while my dad wandered around looking confused and shell-shocked in equal measure. This went on for the requisite nine months, and then, in September 1983, when I was fourteen and Kelda almost eleven, Victoria Jane Holmes arrived, and I'd love to tell you that because she was their natural child, and Kelda and I were not, they immediately formed a bond with her that we could not even hope to emulate. I'd like to maybe here introduce an element of woe to this otherwise jaunty tale, perhaps relating that, on Vicky's arrival, Mum and Dad turfed we two orphans out into the cold and that the rest of this book is now made up of the true story of our survival; me turning tricks for oil rig workers on shore leave and Kelda selling matches to the gentry on the streets before freezing to death in a doorway. I'm only too aware that that's the kind of thing that sells books, but sadly none of that happened. Instead, Mum had been right, it didn't make the slightest difference to how we all were, we just widened the familial embrace to welcome Vicky to the Family Holmes, something I contributed to very early on by complementing her Babygro with a studded belt with

---

2 I appear to have just compared my own mother's womb lining to Godzilla. Again, I don't care how many memoirs you've read, I bet that's a first.

the heavy metal band Whitesnake's logo embossed on it, that I'd bought from the indoor market.

So it was shortly before the arrival of Vicky that Auntie Gladys popped by to say 'Hello' again, despite being not alive anymore. She didn't greet all of us; she didn't suddenly apparate during Christmas dinner or join us on a family day out to the zoo, her no-face worrying the lemurs and her ghostly rain hood making the impalas nervous. Instead she chose to visit my mum, who believes in this sort of thing and occasionally gets 'feelings' about various situations. Even now, occasionally she will ring up just to see if I am still alive, having had a 'feeling' or a dream that I am not. So far, I have always been alive when she's called, which rather makes a mockery of any so-called evidence of her powers, but who knows, one day she might call just as I'm choking on a sandwich, being hit by lightning or being shot while involved in heavy front-line insurgent infighting in a Middle Eastern country. The call usually goes something along these lines:

'Hi, Mum.'

'I'm just calling to make sure you're all right. I had one of my dreams again last night. Well, not dreams, "feelings". Are you all right?'

'Yes I'm fine. Listen, can I call you back? It's just that I'm involved in heavy front-line insurgent infighting in a Middle Eastern country.'[3]

'OK. Do you want to speak to your dad? He's just come in from feeding the chickens.'[4]

---

3 By which I mean in a radio studio recording some bollocks for the radio.
4 He keeps chickens on an allotment. I don't know why.

'No, I'm busy being shot at by ISIS and I can't talk.'

Mum shouts off: 'Les. Les. Les! LES! Jonathan is on the phone. Do you want to talk to him? He's still alive.'

And then my dad will come on and give me an update on the health of his chickens, as though this was the point of the call, rather than it being the upshot of Mum's weird witchcraft. The chickens are regularly killed by foxes too, so it's a shame Mum never gets any of her feelings about them otherwise we could issue the whole coop with a warning.

So, after Auntie Gladys came back the second time, I was having tea (more Findus Crispy pancakes – Mum had branched out from beef and mince and had begun to experiment with cheese 'n' bacon) and just considering how proud I was going to be to be the brother of *two* sisters (but privately thinking that my mum and dad should probably stop procreating now), when Mum announced out of nowhere, 'Your dad is having a vasectomy.' Wearily, I pushed the breadcrumb-covered hot pocket aside, because if there was ever such thing as Too Much Information, this was it. I had been forced to think of my father's semen while cutting into a cheese and bacon crispy pancake, and that is something no one should ever have to do.

'I'm forty-three,' she said, 'and we think that is quite old enough to stop.'

'What? Having sex?'

'Having babies,' she said. 'We'll still have sex.'

'Ewwwwwwww' went my internal alarm system, again.

'It's best to play safe,' she continued, stacking the

dishes,[5] 'so your dad is going for the snip. I knew everything with Vicky would be fine because of your Auntie Gladys, but we think that now is the time.'

Ah yes, Auntie Gladys. My mum's supernatural powers had meant that the late Auntie Gladys had shown up one night and told her everything with her pregnancy was going to be all right. Just like that. No fanfare, no missing face, no rattling of her glasses chain or crinkle of haunted rain hood, just a stroke on the neck and a whisper.

'How do you know that it was Auntie Gladys?' I said, echoing my interrogation of Kelda, after the same ghost had supposedly sat on her bed, years previously.

'At first I thought it was your dad trying it on . . .'

'Ewwwwwwww' screamed the silent alarm.

'But when I tried to elbow him away, I realised he was asleep and facing the other way. Yet someone was stroking my neck.'

If we were to rule out burglars and any head masseurs that happened to be passing, by any stretch of the imagination, this was, of course, bonkers. Again, you and I know that this was probably just a dream, but it had made Mum feel better, so whatever it was, it was OK.

'It was your Auntie Gladys, and she told me everything would be fine,' she insisted.

To be fair to Auntie Gladys and her insight from beyond the grave, everything was fine, and two months later, the four of us became five.

---

5 It wasn't all crispy pancakes in our house. At some point there must have been meals with gravy on our plates, because I remember that my dad liked to put a slice of white bread in it at the end of the meal 'to soak it up'. Obviously he would then eat it – I'm not suggesting he used it as a sort of rudimentary wheat-based J-cloth.

THIRTEEN

. . . in which a vicar almost watches some porn.

The embossed Whitesnake belt that I'd used to accessorise newborn Vicky's Babygro was part of my fashion armoury. Later, I was to embrace what we'll call 'The Miami Vice Years', a time when espadrilles and pastel ruled the earth, and whose sole achievement, in style terms, was to make me walk round looking like a dick. But that was some way off and, for now, I was all about Heavy Metal. I had a biker's jacket despite not having a bike,[1] a cut-off denim jacket (bought from Foster's Menswear boys' department with the sleeves already neatly pre-removed, which I imagined to be the Hell's Angels' method of choice) with an Iron Maiden patch (also from the indoor market) sewn on the back (by my mum, which, again is probably the Hell's Angels' way), white baseball boots and the aforementioned belt. To top it off, I had a studded wristband of the type favoured at the time by Judas Priest frontman Rob Halford. He wore his whenever

---

1 Well, I mean I had a bike, but it was a 3-speed racer from Halfords, rather than one of the 'Silver Black Phantom' variety, as recommended by Meat Loaf in *Bat Out Of Hell*. He used his to 'head down the highway like a battering ram,' while I used mine to either go round my mate Steve's house, cycle to school, or go to hang round the shops.

he was onstage shouting about 'Breaking The Law' at a thousand adoring fans. I wore mine at church youth club on a Friday night whilst snogging girls. I was also wearing it for no reason that I can possibly think of when the vicar came round unannounced, forcing me to frantically cover up some nudity. I am aware that sounds like the opening scene in a farce, and in a way it was.

It was the summer of 1985, school was out forever,[2] and my parents and my sisters had gone on a day out to the Black Country Museum in Dudley.[3] Because my interest in the history and development of canals was, at this time, minimal, I'd opted to stay at home. We were enjoying very different days, my family and I, but we were united by it being the day upon which the God that both my mum and Nana believed in chose this moment to kill the latter with a brain aneurysm at a church coffee morning.

While this was going on, my friend Fat Kev and I were watching a porn film. Well, it wasn't a porn film per se, it was *Fanny Hill*, more a soft-core romp dressed up as historical drama. We knew enough to know it would contain nudity because it had a lady's bare bottom on the cover and that, coupled with the word 'Fanny' in the title, meant that we had had to wait until the most opportune moment to hire it from the local newsagent's limited range of rental videos. And that moment was now.

'This please,' said Fat Kev to the man behind the counter,

2 Well, it was out for around six weeks, after which I was due to start at North Warwickshire College, for a two-year BTEC course in Art and Design. Take that, Alice Cooper.
3 In those days, in the Midlands, you had to make your own entertainment.

slapping down the video case as confidently as he could manage. Kev looked older and was much bigger than me, so he was the designated renter. He was tall enough to pass as an adult, just so as long as he could remember to act as an adult for long enough to get away with it.

'Anything else?' said the man.

'Yes, please. A Curly Wurly and the *Beano*.' said Kev.

Several feet away, lurking out of sight behind the magazines, I mentally facepalmed – despite the trope 'facepalm' having not yet been invented.

The newsagent didn't care though, not in the slightest, so we made our way back to my empty house on our bikes for a feast of Fanny Hill. We had no idea what it was or what it was about; just that it would have one or more naked ladies in it. A cursory glance at the back of the video box had given us an outline of the plot:

'After losing her parents to smallpox, the poor country girl travels to London, where she falls into prostitution under the guidance of an infamous madam. Forced to take a series of lovers to survive, Fanny learns to relish sensual delights – but reserves her heart for her one true love. Starring Oliver Reed.'

It certainly sounded promising, even despite the presence of Oliver Reed. I reached out, popped it in the top loader[4]

---

4 We were old school. Despite futuristic front-loading video recorders being widely available, Dad (who had taken an enormous amount of persuading to even *get* a video recorder in the first place) had just gone down to Radio Rentals and rented the cheapest thing he could find. As a result it was a Mark 1 Ferguson Videostar with chunky buttons that stuck out of the front of it and prevented the door of the cupboard it was in from shutting properly. It didn't even have a remote control, although that wouldn't have worked anyway, because Dad had put it in the aforementioned cupboard.

and pressed play (taking time to note how cool my Judas Priest-style wristband looked on my forearm) and the action unfolded. First gratuitous breast shot in, and both Kev and I put cushions on our laps. Second gratuitous breast shot, and I decided to close the curtains, just in case the vicar came round, which was lucky because about half an hour in, he did.[5] On-screen, Fanny Hill was experimenting with a little same-sex love play and, just as she began to touch herself, the doorbell rang. Kev paused the tape while I went to see who it was. The bell rang again with some urgency just as I reached the door, and when I opened it, I was surprised to see the vicar standing there.

'Hello, Jonathan,' he said. 'Is your mum in?'

I could see him peering over my shoulder, looking for my mum, and I hoped against hope I hadn't left the lounge door open wide enough for him to see the ongoing, faux sixteenth-century lesbianism with his holy eyes.

'No,' I said, 'her and Dad have gone to the Canal Museum in Dudley.'

His eyes flicked back to me. He rightly looked like he wanted to ask why, but instead said: 'Can I come in?'

'Er . . .' I replied.

This was tricky. On the one hand, while I knew the vicar from church, (his name was Andrew and he was tall, balding and kind and I knew him to be fairly sincere about the whole craft of Vicaring) on the other hand, I had no idea of his

---

5 This makes it sound like the vicar was in the habit of popping round regularly, like Derek Nimmo in a sitcom. He wasn't. To my knowledge this was the first and last time he ever 'popped round'.

views on soft-core romping and whether or not it might be a topic of conversation he'd later bring up with my mum at one of the church coffee mornings.[6] This was not something I wanted to happen so, because I was only too aware that we'd paused the film mid lez-up, I was desperately willing Kev to stop the tape completely and turn the television off before the kindly Reverend came into the lounge to bear witness to full frontal nudity and a fat boy eating a Curly Wurly.

'She's not in,' I repeated.

'Yes, but I need to talk to her . . .' He hesitated. 'And you, really. It would probably be best if I came in for a chat.'

'OK, VICAR!' I said the V word as loud as I could in an attempt to alert Kev to the situation. I moved back and he followed me into the lounge. Kev, on the ball for once, had thankfully followed my train of thought and had successfully aborted 'Operation Underage Rental'.

Andrew the Vicar nodded at Kev and then glanced at the curtains that were closed on a bright summer's day. If he wanted to question it, he didn't, instead he just got straight down to his Vicary business.

---

6 'Hello, Dorothy. Have you tried the seed cake? It's delicious. Have some, do.'

'Thank you, Vicar, just a small slice.'

'By the way, Dorothy, I popped round your house the other day while you were out and young Jonathan was watching *Fanny Hill*.'

'Was he, indeed?'

'Yes, I walked in just at the bit where Fanny is enjoying some scissoring with the scullery maid, and then they indulged in what I like to call "anal loveplay".'

'Really?'

'Yes. Would you care for a chocolate finger?'

'It's your Nana,' he said. 'I'm afraid she collapsed at the coffee morning and she's been taken to hospital.'

I know now that he knew that she was dead, but he didn't want to tell me. 'We called the ambulance but I'm afraid . . .' He tailed off and looked sad. I glanced at the TV, just to make sure it was off. No one should have to hear news like this while, nearby, a scullery maid is licking the vagina of a member of the aristocracy.

'When does your mum get home? She needs to call the hospital.'

'I don't know,' I said.

'Well, ask her to telephone the hospital and then to telephone me at the manse. Tell her I will come round and see her later. I'm very sorry.'

He stood up to leave and I walked him to the door. 'I like your wristband,' he said. And with that, Andrew the Vicar was gone.

It's weird, being the sole custodian of news like this. This was, of course, well before the advent of mobile phones so I had no way of getting in touch with my parents on their museum trip, and all I could do was wait until they came back.

'Shit,' said Kev, as I came back into the lounge.

'Shit,' I said and sat down.

We sat in silence for a moment or two, contemplating the transient nature of life. I thought of Nan's house where we'd all lived, squashed up together after Dad lost his building company. I thought of how, one Christmas, I'd taken a photograph of her wearing a hat from a cracker while she brandished a gun in the lounge.[7] I thought of the time I'd taken all the wool out of her wool bag and woven it round her entire bungalow, connecting all the legs of every item of furniture she owned like a yarn spider's web, while she'd been busy in the kitchen. I thought of her watching *Cross-roads*,[8] and then tut-tutting afterwards as I made her watch *The Kenny Everett Video Show*. I thought of her brilliant recipe for scrambled eggs, and the comics she'd buy me that I'd read while lying on the rug in front of her fire eating crisps when I went there every Monday after school. I thought of her lined face smiling with love at me, a grandchild that wasn't hers by blood, but was hers thanks to the random nature of my arrival into the bosom of her family. I knew that I loved her and that I'd miss her enormously.

'Shall I put *Fanny Hill* back on?' said Kev.

'Yes,' I said.

Soft-core costume dramas were all very well, but I must have been about thirteen when I saw my first disembowelling. One minute I was an offal virgin, and the next a man with a leather face had chain-sawed someone's guts off right in front of my eyes. From that moment, like a fresh-faced,

---

7 It wasn't a real gun. After a sherry or two she'd been persuaded to have a go on our new early eighties' Binatone Turn-Your-TV-Into-An-Arcade computer game which consisted of all the action of a white dot moving around the screen which you had to shoot with a plastic gun. She was surprisingly good at it.

8 Hugely popular seventies' soap opera set near Birmingham. It followed the power struggles of two sisters who argued about turning their house into a motel and the Machiavellian machinations of Benny, a bobble-hat-wearing halfwit. It was very much the *Game of Thrones* of its day.

all-American teen getting sliced by a curved spiked blade, I was hooked. It was 1982 and I Know What I Did That Summer, because *Fanny Hill* certainly wasn't the only place that we went for movie kicks. It was six weeks of sunshine that Fat Kev and I completely missed, because we spent it indoors with the top-loading VHS machine and our eyes glued to every single horror film we could lay our blood-soaked adolescent hands on. It was a happy, more innocent time when any quite obviously underage spotty child could walk into any high street video shop and take home an uncut *Cannibal Holocaust*, or a nice splinter-in-the-eye, scene-intact version of *Zombie Flesh Eaters* and no one would, ironically, bat an eyelid. Back then, eyelids would be poked out, eaten, cut off, burned and spiked with impunity, but certainly not batted.

The Evil Dead poster on my bedroom wall (the one that had previously been the lair of the giant spider) meant a lot to me because whichever horror film you'd managed to see impacted heavily on your social status. If you'd seen *Driller Killer* that was one thing, but if you'd seen *Driller Killer* and *Night of the Bloody Apes* then you were moving up the social ladder. To be fair, it was a pretty geeky ladder and certainly not the same ladder as all the cool kids were climbing; the one labelled 'Prowess in PE' or 'On the School Soccer Team', but it was our ladder and we were very competitive. Nick Roser, my friend and main film-rental rival came into school one day and announced that the following weekend his dad would be renting the holy grail of our schoolboy dreams: *The Texas Chainsaw Massacre*.

'Fuck off, no way!' I think was my considered response.

'Bringing it home on Friday night,' he said, with the air of smug condescension of a cat that's not only just got the cream, but is also smearing himself in cream and is flicking the V's to his creamless feline friends.

The Texas Chainsaw Massacre was The One We Had To See. Thus far, not one of us had managed to get hold of it, and it was one that, given its title and reputation, had proved difficult to get past our parents. I could go to the video shop with my dad and bring home, say, *The Last House On The Left* because, if you didn't know any different, it could well have been a property show, but our parents were slowly wising up. On one occasion, ahead of a night when my parents were going out, leaving Kelda and I to watch a film or two, at her behest, I rented the light romantic comedy *Electric Dreams*, which depicted a love triangle between a man, a woman, and a computer. My dad saw it lying on the kitchen table and we both very quickly came in for some intense questioning, largely because he'd mistaken it for a film in the then porn franchise *Electric Blue*,[9] read the words 'love triangle' and simply jumped to the very worst of conclusions. Once satisfied that Phil Oakley and Georgio Moroder were responsible for the theme song and that it was actually a 'science fiction romantic comedy drama', he wandered off, thinking no more of it. He had no idea that I had rented *The Burning* as the other half of the double bill, in which a disfigured caretaker called Cropsy hacked his way through various amorous

9 The *Electric Blue* tapes were sort of designed to be a gentleman's 'art' magazine on your TV. Full of soft-focus close-ups of breasts, this was the porn industry's attempt at keeping up with the times long before the Internet killed its video star.

teenagers. Mind you, one night I found, on the self-same kitchen table, in a bag, the Joan Collins' smut vehicles *The Stud* and *The Bitch*, along with the notorious Roman sex-fest *Caligula*. My mum and dad had rented them for 'after we'd gone to bed'. It was the eighties' video boom, and we were all at it.

It's fair to say that my friends and I were in horror-film heaven. I did indeed eventually see the notorious *Texas Chainsaw Massacre* round at Nick's house, because no one important had yet noticed that truly graphic horror movies were readily available for two pounds a night just next to the crisps in the off-licence. Much to our delight, we'd find sleazy Nazi fun in *SS Experiment Camp* nestling up against the Salt & Vinegar, *I Spit On Your Grave* sitting proudly under the KP Nuts[10] while Luigi Batsella's notorious *The Beast In Heat* had to make do with slightly obscuring the pickled onion Monster Munch. My mum and dad were, at this stage, oblivious to these goings on. In those heady days before the 1985 Video Recordings Act, video releases were uncensored and uncategorised and we were all over it like a rash of indiscriminate killings. There was even (whisper it) *proper porn*. The video shop proprietors, however, were diligent in the policing of this; after all, porn had top-shelf history, so we hatched a plan to send in the kid that looked oldest to get it. He was called Alan, and one day when his

---

10 Ironic, when you consider what happened to the chap in the bathtub. (I realise that this footnote requires a working knowledge of the film and thus this particular footnote may not be for everyone.)

parents were out we all went round to his house to watch *Juicy Peaches 4*. It was rubbish, but we were awestruck to see full-on penetration on a telly and, in one particular scene, a very accommodating young lady tie a knot in her own labia. And remember, this was years before anyone had the fore-sight to invent the Internet and fill it up with smut; such a pornucopia of filth was unimagineable to the twelve horny boys sitting in Alan's parents' lounge watching *Juicy Peaches 4* with cushions on their laps.

Horror films, though, were much simpler to get hold of. Film certification belonged to the cinema and anyway, the sort of things we were watching wouldn't have got anywhere near the big screen in the first place. For cinematic thrills and spills we had *Herbie Goes Bananas*, but if you wanted Herbie to go Bananas with a power tool, then it was to the video shop that you had to turn.

Until, that is, a man called Graham Bright came along and really pissed us off. By 1983 the tabloids in the UK had begun to spot what was going on near the newsagents' snacks and had decided to become outraged about it. Tab-loid journalism was, in the eighties, just coming into its own and, as Nigel Wingrove points out in his book *The Art of the Nasty*, the great video nasty scare was simply 'one of the first contemporary press frenzies, driven by the overriding demand that "something must be done"'. Initially, it was all the *Daily Star*'s fault.[11] It reported that 'the video boom is

---

11 Yes. The *Daily Star*. With its penchant for nude tits and headlines like 'Big Fat Gypsy Upskirt Secrets'. Still, someone's got to take the moral high ground.

giving youngsters a chance to see some of the most horrific and violent films ever made', to which we would reply 'yes, thank you, *Daily Star*, we're thirteen and we could have told you that – and what's more we're quite happy with the arrangement', but then, thanks to the articles, stories and letters that began to pervade the press, the term 'video nasty' was dragged kicking and screaming into the public's consciousness and demanded that somebody save our souls from low-budget European horror.

And that somebody was Graham Bright. 'Our Graham' was a Tory MP for Luton South, and he proposed the Video Recordings Act, which, apart from ensuring certificates for all video films it also, more alarmingly, said that any films that were a bit too icky (in *his* opinion) would be seized by the police, and complicit video shop owners prosecuted under the Obscene Publications Act. A list of thirty-four such films was then drawn up and one by one they began to disappear.

It was at this point that I began to take an interest in politics. Suddenly my carefree life of watching *Nightmares In a Damaged Brain* and *Driller Killer* was being interfered with by Westminster and I was angry. I soon figured out that it was no coincidence of course that 1983 ushered in a General Election and the incumbent Prime Minister Margaret Thatcher, who had just bashed the 'Argie Scum' in a row over some far-off sheep, was keen to secure re-election for her party of blue-rinse film haters. The Tories saw the furore as a welcome opportunity to curry public and tabloid favour and so Leon Brittan, the toad-faced Home Secretary of the day,[12] pushed the act forward via Mr Bright. 'Rape of our Children's Minds' screeched the *Daily Mail*, displaying the restrained, nuanced, liberal journalism that has become its trademark. Next, MPs Jerry Hayes and David Mellor jumped on the bandwagon and derided the 'immoral middle classes' who were allowing these films into their homes, although it's worth noting that both went strangely quiet on the subject of 'immoral middle classes' when they were involved in separate sex scandals a few years later.

By now Mary Whitehouse[13] had thrown her handbag into the ring and the press began to insist that watching violent films directly caused violent behaviour, despite having precisely no evidence to back this up. Although they should have looked our way: Nick Roser and I had several conversations about wanting to nail Graham Bright MP to the ground and put a drill to his lightweight political forehead. We loved these films in all of their toolbox-wielding glory, and he was spoiling our fun. School break times became a competition

---

12 The original footnote here was removed 'for legal reasons'. And then The Right Honourable Lord Brittan of Spennithorne died during the writing of this book. (Not in the same room, I hasten to add.) I haven't reinstated the note; suffice to say that at least this book is published, unlike that dossier containing details of a parliamentary paedophile ring that he somehow lost, back when he was in charge of it.

13 She formed the National Viewers and Listeners Association and was mad. She was a bouffant-haired mood-hoover, sucking all the fun out of TV, stage and film since 1965. Coincidentally, she was born in Nuneaton where we lived so, as teenagers who were growing up there, we thought she'd personally betrayed us all. When she died, sixteen years after the Video Nasty debate, I had a weekend show on Virgin Radio and came out of the news announcing her death by playing the song 'Ding Dong! The Witch Is Dead'. It's fair to say I hold a grudge.

to find out who'd seen the sickest film. Conversations were peppered with things like 'No, I agree that the bit in *Snuff* where the fingers get cut off with a pair of tin snips is incredibly graphic, but, for me, it's *Anthropophagous The Beast* where the cannibal gets smashed in the stomach by a pickaxe and then pulls out and eats his own entrails'.

This, and we didn't even know how to pronounce the word 'Anthropophagous'. And, in fact, I've just discovered that I still don't. But now, play time was over because all of a sudden the man at the off-licence wouldn't rent anything with a lurid cover to us any more in case he went to prison. This was the end of our world. I was furious. This Bright man had ruined my life.

And then I discovered girls and forgot about it. But, ever the film buff, in my later years I tracked down every single one of those banned films – some of which I'd never seen – and collected them until I had them all on slightly dodgy VHS. Fast-forward to now and you can more or less buy all of them uncut on DVD in HMV. Just the other day I saw Lucio Fulci's *The House By The Cemetery* in the sale for £5.99 and *Driller Killer* doesn't cost a lot more. Even *Cannibal Holocaust* is there, resplendent in all its someone-impaled-on-a-spike-through-their-hoo-ha glory. Well, almost. In 2011 it was resubmitted to the British Board of Film Classification who reinstated the gruesome five minutes they'd previously taken out, but to this day, there are still fifteen seconds missing, and they consist of a man stabbing a raccoon. So, fair enough, really.

FOURTEEN

... in which a gerbil is murdered by accident and a sheep is mistreated.

Despite Mr Bright's and the *Daily Mail*'s insistence that watching these films would make me go out and stab a raccoon, I have never done so, although I did once accidentally kill a gerbil. It was my sister Kelda's and, technically, it wasn't my fault, although to this day she maintains that it was. I say, Let God Be My Judge, and in case God is reading this, and weighing up the evidence before passing any kind of verdict that could see me cast into the special pit He reserves for sinners who have once accidentally broken a rodent's spine with an armchair, here are the facts of the case.

My sister had a gerbil. Two, in fact, but gerbils are notoriously territorial and, a couple of days after they arrived in their new home, one of them bit off part of the other one's tail. We should have seen that as a warning, but no one did and, despite a bloodied stump, the weaker of the two little creatures seemed to be fine until, one day, it wasn't and instead it was dead. It wouldn't have taken Poirot to deduce that this death could be placed squarely at the door of the surviving gerbil who, despite being a murderer, simply carried on eating his sunflower seeds and running on his stupid wheel as though nothing had happened. So when he later lost his life to a bigger opponent (in this case, furniture) in a way he got what was coming to him.

It's fair to say that this argument was lost on my sister, even when we had it thirty years later, when I finally admitted that I *may* have been present at Albert's[1] death. We were reminiscing about childhood, as siblings are wont to do.

'You once tripped me over and I fell into the stone fireplace and damaged my teeth. You were evil to me.'

I wasn't evil to her; her memory is clouded.

'And then once, while we were jumping up and down on Mum and Dad's bed, you pushed me off it.'

It didn't happen like that, her memory is clouded.

'But when I was fourteen you grassed me up for smoking by buying me cigarettes and a lighter, wrapping them up and then giving them to me on Christmas morning so that I opened them in front of Mum and Dad.'

Yes, fair enough, I did do that.

In my defence, I was simply concerned about her health. It was in no way a cheap shot of the type that would a) be amusing to seventeen-year-old me and b) get her into trouble.

'And then when I was sixteen you TOTALLY embarrassed me in front of EVERYONE I knew at my own party by throwing all my friends out of the house.'

Again, true. And, again, in my defence, what had happened was that my parents has gone away for the weekend and, in what turned out to be an ill-judged experiment, had left us to fend for ourselves for the first time. On the Saturday night,

---

1 Yes. The gerbil's name was Albert. Deal with it.

I fended for myself by going to the pub with some friends and, not to be outdone, Kelda fended for herself by inviting some psychopaths round to have a party. She then further fended for herself by drinking all of the beer in the fridge (my beer, as it happens) and whatever she could glean from our parents' drinks cabinet before eating an entire pack of paracetamol because one of the attendant psychopaths had told her it was 'a good way to get hammered'. I arrived back to find that our house now appeared to be a cross between National Lampoon's Animal one and Ancient Rome. This, I reasoned, would reflect badly on the skills entrusted to me as 'the older brother in charge' so, once I'd prised apart the couple copulating in the bathroom, I set about stopping the party.

'Er, could you stop the party, please? It's time to go home.'

If you've ever tried to stop some sixteen-year-olds from having a house party you'll have some idea of the tenacity with which they try to hang on to it, especially if they are, as previously indicated, psychopaths. My sister was at once mortified and furious. Mortified, furious and full of sherry and paracetamol.

'Whaaaathfucsssfucpartieee,' she said, waving her arm at the carnage. Nearby, someone with curious hygiene, a beanie hat, and an attitude problem noisily opened a beer. My beer. It was a can of mild I'd got Mum to buy me from Sainsbury's before they'd left. This was the final straw. Nobody drinks my mild. I grabbed the can from his hand and, as he made a lunge for me, I kicked him hard in the knee, knocking it backwards. He went down. His friend, the one who'd been mating under the Matey[2] in the bathroom stepped in but I used the can of mild as a weapon, smacking it into his nose. My sister shrieked and two more of them came at me. One had a knife. His first attack missed and he wasn't going to get a second because I grabbed his knife hand as it went by, spun round and using his own weight against him flipped him on to the coffee table which shattered as I kicked the knife under the sofa and turned my attention to the next idiot.

'I'm going to tell Mum you broke the table!' shouted my sister, except it came out as 'Imgnumuumble', but her cry was lost under the yell of pain from the six-foot skinhead whose arm I broke while simultaneously punching him hard in the ribs.

By now, the music (I think it was Go West's eponymous debut album) had stopped. The room was quiet, except for the whimpering of Those Who Had Been Vanquished.

'I said it's time to go home.'

And they went, dragging their bloodied friends behind them.

Or at least, that's what happened in my head. In reality one of them (the copulating one) had, while fully nude and semi-erect, tried to push my head down my own parents' toilet and would have succeeded had it not been for the fact

---

2 Bubble bath. Advertised with the memorable refrain 'Matey's a bottle of fun / You put it in the bath / It's fun for everyone / It's always good for a laugh.' The bottle had a sailor's face. The suggestion was that you were bathing with a sailor.

that I wasn't alone, and fortunately had got four university[3] friends with me who were staying for the weekend. One of them was 'Big Pete' who was true to his name and played a lot of rugby and it didn't take long for the partygoers to realise that Big Pete probably wasn't to be messed with. He was good in a crisis. To defuse a 'situation' in a pub, I once saw him eat a pint glass and then set light to his own arm. So once he stepped in, bar some shouting from the other side of the garden gate, the property was clear and my sister was soon to be in a whole heap of parental shit.

'What the fuck are you doing?' I asked, possibly not that good-naturedly.

'Issparyyandyouveruinedit,' she replied.

'Where's all our beer?'

'Isspartydrinkily.'

She went to bed. I secured the house against any further invaders and, barring the arrival of more idiot troops trying to gain access to our abode by hiding in a Trojan Twat that they'd built, I settled down for a quiet night, my university friends and I all opting to sleep in the lounge for reasons that escape me.

At around 2 a.m. I woke to the sound of my sister leaving the house by the front door. It was an old-fashioned door with a mortise lock, rather than a Yale type, so once locked from the outside and the key taken, it couldn't be opened from the inside. She'd left, and the rest of us were trapped

---

3 Christ Church College at Canterbury, Kent. I was reading Radio, Film and Television and English as a joint degree. My lecturers included an elderly nun and a man who would repeatedly and absent-mindedly scratch his testicles while speaking.

in the house at the mercy of any fire and Big Pete's appalling snoring. This made me angry – I'd go so far as to say livid. Without thinking, I pulled on some jeans and climbed out of the lounge window and followed her up the lane in the dark. I rounded a corner and there she was, in the back seat of a two-door Ford Capri, which was full of the irksome sixteen-year-olds from the party. As they saw me appear, one of them made to get out of the car to deal with me in what I imagine to be a violent manner, but because I was cross I didn't give him the chance and pulled him from his seated position and trod on his head. This time it really happened. As he squirmed in wet grass, I flipped his seat forward, grabbed my errant sibling by the arm and dragged her out of the car before anyone really realised what was going on. Within minutes she was back in the house and, within moments of my parents' return two days later, was grounded. First the grassing her up for smoking via the gift-wrapped tobacco, and now this. No wonder she thinks I'm a dick. Which brings us neatly back to the incident with the gerbil. You may remember it's now thirty years after it happened, Kelda and I are reminiscing about our childhood and I've just admitted that maybe I did have a hand in Albert's demise.

'You did *what*?'

I'd misjudged it. I had light-heartedly mentioned that the gerbil that had been found injured all those years ago might have been down to me.

'Er, it wasn't on purpose. Mum had let it out for a run and it ran under the armchair and so I lifted the armchair to look for it just as it was running out the back and the lifting armchair trapped it as it ran out and, erm, maybehurthis-backabit.' Now I was slurring and difficult to understand, not because I was drunk on painkillers and sherry, but because I was scared of my sister.

'Let me get this straight. You killed Albert? Albert the gerbil?'

'No, I didn't . . . well, yes, kind of. But it was an accident.'

'You said you'd found him like that. You said you'd found him twitching on the floor.'

'Yes but . . .'

'You killed my gerbil.'

'Well . . .'

'You said you'd found him like that. You came in and *Rentaghost* was on. You brought him into the kitchen on your hand while me and Mum and Dad were having tea which was crispy pancakes[4] and chips and beans and Dad had brown sauce.' Her eye for detail is uncanny, even when furious.

'I used to love *Rentaghost*,' I said.

'You killed Albert,' she repeated.

At time of writing, she still hasn't forgiven me. For any of it.

Not long after I killed my sister's gerbil, I was sick on a stranger's sheep. Disclaimer: I didn't know it was there and it wasn't on purpose. It happened on the long road out of North Wales that led from Dolgellau to Welshpool and beyond, all the way to the Midlands; a well-travelled route by the Family Holmes on our way back from the annual

---

4 Of course it was.

holiday jaunt to Shell Island, which was notable for having very few shells, and not being an island.

For some reason (which I now know to be mainly financial) our annual breaks were spent either in Wales or Norfolk. Nuneaton was roughly equidistant from either, so whichever way my dad turned out of the drive, a big frame tent strapped firmly to the roof rack, dictated our destination. My parents liked camping in roughly equal amounts to the level at which Kelda and I hated it, largely because we could not see the point. Why, when we had a perfectly serviceable house that was dry and had a toilet and electricity, were we 'holidaying' in a damp cloth cube that had a large polythene bag as a floor, a bucket for a toilet and was seemingly an incredibly powerful magnet for rain. Lots and lots of rain.

'Don't touch the sides of the tent!' Dad would say on a constant basis, as we huddled in it, staring out through flapping plastic windows at Wales or Norfolk coming under siege from the weather. For some reason (and surely a major design flaw in tents) if you touched the 'walls' it rendered them permeable and the rain would detect this and would then concentrate its full attention on coming through and running down the inside to pool on the undulating polythene floor, mixing with the wee where my sister had accidentally knocked the bucket over. And we'd sit and sip tepid tea brewed with never-quite-hot-enough water from a camping stove and whitened with powdered milk out of plastic beakers. Plastic beakers full of tea made with 'Marvel' milk became the taste of camping and this was something else I could never understand, given that proper milk was widely available.

'Proper milk won't keep,' Mum would say. 'We don't have a fridge.'

'But the inside of this tent is colder than the inside of the fridge we have at home,' I would argue.

'We're not *at* home; we're on holiday,' would come the reply.

'Yes, and if we'd stayed there, we'd be dry and there'd taps,' I'd complain to deaf ears as I was sent with a large container to fetch water from what was nothing more than a muddy standpipe with a queue of other miserable-looking campers pretending to be enjoying themselves – a container that, when filled with water, was too heavy for me to carry back, resulting in me traipsing back and forth from the tap all day, in the rain, because I couldn't move it when it held any more than a third of its capacity. Back at the tent, my dad was organising some family 'fun'.

'Let's go for a short walk,' he would say, handing out cagoules, and we would sigh, knowing that his idea of a short walk was a nine-mile trek up Mount Snowdon. And as if camping itself wasn't bad enough, then there was the drive home. Which is where I met the sheep.

In all honesty, I was partially to blame for what happened to it. I was probably around nine or ten and, at this forma-tive age, was fairly susceptible to travel sickness. Barely a holiday-length car journey would go by without something or other welling up inside me, an affliction that became such a regular part of our journey that all manner of anti-travel sickness techniques were regularly bestowed on me by well-wishing elderly relatives for whom the phase 'old wives tale' was tantamount to documentary evidence. By age eleven I had been sat on folded newspaper, force fed barley sugars and ginger nut biscuits (though not at the same time), had my tummy wrapped in brown paper, worn an elastic band round my wrist, held a live guinea pig under my armpit between Telford and Welshpool and wore pants made of nettles before we'd even made it through Wolverhampton.[5] It's fair to say that not one of these methods worked. At times, the rear of our family car was so vomit-splashed that it was less like a passenger space and more like the aftermath of a Roman feast, except without the buggery.[6] It wasn't just one car either; in fact, a number of cars were tried, tested and vomited on during this time. At one point my dad even changed his car from a classy Renault 12 (French engineering) to a more upmarket second-hand Triumph Dolomite (British technology) because Grandad had told him that French cars had poor suspension. Sadly, this turned out to be somewhat of an old grandad's tale as, on its maiden voyage, the proud seventies' flagship of the Coventry carmaker's range suffered exactly the same fate as the Renault,[7] becoming more of wheeled vomitorium than a vehicle.

_____

5 The guinea pig and nettle combo may not be strictly true, but I'm fairly sure they were suggested.
6 Although occasionally it could boast a nude boy, given that when I'd been sick all over my own clothes, I could well spend the rest of the journey wrapped in a duvet and little else, much to the horror of my sister.
7 My grandad also had a Renault 12 and first suspected its poor suspension when I was sick all over the back of his seat on a day out with him and Nana Holmes to go fruit picking in Litchfield. In reality, Litchfield was only twenty-two miles away from Nuneaton so he'd reasoned that suspension, rather than distance, had caused the problem. He was wrong.

Looking back, one possible catalyst was the fact that both my sister and I were not actually sitting on the seats of the car, but rather on any number of teetering pillows, blankets, sleeping bags and (when I wasn't wrapped in them) duvets. This made for a travelling experience somewhat akin to being buffeted around in the guts of a flump. It was also in the days before rear seat belts were a 'thing', so the fact that I was giving the story of the 'Princess and the Pea' a run for its money in a series of cheap runabouts may have had something to do with it. My own personal technique to try to combat the wobbling, soft-furnishing nausea was to try to go to sleep, which I would do by curling up in the corner with my head down near the door handle. Unbeknownst to any of us, this would actually make it worse as, of course, you tend to feel less sick if you can see out of the front of the car, staring at a relatively steady horizon, but given that we were a family that believed in the scientific principle of barley sugar, it's fair to say that technical knowledge in this area wasn't necessarily our strong point.

It all came to a head on one ill-fated journey back from Wales, where on this occasion we'd been staying in the small village of Brithdir, near Dolgellau in Snowdonia National Park. We'd been camping (of course) and before the massive, almost insurmountable, two-and-a-half-hour journey back, I made the mistake of drinking a banana milkshake. No one thought to stop me, no one thought it through and all were oblivious to the coming lactose storm as my dad bought it for me in a seaside café in Barmouth without considering the consequences.

'Can we stop?' I asked from the cocoon of bedding on the back seat. We had travelled less than ten miles, but the combination of tropical dairy beverage and the ups and downs of narrow Welsh lanes was not a good one. From the tone of my voice, my dad knew what was coming.

'Pull over, Les,' said my mum, a hint of a note of rising panic in her voice. And it was then that poor Kelda, who was in the back with me, began the process of squeezing herself into the corner of her side of the back seat, a look of unadulterated fear on her face.

Earlier, in Chapter Four, where we took some time to consider the sheer horror of being attacked by spiders, you may recall a reference to the scene in John Carpenter's 1982 remake of *The Thing*, when a man's head detaches itself from his torso, sprouts spider-like legs before scuttling off, screeching. Well, the rear of my dad's car was now tackling its own remake of the original 1954 Howard Hawks' classic. There's a scene in Carpenter's version when Kurt Russell, trapped in a remote Arctic base, is testing the blood of his trussed-up colleagues for alien infection by sticking a hot wire into a number of petri dishes that are full of it. They know *one* of them is The Thing, but the question is, which one? The men's blood is hotwired one by one, until Palmer has his plasma jabbed, and his blood yelps and leaps from the dish all full of alien DNA, which is when Childs, Nails and Garry (alongside him and all tied to the same bench) begin to try and frantically get as far away as they can, pulling at their bonds but unable to move fast or far enough, while Macready tries hopelessly to light his faulty flamethrower. It's a smart, effective, brilliant scene in which you know that the inevitable is going to happen; which is exactly how Mum, Dad and a terrified Kelda must have felt, trapped in a remote Triumph Dolomite.

Yet my dad acted fast. Deftly spotting a passing area in this single country lane, he pulled in as I grappled for the door and stumbled out. In front of me a dry stone wall, of the type painstakingly built by a farmer; a hardy son of the soil had worked come rain come shine out here in the hills, meticulously constructing this field boundary using skills and techniques dating back to the dark ages, all of which passed me by as I gripped it and threw up banana milkshake over the top of it and into the field beyond. I was dimly aware through the tears that Mum was asking me if I was OK, and that Kelda was yet to emerge from beneath her sleeping bag shield. Eventually, the retching stopped and the watery mist cleared, which was when I looked down and saw that I'd been fully sick straight on to the woolly back of a sheep. There was a three-foot drop on the other side of the wall, and the beast had taken shelter there from the mandatory drizzle, little expecting that it would be hit by precipitation of an altogether more yellow, bananary nature – a tropical downpour, if you will, rather than a Welsh one.

The confused sheep wandered off and, from a distance, now really just blended in with the others that had been similarly marked with dye to denote which farm they belonged to. Mum and I got back in the car. Four miles further on, Kelda was sick and covered the back of my dad and all the bedding in strawberry flavour. It was a long drive home.

*

Of course, being sick on holiday doesn't stop with childhood car journeys, or sheep. It's a rite of passage for any teenage drinker finding his or her feet while spending a week or more on foreign soil with their peers. And it's not just teenagers either, as it was in a far-off land (during my mid-twenties, when I should've known better) that I found *my* feet heading drunkenly out of a nightclub and into an awkward situation that taught me a valuable lesson about the evil power of peach schnapps. The occasion was a cheap 'lad's' holiday to Gran Canaria,[8] much of which was spent trawling the horrific bars and sunbeds of one of Europe's premier destinations for twats. Having run the gauntlet of drinking establishments that tried to lure us inside with free shots of the fruity booze (and oft succeeded), it was still early evening when we staggered into a nightclub whose name I have long since forgotten,[9] and continued to partake of the traditional drink of the indigenous Completely Pissed people who seemed to inhabit the island.

At some point, I think I knew I was going to be sick. The air had become thick with the stench of mid-nineties trance and the peach, like the banana before it many years ago in Wales, was on the verge of making a comeback. And so it

8 I have been on precisely three 'lads'-style holidays over the years. There was Gran Canaria, a Club 18-30 holiday when I was seventeen and finally a trip on the Norfolk Broads in 1985 when five of us hired the biggest boat in the brochure (because we thought it looked a bit like the ones in *Miami Vice*) only to find it was too large to go under any bridges, thus trapping us for seven days in one square mile of water, unable to go anywhere. And then we broke the boat hook, and lost our deposit. And you thought *Ibiza Uncovered* was exciting.
9 Possibly 'Shitheadz' or 'Chavvy's' or something.

was that I left my friends and staggered up the stairs out into the fresh air. A few gulps of the smell of chips and sunburn in the street outside did nothing to alleviate the inevitable and so, bile rising, I saw some tall, dense bushes in front of me and headed straight in. My eyes had begun to blur and, as I made it through the foliage, I put out my hopelessly flailing hands towards a wall and, leaning heavily against it, began to vomit up the schnapps, beer and any food that I had eaten that day which, given our locale, was unlikely to be gourmet.

For what seemed like an age, everything came out of me. Eventually, exhausted by the self-inflicted ordeal, I rested my forehead against the cool, shaded surface of the wall. I opened my eyes to see that my trousers, trendy espadrilles and the sandy ground beneath them were covered in sick and I groaned. It was then that I gradually realised that the reason I could see this carnage quite so clearly, was that it was a lot brighter beneath these dense trees than it perhaps should've been, and it was then that my eyes began to trace the line of the wall upon which I was resting my sorry brow. It was light, very light. It was the lightest wall I'd ever seen, in fact I'd go so far as to say it was transparent and made of glass. I raised my eyes further, spitting some residual liquid out of my mouth. My gaze continued upwards, as slowly I was able to make out shapes, and various items began to swim into focus; tables, plastic chairs, people's legs, a polished floor with bits of lettuce on it, a counter, a large pair of golden arches forming the letter M, and finally the shocked, frozen faces of a family of four, a selection of burgers, fries (and my early nemesis, the milkshake) halted, poised and suspended halfway between table and mouth. As I watched, the mother of two put down her Filet o' Fish, while father slowly prised the cheeseburgers from his small daughter and son's hands. I had vomited up a full-length floor-to-ceiling window in full view of all the patrons of a busy McDonald's.

I can't be sure, but I think I waved. To this day I don't know why, but it was all I could think of to do. As the tableau broke, and the dad started angrily calling over a member of staff and pointing, I legged it.

If you're reading this, and you are the nice, yet horrified, family who were on holiday in Playa des Ingles circa 1995–6, and had your evening ruined by a man being sick on your window, I can only apologise. It was probably the unhappiest happy meal that anyone's ever eaten.

FIFTEEN

*. . . in which I encounter some politics and lie on the floor,
while my mum smashes up a hotel.*

The year 1982 saw a wind of change blow through the holiday plans of the Holmeses. Amid much excitement, there came a big announcement.

'We're not going to Wales this year,' said my mum. 'And nor are we going to Norfolk.'

What crazy talk was this? We always went to Wales or Norfolk. Mum was messing with the Matrix.

'Greece,' said my dad. 'We are going to Greece. And we're staying in a hotel.' It was to be our first holiday abroad and it sounded dangerously ambitious.

Meticulous planning on my parents' part meant that we were to spend a week on a Greek island (Aegina, which no one's ever heard of) and then a week in Athens (which they have). Mum had always wanted to see the Parthenon and all the ancient trimmings that Greece has to offer and was over-excited to be doing so, which possibly explains why, two-thirds of the way through the holiday, she was thrown off a roof. In fact, we all were. Apart from my dad, who had gone to fetch his camera.

What happened was this. We'd made it intact through the island part of the holiday, excursions to various notable sites of antiquity had been successful and enjoyable and the beach had been our playground. We'd eaten sandwiches beneath the Temple of Aphaea, walked through the ancient olive trees of Eliones and had built sandcastles in the shadow of Apollo's sixth-century holy hangout, so when we arrived in Athens, hot and sweaty from the Piraeus hydrofoil, we went straight to the hotel. As a family from Nuneaton where the most exotic place you could swim was a toss up between the Pingles Leisure Centre or in a dangerous disused quarry, what we were especially looking forward to was seeing for ourselves something that people like us had never seen the likes of before: a pool on the roof.

We knew from the brochure that it had one, but the very concept boggled our Midlands' minds. Swimming pools that we were familiar with were verruca-filled chlorine pits that resonated with the shouts of horny teenagers wilfully ignoring the signs that forbade any form of 'heavy petting' or 'bombing'. Often, in fact, people wouldn't even wait until they'd got to the pool to break the rules. On one memorable trip to the Pingles Leisure Centre with my mum and Nana, aged around nine (me, not her), we'd not even made it to the entrance before we caught sight of an amorous couple enjoying the first stages of romantic congress on the slope of a golf bunker on the adjacent course. They were yards from the pavement, and the loving gentleman in question, his tongue deep in his charming partner's mouth and his hand firmly in the gusset of her tights, was working at his task furiously and quite openly in full view of me, my sister, Mum and Nana. Being nine, I was unsure of what he was doing, six-year-old Kelda even less so.

'What are they doing, Mummy?' she said. She'd been the first to spot them.

'Oh dear,' said my mum, 'let's hurry up and get inside', which was a fitting thing to say, given that that's exactly what the golf-course Romeo was trying to do.

'It's disgusting,' said Nana, and I realised that she was talking to the couple. But because they paid no heed, she assumed they hadn't heard her, so she raised her voice and said it again.

'I said it's disgusting!' she repeated, only louder, while pointedly staring at their love. It was an odd scenario; watching your elderly grandma watching someone getting fingered on a golf course.

'You should find somewhere else to do that,' she called to them, which was basically the granny equivalent of telling them to 'Get a room', years ahead of that particular phrase's time. By way of reply, Loverboy decided to completely ignore her and up his pace, and now I was really curious.

'Yes, what *are* they doing?' I said.

'Has she got an itch?' said my sister.

Faced with the unhappy prospect of having to explain what was actually going on, my mum leapt on this account of the situation with visible relief.

'Yes!' she said. 'She has an itch and her . . . friend . . . is helping her with it.'

We all looked at them in silence.

'Why can't she scratch her own fanny?' Kelda asked.

We went swimming. It was never mentioned again.

*

Four years after this, the pool on the roof of our hotel in Athens threatened no such horrors. We'd never seen such luxury, and compared to camping in Wales or Norfolk in the rain this was holiday heaven. There was a poolside bar, tables, comfy chairs, trees, plants, and a view across the city to the Parthenon itself. But at the centre of it all was a glorious, shimmering, verruca-free slash of blue that was, incredibly, ON A FUCKING ROOF. We couldn't wait to get in it, but before we did, and while Dad went to fetch his camera and his 'bathers',[1] the rest of us sat down for a drink. Mum spotted a swinging garden chair with room enough for three and we all had freshly squeezed orange juice, although Mum added a cheeky Ouzo to hers 'because I am on holiday.'

Now, depending on whether you are reading this book avidly cover to cover, just dipping into it or are just glancing idly at it while sitting on the toilet, you may or may not already be aware that my mum is not a big drinker. In fact, she's not even a small drinker, only very occasionally agreeing to a small glass of sweet white wine on a special occasion, but nothing more. But, as she rightly pointed out, she was on holiday, and she was in the sunshine, so why not enjoy a glass of the local beverage while enjoying the ambience of a roof? Maybe she had one, maybe she had two, I'm not sure, but at some point she noticed that together we could swing gently back and forth on this chair and ruddy well have fun doing it. In front of us was one of those al fresco lightweight aluminium tables, and on it five or six glasses of juice and/or juice with added anise aperitif, a bottle of

---

1 This is Midlandish for 'swimming trunks'.

water and some extra water tumblers, just for good measure. You can probably figure out what's coming next but, to cut a tipsy story short, one slightly too overenthusiastic swing later, Mum's outstretched feet caught the table on its underside and, with a flourish worthy of a seasoned rugby fly half, she drop-kicked the whole thing into the pool.

My dad arrived back to a scene of shattered glass, orange juice, Ouzo and the complete evacuation of a rooftop recreational facility. An army of Greek waiters were struggling to help men, women and children out of the water and into towels, while a few more were trying to hook the table out. There was juice dripping down the tiles and the glorious blue shimmer of before had taken in a distinctly orangey hue at one end. It had also gone partially cloudy, where the Ouzo and broken glass had hit. We didn't get our swim and were asked to leave the roof, but everyone was very good about it, given that it took two days to drain, clean and refill the pool. The following year, we went back to Wales.

Around this time, one of the must-watch TV programmes for any thirteen year old who didn't quite understand grown-up jokes was *Not the Nine O'Clock News*, the BBC2 comedy that launched the careers of Rowan Atkinson, Pamela Stephenson, the late Mel Smith and the Welsh Griff Rhys Jones. Because of our regular holidays across the border in the Valleys, I was especially intrigued by one particular sketch that mocked the then ubiquitous TV adverts for the National Coal Board; and their invitation to 'Come home to a real fire'. To this, the writers had added the punchline, 'Buy a cottage in Wales.' I knew the advert, but had no idea why this was funny, so I asked my dad, who used to watch the programme with me, and was laughing at the joke.

'Why is that funny?' I demanded, interested but ignorant.

'Politics,' he explained.

Pressed further, he told me that some Welsh people were against the English holidaying in their country and so, to vent their anger, they had taken to burning down everybody's holiday homes. Suddenly I understood. It was a clever joke with a point, and now not only was it funny, it was also my first real inkling that you could take the piss out of politics.

Growing up in the Holmes' household meant growing up straddling the political divide. On one side of it, my mum, a staunch Labour supporter from working-class stock, born and bred in Nuneaton; her mother had been a nurse and so too was she, and she would routinely, and vocally, blame Mrs Thatcher, who she disliked enormously, for all of the country's ills and woes. My dad, on the other hand, was a Conservative voter, staying that way even when his small building business went bust under Thatcher's auspices, yet continuing to maintain to anyone who'd listen that she was 'good for the country'. For my part, I was entirely politically naive, yet like most teenagers, I knew for a fact that I knew best and given that I *was* a teenager – and therefore the rules said I HAD to rebel against those in a position of power, whoever they were – I too was a Labour supporter, even though I had no idea what they actually stood for. I knew Mum disliked Mrs Thatcher so I did too, plus I had seen some of her policemen beating up some miners on the telly and it all looked a bit unpleasant.

'Going to the dogs,' my mum would say, referring to the country as a whole, rather than suggesting a Holmes' family day out to Battersea.

She'd say it to try to elicit a response from my dad who, despite his support for Mrs Thatcher, wasn't really one for intense political debate.

'This country,' she'd say, 'is going to the dogs' and look at him, pointedly.

She was unspecific about what breed of dog. In the event, my dad would have argued that Thatcher's dogs were probably St Bernards; powerful animals that came to the aid of those who were stricken in their time of need, dispensing not brandy but a reduction in the national debt from their barrels. I knew this, just as I knew that the dogs my mum had in mind were more unlicensed pit bulls chewing through miners and unions like they were a slipper or a child's arm.[2] In truth, I had no real idea. I was interested in politics, but at the time the more pressing arguments in my world were all to do with whether Iron Maiden were a better band than Magnum.[3] Like many kids my age in the mid- to late 1980s, after a brief introduction to it from *Not the Nine O'Clock News*, I began to gain an understanding of politics from *Spitting*

---

2 The National Coal Board's advertising campaign didn't last long into Mrs Thatcher's tenure.

3 They were, something to which their longevity is testament. Magnum were undoubtedly a powerful force; *On A Storyteller's Night* is a mighty piece of work, the cover depicting, as it does, various fantastical creatures and goblins huddled around a table listening to tales of Yore in front of a log fire. But, having just checked, at time of writing Iron Maiden have sold 85,000,000 albums and are currently touring the stadiums of the world on their own private jet. Magnum are at the Assembly Rooms, Leamington Spa.

Image, the satire that nothing has come close to since. In America, there's a statistic that says that most young people aged between eighteen and twenty-four get their news from *The Daily Show*, but in Nuneaton, when I was a teenager, it was monstrous rubber versions of Douglas Hurd and Nigel Lawson that helped us figure out how Government worked. At the time, Nigel Lawson was the Chancellor of the Exchequer and the father of Nigella Lawson who went on to become the TV chef famous for indulging in foreplay with food and being strangled by Charles Saatchi. Actually, let us just take a moment to ponder a question that has long been bothering me: if your name is Nigel, how cruel do you have to be to give your child your own name? Not only that, but this tiny baby is a girl. Why aren't you thinking 'Ah, I have sired a daughter, yet I cannot give her my name because it is a man's one. To do so would be unkind.' And before you say 'Hang on a mo, Jon. At least he had the decency to put "Ella" on the end of it to give it an air of femininity,' consider this: nobody in the long history of anyone has ever looked down at a beautiful tiny girl handed to them by a midwife, in the hospital,[4] and looked into her fragile, newborn eyes and thought 'Yes. Nigella. Let's call her Nigella. She looks like a Nigella.'

No one looks like a Nigella. Not even Nigella. In fact, it's not even a name at all; quite plainly all it is, is the suffix 'ella' on the man's name 'Nigel' and so is, without any shadow of a doubt, a shit name. Sure, we've sort of come to accept it now through endless TV shows and cookery books but if you

4 Private, probably. He's a posh Tory.

take a moment to step away and consider it, can you honestly say Nigella is anything other than a word lazily lobbed at a baby girl by someone who clearly wanted to pass his name on to a boy. Do you know *anyone* else called Nigella? No. No you do not. If you're reading this on a train or a plane or in any otherwise public place, just take a moment to glance up from these words and have a look around. Go on. Do it now. I'll give you a moment to do so . . .

[. . .]
[. . .]
[. . .]

There. See? See all those people around you? Not ONE of them is called Nigella. Not a single one. And, let's be honest, even before you add the 'Ella', Nigel is a bit of a crap name. The only Nigels you've ever heard of are Nigel Mansell and the one that XTC were famously making plans for, and those plans were (I hope) to take Nigel aside and tell him that if he ever had a daughter then calling her Nigella would be a really stupid idea and would forever be construed as the vainglorious actions of a egotistical, lazy climate-change denier.[5]

But it was thanks to the likes of Lord Lawson, Baron of Blaby, and his rubber puppet that I was starting to become interested in Westminster. Plus, I'd joined Youth CND, partly because it was mandatory for fifteen-year-olds in 1984 to think that nuclear weapons were a Bad Thing, but mainly

---

5 One of his other daughters is called Thomasina. I mean for fuck's sake.

it was because all my mates had joined and it was seen as a cool thing to do, which is why I confidently drew a CND sign on my school rucksack and pretended that I knew what unilateral disarmament was. In fact, being a member of Youth CND was, crucially, really just a way for us all to get into a pub while being underage. Handily, meetings were held in a tatty room above the Crown pub in Nuneaton and I reasoned that if I sat up there on a Tuesday evening, out of view of the bar downstairs, and pretended to disagree with the Government then someone would eventually buy me a pint of mild.[6]

'The thing is,' I told my mum and dad, sagely, 'is that when the bombs went off in Hiroshima and Nagasaki, those standing directly underneath the blast in the epicentre were vaporised, and the scorched outline of their bodies was for-ever seared on to the walls and floors where they'd been standing.'

'That's nice, dear,' said my mum who wasn't really listening. We were having tea, as a family, and I was demon-strating my political nous by explaining in quite some detail what I was going to be doing at the weekend in the town centre.

'So we're going to recreate the horror by lying on the floor and drawing scorch marks round each other in charcoal and chalk.' One sister rolled her eyes. The one that was at this time too young to roll her eyes smeared some jam across her own face. That was gratitude for you, given it was their

---

6 I have racked my brains but cannot for the life of me figure out why, as a teenager, I drank mild.

nuclear-free futures that I was fighting for. My dad took another oatcake.

As he chewed it, I was doing my best to sound knowledgeable regarding the nuclear horrors of the Second World War, but I was essentially just regurgitating the propaganda from the previous evening's Youth CND meeting, where I had memorised the gruesome details of the terrible incident because they'd been handed to me on a leaflet. Yet though I was as clued up on the Second World War as the next fifteen-year-old and certainly knew of Hiroshima, my main interests around this time were Bon Jovi and wanking,[7] so I had no real idea of why the Americans had dropped a nuclear bomb on it. Sitting at the table, idly pushing a boil-in-the-bag cod in parsley sauce around my plate, I still hadn't, but the idea of disrupting shoppers in Nuneaton town centre to protest about an event that had happened forty years previously appealed to my rebellious nature. My chief understanding of the conflict and how Japan got drawn in and how and why the Americans launched their attack on them was based mostly on listening to 'Enola Gay' by OMD, with my in depth academic research supplemented just two years later when Deacon Blue also wrote a song about it on

---

7 Although not at the same time. That would have been weird, and probably resulted in me being thrown out of a Bon Jovi concert by their angry Head of Security, something which did happen, but only much, much later. And it wasn't for wanking. It was more for climbing up the drum riser during the gig and taking a photograph of the band from behind them while they were onstage at the O2.

their debut album *Raintown*.[8] Clearly, the bombing of foreign soil and the subsequent deaths of two hundred and fifty thousand people from the explosion itself and then burns, radiation sickness and injuries caused by the detonation of a uranium gun-type fission weapon (Hiroshima) and a plutonium implosion (Nagasaki) is fertile songwriting ground.[9] Rizzle Kicks – take note.

The following Saturday (always a busy shopping day in Nuneaton what with everyone from school going into town to steal pick 'n' mix from Woolworth's) I found myself splayed out on the floor in front of Superdrug while my friend Fat Kev and a couple of others drew round me with chalk, scoring out blast marks on the pavement and leaving my imprint forever scarred into the floor. Or at least until it rained in our Raintown.

'Who's going on the floor?' said Rob, who was a bit older than us and the Leader of Youth CND. 'I can't, because I'm the leader.'

Everyone else refused to as well, and eventually all eyes turned to me. This was because, immediately prior to turning their eyes to me, they'd all turned their eyes to the ground and seen bits of chewing gum and dirt all over the floor of the only recently pedestrianised shopping centre.

'Why me?' I said.

---

8 This is 'He Looks Like Spencer Tracy Now', written about Harold Agnew, the physicist and scientific observer who flew on the Hiroshima bombing mission in 1945. 'Harold Agnew' is a proper name. Unlike 'Nigella'.
9 Ironic, given the state of the soil in Hiroshima and Nagasaki for years afterwards.

'Because you are small and we'll use less chalk so we can do more shadow blasts,' said Rob. Annoyingly, he had a point, which is why he was our Leader. 'Besides, I'm not lying down there; there's all chewing gum plus it's really busy I might get stepped on.'

'What about if I'm stepped on?' I said.

'You won't be, they'll just step over you because you are small. Lie down.'

As the designated 'blastee', my job was to splay myself across the ground in roughly the same pose as someone who'd just been obliterated by an atomic bomb, my chalky charcoal image 'burned' on the ground for everyone shopping at Superdrug to see. It's worth mentioning that at this point in my life I had long hair, fashioning myself after TV's *Robin of Sherwood*, played at the time by Michael Praed,[10] and it soon became clear that the combination of Robin of Loxley-style locks and lying on the pavement in a pedestrianised high street on a Saturday morning was a bad one. My hair trod on at every turn, we moved around a bit, sometimes on the floor, sometimes against walls, all the while realistically simulating the horrors of nuclear armaments, though explanations as to the humanity of it all fell on the deaf ears of Superdrug's manager who came outside to move us on. He was so ignorant as to the terrible theatre of war that he first called us 'bloody hippies' and then called

---

10 I longed to be TVs Robin of Sherwood. Saturday teatimes were his playground, as he romped around righting wrongs with Ray Winstone (in an early role as Will Scarlett) and Clive Mantle off of *Casualty* as Little John. Michael Praed was very good-looking, a hit with the ladies and had long hair. He probably looks like Spencer Tracy now.

the police. Our Glorious Leader Rob, meanwhile, called the local paper. The resulting photograph was quite effective: a man with gum in his hair lying in the street while his mates kneel next to him holding chalk. For their part, the police, having decided that our little demonstration was never going to rival the one at Greenham Common, simply let us carry on. I think they were more concerned with the manager of Woolworth's who'd come out to complain about ongoing theft of his pick 'n' mix.

Did our protest that day successfully draw the attention of Nuneaton's shoppers (and shoplifters) to the notion of War being a very poor chisel with which to carve out a peaceful tomorrow? Well, think on this: to this date, the Midlands has never been hit by a nuclear weapon. And I like to think the good people of Nuneaton have us to thank for that.

SIXTEEN

. . . in which I dress up as Miami Vice *and get thrown out of a party by Mrs Thatcher's security detail.*

So I was curious about politics but, at this age, I was also quite interested in going out and learning how to drink alcohol until I fell over, so it was sort of fitting that, years later, the two things came together during one disastrous evening that we shall quietly refer to as 'The Thatcher Incident', something which we shall get to in a very short time.

In my teens, though, when it came to buying anything to drink that looked even remotely interesting, I was at a disadvantage amongst my peers because I was short and looked like I was about seven. This meant that my choice of drinking establishments was limited to a) the park, or b) the aforementioned room above the Crown on a Tuesday. Occasionally we would try a nightclub – and trial and error had revealed that the one place I could generally get into was Rumours, a terrible place that had stolen the font from the Fleetwood Mac album of the same name for its neon sign, and enjoyed the general atmosphere of a plague pit. I could get in, not because I looked old enough, because I didn't; it was more because the bouncers on the door were thick. On more than one occasion Fat Kev and I would turn up at Rumours and take advantage of this, attempting to befuddle them with maths. In the main, this worked, including on one occasion when Kev let his guard down and accidentally demonstrated a bouncer-like level of stupidity all his own, but handily the door fascists were more stupid than he was. On the evening in question we'd arrived, dressed in our finery. My finery (given that this was 1986) tended to be whatever Top Man were selling that slightly resembled what Don Johnson was wearing in *Miami Vice*; a white jacket, a pastel-coloured T-shirt and espadrilles. Kev, meanwhile, was wearing a lemon-yellow Marks & Spencer's jumper that his mum had bought him. We were at the cutting edge of fashion.

There has been much written about the vogue of the eighties with its legwarmers and its snoods and its golliwog on the side of a jar of Robertson's Jam.[1] It was also cool to roll the sleeves of your white or pastel-coloured jacket up to your elbows, which was a handy look for me as, had rolling your suit sleeves up not been fashionable, they would have been far too long and would have hung off the end of my hands like the melty clocks in that Salvador Dali painting. In short, I looked like a twat. But then so did everyone else, so it was fine.

Kev, as we established in an earlier chapter, was even then about six feet tall and I, er, wasn't. We were both sixteen, but where Kev looked about nineteen, I, er, didn't. I think the Sonny Crockett-look had probably lifted my appearance

---

1 Discontinued in 2009 and replaced with Roald Dahl characters. The 'Golliwog' image was considered racist by this time. It probably didn't help that the jam jar illustrations were collectable and thus, beneath each depiction of a black stereotype was written the word 'token'.

to somewhere around the age of twelve, but it was still far short of the 'eighteen' entry rule.

'How old are you?' came the familiar mantra of the chap on the door. He was one of two, and they were both sporting new fangled federal agent-style walkie-talkie earpieces to communicate, despite them standing next to each other. These, too, may have been from Top Man, part of their *Miami Vice* collection.

I went first.

'Nineteen,' I said, confidently, surreptitiously moving one espadrille-clad foot closer to the door. (Because *Miami Vice* was such a 'thing' in 1986, the 'no trainers' rule was relaxed because sockless canvas beach shoes were seen as the height of cool. Not on me, obviously, but certainly on Crockett and Tubbs.)

'Nineteen,' he repeated. It wasn't a question; he was mulling it over. I shifted my weight so that my espadrille caught the light of the Fleetwood Mac-fronted *Rumours* sign. Plus, I was wearing a pink shirt. I may well have been standing in a doorway in Abbey Street in Nuneaton, near Kwiksave and opposite a fabric shop, but I was screaming '*Vice*'. For all this guy knew, I'd just parked my Ferrari Testarossa round the corner outside the Co-op and had come straight from the beach where I'd taken down some perps who were shipping bad sunshine into the Midlands on a yacht.

'When were you born?' he said. He exchanged a glance with his friend, the other doorman, as if to say 'This'll fox him. All the rolled-up Top-Man suit jacket sleeves in all the world won't help him now.'

But I was way ahead of him. Using an ancient and mysterious system known as 'maths', I'd cleverly worked out what the year of my birth would have been if I was genuinely to have been nineteen. It was fiendish this system, as it involved pretending that my birthday was a whole three years before it actually was. To make it even more undetectable as a trick, I kept the day and the month the same.

I smiled. '24th April 1966.' I said.

He looked at me, and I could see him struggling with the mental arithmetic. After a few seconds he either worked out that that did indeed make me nineteen, or he gave up. Either way he waved me through. Behind me, Fat Kev stepped up to the oche.

'How old are you?' said the bouncer, no doubt taking in Fat Kev's lemon M&S jumper that couldn't have screamed 'My mum bought this' any more than if it had had those words knitted into the front.

'Nineteen,' said Fat Kev. Nineteen was our standard getting-into-nightclubs answer. It was a technique we'd honed based entirely on the unproven theory that saying 'eighteen' would immediately arouse suspicion. Our reasoning went something along the lines of 'They expect us to say eighteen because that is the minimum age at which I am legally allowed into their establishment to partake of the alcoholic beverages. Thus, if I say eighteen it will not sound convincing. Nineteen, however, sounds eminently more believable.' This was bollocks, clearly, but it always worked. And now Fat Kev was deploying the weapon.

'When were you born?' Same question to Kev, another glance to his door pal. It was a foolish question really, given that Kev was totally in earshot when I'd flummoxed them with hard sums. All Kev had to do was pull up his actual day and month of birth and append it with the already tried and tested '1966'. I'd done all the hard work. It was simple.

'20th June 1964.' said Fat Kev.

I froze, poised on the threshold of Rumours, so close that I could almost taste the Fosters.[2] I could hear the sounds of Simple Minds' 'I Travel' beating out its infectious rhythm from inside, and my heart began to match it as I realised that we were rumbled. Fat Kev had made a fundamental mistake. He'd, quite literally, made a schoolboy error. Looking back, this must have been how Gordon Jackson's character had felt in *The Great Escape* when the Gestapo ask him for his papers and then, when they'd wished him 'Good Luck' he accidentally replied in English. Flight Lieutenant MacDonald, aka 'Intelligence', was thus recaptured, and now we were going to lose the Battle of Getting into A Crap Nightclub. War is hell.

I was halfway through the door, I could see the stairs up to the club and I could also smell the freedom that comes with underage drinking, yet the whole evening was being ripped away thanks to Fat Kev's fat idiocy and poor grasp of basic subtraction; he'd told them he was nineteen, yet his birthday placed him somewhere around twenty-two. We had both said we were nineteen yet were seemingly born in wildly different years. One of us had to be lying, and if one was, then it stood to reason that both of us were. I stood

---

2 By this time I had developed quite the cosmopolitan taste and had moved on from drinking mild.

there, sweat breaking out on my brow as I waited for the hand upon my shoulder and the cry of 'Achtung! Schnell! Schnell!' as were dragged into the street and shot.

It didn't come. The bouncer's understanding of maths was even worse than Fat Kev's. As far as he was concerned we were both nineteen despite having been apparently born two years apart. We were in.

And, in common with all nightclubs, it was shit.

We didn't really enjoy it at all, not ever. Nightclubs were a thing that we just thought you were supposed to do, and so we did, but in truth Nuneaton's entertainment scene for teenagers had far more to offer. There was, for example, 'hanging around in the park', which has always been a rite of passage in towns up and down this fair land. Down the 'rec', sitting on the swings in the children's play area is where I first tasted the sweet, sweet taste of sweet cider and then tasted the bitter, bitter taste of sick when I vomited it all up again near the slide. The first time I was sick with the help of alcohol was on Christmas Eve 1984, at Dawn Harper's house. It was a school house party and, for reasons that have since become lost, Dawn's parents let her have a houseful of fifteen-year-olds round while they went out. 'Twas the Night Before Christmas at Dawn Harper's when all through the house, plenty of creatures were stirring . . . not least me drinking whisky that I'd smuggled out of Dad's drinks cabinet not two hours previously, and Nick Harrison who was fingering Helen White in the bathroom. As it was Christmas, it's fair to say that her stockings were quite likely lobbed on the floor without care, in the hope that St Nicolas Harrison soon would be 'there'. I don't recall much of the evening, but I do remember that the whisky in question was Bell's, a brand that I know now would make the whisky connoisseurs amongst you make the sign of the cross and whisper of its evil. In my dad's defence, he's never been much of a drinker and I imagine it was a gift, or something that he thought to keep in the house in case any non-discerning guests popped by. Whatever the reason, he now hadn't got any left because I had decanted it into a series of empty miniatures and smuggled it out. And I was drunk on it. Very, very drunk.

I also don't remember the walk home, if it even was a walk. It was more than likely a crumpled weaving between parked cars and, at some point, it must have involved a crawl because my new Christmas jacket (white, incredibly fashionable circa 1984/5) that I'd begged to be allowed to wear to the party on the day before I was supposed to be unwrapping it was irreparably grass stained when I found it on the floor of my bedroom on Christmas morning. I was lucky not to add 'vomit-encrusted' to its collection of immovable marks too, as I spent the whole night curled like a cliché around the bowl of the upstairs' toilet.

I was dimly aware of my dad peering round the door, a bit like the man from the aforementioned 'Night Before Christmas' poem peeking into his lounge only to find Jolly Old Saint Nick, 'dressed all in fur, from his head to his foot'. Except, where Santa's eyes had

> *'twinkled! his dimples, how merry!*
> *His cheeks were like roses, his nose like a cherry!*
> *His droll little mouth was drawn up like a bow,*
> *And the beard of his chin was as white as the snow'*

my eyes looked like someone had jabbed them with a stick. My dimples now droopy, my cheeks pale and drawn, my droll little mouth was all soupy and I looked quite forlorn. And the beard on my chin was the bumfluff of a fifteen-year-old and contained traces of half-digested whisky, Bailey's and After Eight mints. Yes, After Eight mints and Bailey's. It was Christmas.

'That'll teach you,' said Dad. It didn't, of course. Far from it. Although I did learn to never drink whisky again, which is probably why, twenty years later, when I sat next to former UK Prime Minster Margaret Thatcher at a birthday party and got hauled away from her by security at the behest of another former Prime Minister, John Major, I'd been mostly drinking gin.

It was Lord Ashcroft's sixtieth birthday party. I wasn't in-vited exactly, and neither did I gatecrash, but rather it was a job of work, hired, as I was, to write a bespoke set for the impressionist Jon Culshaw to base around Ashcroft's life and career. I know, it sounds exhilarating, doesn't it? If you're not familiar with Lord Ashcroft, he's the Tory party donor and life peer, a former Deputy Chairman of the Conserva-tive Party and a man who was 37th on the *Sunday Times* Rich List 2009 with an estimated fortune of £1.1 billion, not all of which he appears to have paid tax on in the UK. Having dual citizenship, he spends what we can safely call a 'tax loophole' of his time in Belize but, on this occasion, he was celebrating in London, along with the higher echelons of the Conservative party. The entire shadow cabinet was going to be there, along with Tory grandees such as John Major,

Margaret Thatcher, Ken Clarke, Douglas Hurd and Norman Tebbit; all the people I'd ever seen on *Spitting Image* all together in one room, off duty, getting smashed in a hotel on Park Lane.

To give you some idea of the budget, the whole Great Room at the Grosvenor House Hotel in London[3] had been decorated to resemble a Belizean jungle. It was an expensive, fairly accurate recreation too; there were trees, waterfalls, rocks, exotic plants and pretend parrots as far as the eye could see; it genuinely had the feel of a South American rainforest – though they'd stopped short of illegal logging. At one end was a stage worthy of the O2. Top of the bill was Tom Jones and his full showband that Lord Ashcroft's family *had secretly flown in from Las Vegas* to play for the partygoers. Sir Cliff Richard was performing; Lulu was on the bill, and Denise van Outen was genuinely jumping out of a cake to sing 'Happy Birthday' to the celebrating peer. It was rumoured to have cost more than £2 million and at least £7.50 of it went on the gin and tonic that I was currently enjoying in the company of the eighties' TV magician Fay Presto, who had been hired to perform close-up magic. I was enjoying it because I was curious as to what crazy hijinks the Conservative Party might get up to at their own private party, hidden away from the eyes of the press, and was eager to see Lady Thatcher get mashed on Jägerbombs and be sick on John Selwyn Gummer. It didn't quite pan out like that. There

---

3 If you are unfamiliar with it, it remains one of the largest ballrooms in Europe. It's underground and, in its time, was graced by royalty. Nowadays it mostly hosts any number of corporate ceremonies, such as the Garden Furniture Awards.

was embarrassing behaviour and there was drunken revelry and I'd even go so far as to say there was rude, obnoxious, alcohol-fuelled full-on disorder, but it turned out that all of it was done by me before I was removed, on former Prime Minister John Major's instruction, by some men in suits.

It started well. Jon Culshaw (ever the professional, he was in no way involved in anything that followed) performed his set and oh, how they laughed. From the side of the stage I saw William Hague laughing heartily at his own stupid voice coming back at him though Jon's magical mouth, and I witnessed first-hand Iain Duncan Smith chuckling along as Jon 'did him' saying something I'd written criticising one of his own policies. Brimming with success, I went to the bar. It was there I saw Fay Presto,[4] found her to be most pleasant company, and before I knew it I had had way too many gins followed by quite a lot of wine.

The Great Room at the Grosvenor House is so called because of its enormous size. It comfortably sits twelve hundred persons for dinner and is the largest entertaining space in London, which is unsurprising as when it opened in 1929 it played host to a massive indoor ice rink, whose pipes and refrigeration equipment still lie beneath the floor. It was here, apparently, that the young Queen Elizabeth learned

---

4 Fay Presto. You know? Fay Presto. Noted magician. She was on *Wogan* a lot in the eighties. And by that I mean his BBC1 chat show, rather than that she could be regularly seen straddling the genial Irishman. Her 'Bottle Thru table' trick was voted 37th Greatest Magic Trick of All Time. Remarkably, Fay Presto is not her real name. Her real name is Oliver, because she used to be a man.

to skate, and, according to my research,[5] international ice hockey matches were held within. I'd like to think the frosty atmosphere that I was about to encounter was something to do with the history emanating from its hallowed walls. It wasn't, though, it was more to do with my ill-considered gin-and-wine combo. The Great Room also has a balcony that runs all the way around it, from which spectating ladies and gentlemen of the twenties and thirties could look down on the ice skaters and marvel at their skill. Fast forward seventy or eighty years and Fay Presto and I were looking down on the Conservative and Unionist Party of Great Britain and Northern Ireland, past and present, enjoying coffee and petit fours, and it was from this vantage position that I spied John Major weaving his way through the crowd. I watched him, mildly fascinated. To my generation he was the grey politician from *Spitting Image* who ate only peas and tucked his shirt into his underpants, underpants that Edwina Currie had famously removed in order to get at John Major's minor.[6]

Edwina Currie was also present. This was years after their affair and, as I watched, John Major studiously avoided her table and wove his way through his friends and colleagues back to where he'd been sitting with the likes of Kenneth

---

5 Wikipedia.
6 In 2002 it was revealed that former Prime Minister John Major had had a four-year affair with later-to-be health minister Edwina Currie. The mental image of them having sex that was subsequently shared by the nation was absolutely horrific. It was probably the last time that quite literally everyone in this country was 100% politically united, as together we all pictured John Major and Edwina Currie, she tugging his shirt out of his famous underpants and he licking peas off her tits.

Clarke, Michael Howard and Douglas Hurd and – to my delight – Lady Thatcher. Margaret Thatcher was sitting chatting to former Chief Secretary to the Treasury and Heritage Minister, David Mellor, himself noted for allegedly wearing a Chelsea football strip and sporting it during sex with a 'soft-porn' actress called Antonia de Sanchez in 1992. Through a filter of Tanqueray and Pinot[7] I saw John Major sit down and take his place on the other side of Lady Thatcher and then I spied (the tables were round and seated ten) an empty chair. It was at this point that things began to go wrong. My mildly tipsy state saw me emboldened with a courage beyond my means and so it was that I saw this for what it was; an opportunity to converse one on one with some of the finest political minds in the country on anything from the state of the NHS and the Education system to taxation, the environment, transport and welfare reforms. Perhaps they would even like the story of my political background of lying on the floor of a town centre and being drawn around with chalk as a member of Youth CND. I bade a good evening to Fay Presto and headed down the grand sweeping staircase and made a drunken beeline for the Tory Cabinet circa 1990–1995.

Here's what I remember: first, sitting down and helping myself to wine in front of a surprised Virginia Bottomley, and I'm quite sure I then waved across the table at Sir Malcolm Rifkind. I then leaned round David Mellor and introduced myself to Lady Thatcher because I knew I had quite a lot of

---

7 Also, coincidentally, I've just realised, quite good names for soft-porn actresses.

thoughts about her tenure as Prime Minister that I wanted to share with her. And so it began.

Probably.

I like to think that I had become a welcome guest at this birthday Algonquin Round Table and had dazzled the Government who'd shaped my growing up, my formative years, with insight, wit and passionate debate; after all, I was one of Thatcher's children so surely the Matriarch at the table would love to hear of how she had shaped me, just as any mother would listen to her son. In many ways she was my third mother, after my birth one and my adoptive one. Margaret Thatcher probably did more to shape the world I grew up into and thus had come to have a bearing on my life and the lives of my generation and, I felt, would only be too pleased to hear from me, her Child, who was, at this time, full of booze. I'd like to think that, but I can't remember. In fact, I was so drunk, that thinking about it now, it may not have been Mrs Thatcher. Or John Major. Or any of them.

The next thing I do remember is waking up in my hotel room, fully dressed face down on the bed with the sun bearing down on me through the windows, and sweatily heating up my hungover face. I couldn't for the life of me work out how I'd got there, but between the stabs of searing head pain I began to have flashes of gin, wine, a table, a man in a suit with an earpiece, an argument, another man in a suit with an earpiece, and then some sort of frogmarch up some stairs.

A day later I received a phone call at home from the Important Man who had got Jon Culshaw and I the gig in the first place.

'What the hell happened at the Ashcroft party?' he said, without even bothering to say 'Hello'.

'Eh?' I replied, genuinely nonplussed but with a sudden unease in my stomach that I thought was perhaps the latest rumbling from the hangover I was still suffering from, but in all reality knew wasn't.

'The Ashcroft thing, at the Grosvenor?'

There was no more information forthcoming and, to be honest, I didn't want to hear any. The flashbacks had been increasing of late and I was living an existence somewhere between hell and reality, not unlike Tim Robbins in the film *Jacob's Ladder*, only the demons I kept seeing had the faces of the mid-eighties' Conservative Government.

'Yeah, it was fine,' I ventured.

'There's a story going round of an incredibly pissed bloke who sat down uninvited at a table and was offensive. Apparently he was rude to the guests, asked John Major if he ate peas off Edwina Currie, rambled about lying on the floor covered in chalk, and then whoever it was drank William Waldegrave's wine.'

'Well, he was Health Minister so that's actually doing him a favour—' I started.

'Was it you?'

'No. Absolutely not.'

'The description fits you.'

'It can't have been me, I would've remembered.'

'You don't remember being escorted from the party?'

'No.'

This was true. I didn't remember it at all. The flash-backs had tended to be grouping themselves more around the whole 'shouting into a former Prime Minister's face' thing.

'She won't remember that, she's got early-stage Alzheimer's,' I said.

'What?'

Shit. I'd said it out loud.

'Nothing. If it was me, which I'm sure it wasn't, then I'm really sorry. Shall I write to the Conservative Party and apologise?'

'You are a very stupid idiot and you fucked it right up.'

'Yes. Sorry.'

An invitation to Lord Ashcroft's 61st birthday party came there none. And then, seven years later, Lady Thatcher's failing health caught up with her and sadly she died.

It was nothing to do with me. I wasn't there.[8]

---

8 As far as I can remember, but, y'know, gin.

SEVENTEEN

... in which I fail to have a fight.

I take scant solace that the evening didn't end in what a tabloid newspaper would call 'a brawl'. I'm not sure I'd have got off quite as lightly as I did if, say, if I'd punched John Selwyn Gummer in the guts while Virginia Bottomley screamed, 'Leave it, Sir Malcolm, he's not worth it!' at a livid Rifkind who was itching to pile in. Perhaps if famously fist-handy John Prescott been there and had had my back, we could have taken them, but then again, seeing as how I have spent my life studiously avoiding any kind of physical violence, probably not.

Absent from this memoir will be a story about a fight. If you want to read about fighting then I politely suggest you look elsewhere, such as former SAS hardman-turned-author Andy MacNab's book *Bravo Two Zero* in which he continuously talks about 'slotting towelheads',[1] or even *Against the Odds*, the autobiography of boxing legend Larry Holmes.[2] Or why not leaf through *My Story*, the autobiography of Cheryl

---

1 Presumably some sort of DIY bathroom renovation technique? *Note to Editor: Can we check this one?*

2 No relation. Although, as far as I know, of course, he could be.

Cole,[3] who once punched a nightclub toilet attendant in the face during an argument about lollipops. When she was convicted of assault occasioning actual bodily harm in the ensuing court case, the judge summed her up saying she had committed 'an unpleasant piece of drunken violence', for which she showed 'no remorse whatsoever'. She is a thug, something I only mention because everyone seems to have forgotten it.

EVERYONE: Ooh, have you seen that Cheryl Tweedy-Cole-Fernandez-Versini is back on *The X Factor*?

ME: She's a thug.

EVERYONE: I love her! She's the nation's sweetheart.

ME: No she isn't, she's a danger to others.

EVERYONE: But she's got a million billion trillion followers on Twitter and when she tweeted that she was 'feeling down' recently they all started tweeting her back with the hashtag #cherylisahero

ME: She's not a hero – unless the definition of hero is 'someone who violently punches a toilet attendant called Sophie Amogbokpa in the face in a nightclub', an act for which she was charged and then tried and convicted in a court of law.

EVERYONE: She's a judge on *The X Factor*. I love *The X Factor*.

ME: The only judge we should be remembering is the

---

3 At time of writing she's now the people's princess, Cheryl Fernandez-Versini, but back when she violently punched a black lady in the eye for no good reason, she was Cheryl Tweedy. She can change her name as many times as she likes, We Will Never Forget.

one that sentenced her to pay costs and damages to
her victim and undertake 120 hours of community
service.

EVERYONE: Yes, but she's the face of L'Oréal.

ME: Are you sure she didn't *punch* the face of L'Oréal?
That would make more sense.

Everyone has forgotten. If you do anything else today,
remind at least five people of what the Nation's Sweetheart
is capable of and tell them to pass it on. Together we can
do this. Personally, I tend to shy away from actual physical
fights and fighting, in much the same way that a fox might
'shy away' from rich people on horses who want to kill it with
dogs or a toilet attendant in a nightclub in Guildford might
'shy away' from Cheryl Tweedy-Cole because according to
Judge Richard Haworth in The Crown vs. Cheryl Tweedy-
Cole she committed that 'unpleasant piece of drunken
violence [for which she] showed no remorse whatsoever'
while also apparently calling the toilet attendant a 'fucking
bitch', which is why he convicted her of assault occasioning
actual bodily harm, which I only mention here in passing, in
case you have forgotten.

Something that nearly ended in a fight, but didn't, was
the time that I accidentally got on the wrong side of a fat
man – figuratively and literally, as it turned out. We were
on yet another church youth group outing, this time to
see a vaguely amusing singing guitar duo called Phil and
John at the Derby Assembly Rooms. Phil and John were a
Christian twosome whose signature live moments involved
singing about gnomes and then, during a cover of Simon and

Garfunkel's 'The Boxer' after the bit that goes 'Lie-la-Lie', one of them would lean forward and hit the microphone with his head. They were not exactly Run-DMC, but we loved them.[4] On the way home, the minibus, in which we were all trying to get off with each other, stopped at Corley Services on the M6. Sustenance was decided upon, and we all dutifully queued up in the restaurant bit, sliding our trays along those metal runners that seemingly skirt the entire perimeter of such establishments like disappointing mono-rail systems. We were riding the Crap Food Train and we weren't going to stop until we had a can of Lilt each, and a biscuit. I was in front of Fat Kev who, you may recall, was called Fat Kev because his name was Kev, and he was fat.[5] He was, remember, also around six feet tall, and over his lemon-coloured jumper from M&S was wearing a padded red and blue striped puffed-up skiing coat, of the type which he would now argue was fashionable at the time but really wasn't. Back then he used to make the same argument about his glasses, which were of the type sported by Christopher Biggins.[6]

Because he was quite a bit taller than me, my peripheral view of him whilst perusing the service station's offerings of

---

4 To balance things up in religious terms, roundabout this time I was also listening to Black Sabbath's *Live Evil*. Equally evil in 1983 was *The Kids From Fame*, which I also liked. 'Starmaker' remains a magnificent piece of work.

5 Looking back, this is definitely more evidence, if it were needed, of my early creative streak.

6 Terrible big-framed things, like zany scaffolding for the face. See also Sue Pollard, Elton John and 'Brains' from *Thunderbirds*.

'under-flap' snacks[7] was really just a flash of garish jacket, so I was dimly aware that he was next to me, but I was concentrating on paying because we'd reached the till.

'Lilt and biscuits,' said the disinterested lady. If she was concerned about my lack of vegetables, she didn't show it. Mind you, she probably thought I was fine because back then, according to the advert, Lilt had a 'totally tropical taste' because it supposedly had real pineapples in it. Yeah. Sure. Did it fuck.

As I was fishing for coins, there was a flurry of movement from Fat Kev. Between me and the till lady were three or four wicker baskets, each containing a selection of biscuits in packets of three, of the type that you still find next to the kettle in a Travel Inn. I remember exactly what they were too, because it was at this point that everything seemed to drop into slow motion. On offer were shortbread fingers, fruit shorties and bourbons. Fat Kev reached over in front of me, quite rudely to my mind, and with his pudgy grasping hand at the end of his red and blue stupid Puffa-jacket sleeve, picked up a packet of Bourbons and put them on his tray. I looked at his tray. It already contained the gateau and a plate of chips. And now he wanted biscuits. I snatched them up, wheeled

---

7 You had to lift those flaps up to get the food out of the Perspex cave behind it. It was like looking at slices of gateaux in transparent veal crates. What's more, the whole self-service system was never properly thought through. It took two hands to lift a flap, hold it open, and take out the gateaux or whatever was inside; yet somehow you had to also keep your tray balanced on the slidey railway. This involved pushing your body against the tray to keep it in place while you helped yourself to cake. From a distance, and from behind, it looked like a row of people trying to frot with their own dinner.

round to face him and shoved the packet of Bourbons under his nose shouting, 'What the hell are these, you fat bastard?'

It wasn't his nose. And what's more, it wasn't his face either. It also wasn't his jacket, because it also wasn't him. At some point a bigger, fatter big fat man in a similar coat had cut in line and I hadn't spotted the swap. He was taller than Kev too. And angrier.

'What?' he said, and stepped forward.

A lot has been written about the response of fight or flight. Various journals describe it 'a physiological action that is triggered in times of acute stress; the body's sympathetic nervous system is activated due to the sudden release of hormones, stimulating the adrenal glans which in turn trigger the release of catecholamines, which include adrenalin and noradrenalin.' It was first described in the research of the American physiologist, Walter Bradford Cannon, as a theory that 'animals react to threats with a hormonal cascade that primes the animal for fighting or fleeing.' My research at this time was indicating that there was a third response, which was shitting yourself.

'What the fuck is your problem with my biscuits?' said the Man Who Wasn't Kev, somehow appearing to grow bigger and fatter, like someone had pumped meat into a dinghy.

By this time, all eyes were on the queue and it had gone very quiet. The woman on the till may not have been interested in my Lilt, but she was certainly interested in this. I was desperately trying to figure out what had happened. One minute Fat Kev had been next to me loading cake on his tray in his stupid STUPID, highly distinctive jacket and the next he was nowhere to be seen and a giant was wearing it. I cleared my throat as the whole of Corley Services waited. A hush had fallen over the place, from the racks of Curly Wurlys, Texans, and Star Bars in WH Smith to the inexplicable and mostly empty roomful of arcade games that they always had – and still have – in these places.[8] Even Asteroids had stopped beeping.

I cleared my throat again. I'd like to say it was for dramatic effect but it wasn't, it was because it had decided to close itself of its own accord; my own body deciding to spare me the humiliation and pain of being punched by actively assisting in my suicide by asphyxiating me. I've added another response to the theory of Walter Bradford Cannon; we now have 'fight, flight, shitting yourself *and* being autonomously killed by your own pharyngeal muscles'. There was nothing else for it. It was time to speak. I am not a fighter so the only thing to do was to summon all of my intelligence, humour and highly respected skills of diplomacy and talk my way out of it. I indicated the Bourbon biscuits.

'Er, it's just that I've never seen them in packets like that before,' I said. That was it. That was all I could manage.

'They've changed the design,' said my nemesis.

I couldn't believe it, I'd said a meaningless shit thing, and it had got me out of a hole. Careers in broadcasting have been built on less.

---

8 Why? Why are they here? I'm on the way to the North, I only stopped here to fill up with petrol and have a poo and a pasty. Why would I want to have a game of Fatal Fury: King of Fighters? At best it's an unlikely scenario. 'Come on, Graham, if we get a move on we can make Kendal by late afternoon and perhaps make your terminally ill mother's bedside before she passes.' 'Hang on, love, I just thought I'd pop in here first to see if I can get the high score on Ridge Racer.'

'I thought you were my friend, sorry,' I added, a riposte worthy of Oscar Wilde. He shrugged.

With the chance of violence fast fading, Corley Services on the M6 returned to normal. There was an audible 'ping' as, across the walkway, out beyond the Star Bars, Asteroids started up again.

'But you called him a fat bastard,' said my friend Woody, later, struggling to get his words out in between crying with laughter as we made our way back to the minibus.

'Perhaps God was protecting me,' I said. 'Or maybe he didn't hear me properly?' Which was really the only logical explanation for how I'd escaped having the totally tropical taste of a Lilt can shoved firmly up my arse. This was my first, formative lesson in being careful what you say to people bigger than you are.

'If you called me a fat bastard, *I'd* punch you,' said Fat Kev, spilling cake down his Less-Than-Amazing Two-Colour Dreamcoat.

'Shut up you fat bastard,' I said, and we drove off into the Midlands' night.

The second time I didn't have a fight was at a school leavers' disco. I had school friends and I had church youth club friends and though this involved a church hall, it was a school event. We'd hired a dusty old hall in Nuneaton town centre and stuffed it full of borrowed equipment and lights. There was also quite a lot of booze so a good time was certainly being had by all, but the good times all came to a bit of a sudden end when, just before the allotted kick-out time of 11.30 p.m., the front door banged open and in came some older kids. Five or six of them, they were probably eighteen or nineteen, were a bit drunk and were looking for more lager and a fight in that order. Almost immediately a tense stand off ensued, like the one between North and South Korea, except with drunken teenagers. The 'hard' kids in my year, Richard Hudson, Mark Bodill and a couple of others, stood their ground, forming a defensive line between the rest of us and the invaders. A few words were exchanged and then it all kicked off. Rich Hudson got headbutted, Mark Bodill pushed the older kid into one of the many nearby stacks of chairs[9] (which collapsed) and a melee broke out. Within seconds, despite hovering at the back near the disco equipment, I found myself faced with a chunky spotty kid in a leather jacket looking to punch something, and upon seeing me, decided I was it. So he punched me. I'd never been punched before so it came as a bit of a shock, so much so that rather than fall down I just stood there in surprise. He'd aimed for my face and pretty much nailed it, getting me straight in the right eye. When I didn't fall down he looked as surprised as I did but quickly recovered his composure and made to do it again. He didn't get the chance though, because that was when someone smashed him across the face with a mop. As he staggered backwards my rescuer grabbed my hand and pulled me away, and my sight of him was lost in the general brawl that was going on in and around an increasing number of falling chairs. I turned and looked into the eyes of Sarah Peatfield, Mop Warrior.

'All right?' she said.

'Thanks,' I said. 'He hit me in the eye.'

She peered at it.

---

9 Yes, we'd tidied up. We were brought up proper.

I had a quick flashback to when I'd had stitches in my head, specifically remembering that injuries could provoke a level of sympathy in girls completely at odds with the fact that until you'd been wounded, they hadn't really even been aware that you exist. I quite fancied Sarah Peatfield, so I'd like to tell you what followed was like that scene in *Raiders of the Lost Ark* when Indiana is injured after being beaten up by a Nazi, and, as he points to his various injuries, Marion kisses them one by one until he points to his lips and they lock with hers in a passionate embrace.

'Can't see anything,' she said. 'Looks fine.'

'He hit me quite hard,' I said.

'Nah. Not really,' she replied and went back into the fray. I'm ashamed to say I didn't go back into the fray, and in truth the fray was over as quickly as it started as by then the older kids had managed to grab two-thirds of a bottle of cider from the booze table and had legged it. There were plenty of proper injuries. Rich Hudson had a nosebleed, Mark Bodill had a split lip, and at least two of the hall chairs would be confined to a life where one of their four legs would never again sit flush on the floor. I already knew that, come Monday, this tale would be turned into something resembling the *Gunfight at the OK Corral* and, if I could big my part up, I would appear cool like Rich Hudson and Mark Bodill. This depended on two things:

1) My injury needed to develop into a fully fledged black eye.
2) No one must know that I was rescued by a girl with a mop.

The evening was over. Examining my punched eye in the mirror in the toilet, I could see that Sarah Peatfield was right, there was not one indication that I'd taken a hit and thus there was zero evidence that I'd played a big part – a major part, a front-line soldier's part – in the Assault on The Leavers' Disco. Yet I had taken hostile fire, and this put me up there with the hard kids. Except it seemed that I had nothing to show for it. And that's why, right there, in the male toilets of St Nicolas Parish Church Hall, I hatched a plan. Bruises and black eyes take a while to develop, I reasoned, so despite there being nothing visible now, by Monday there could well be – especially if I helped it along. And that's why I punched myself in the eye.

It's quite hard to effectively punch yourself in the eye. The chief problem is that because you know you're doing it, it comes as no surprise, so the part of your body that you're trying to punch is quite ready to flinch from the part of the body that's trying to hit it. My eye, being my own eye, clearly didn't want to be punched, and so each time I did it, tentatively increasing the force of the punch, my own face shied away, despite me trying to make it not. My own face knew I was an idiot, even if I didn't. I appreciate that you may well be unaware of this biological fact, because the chances are you've never been so stupid as to try to punch yourself in the eye, but take it from me, it's nigh on impossible. I didn't want to actually hurt myself, either; I just wanted just get enough of a bruise to make it look like I'd had a proper fight. I peered in the mirror. Nothing. Not a mark. It was now 11.40 p.m. My dad had arranged to pick me up near the library, a five-minute walk away, and that gave me more time. More time to also impress my dad. Five minutes to be precise. Five more minutes of walking along punching myself in the eye. Which is what I did, all the way to the car. I really needed this to be a bruise by Monday, because at school the fight would be all anyone was talking about. Eventually, by moving my head forwards to meet my fist I managed to get one good hard shot in and, as it really, really hurt I was sure I could feel it swelling up. Out of the other eye, I could see Dad's car parked next to the video shop opposite the library so I limped as well, for good measure. I opened the passenger door and got in. He was going to see the eye, and I, Son to my father, could tell him I'd been in a fight. It would be a rite of passage, a moment between us. We were Warriors.

'Good party?' he said.

'Some older kids gatecrashed,' I said. 'There was a fight.'

He turned to look at me, and in the sodium arc glow of an eighties' streetlight, and the faulty alternator light from the dashboard of a Vauxhall Cavalier, I could see concern on his face.

'What happened?'

'I got punched in the eye.'

He looked closer. It wasn't dissimilar to the eye examination my mum had given me all those years ago when our neighbour Rob had shot me in the face with his starting pistol. He also came to the same medical conclusion that my mum had.

'Can't see anything,' he said. 'Looks fine.' And we drove home.

On Monday morning, by the time I got to school, everyone knew about the mop.

EIGHTEEN

... in which an Oscar-nominated screenwriter sticks a pair of scissors in my ear in Graham Norton's disabled toilet.

As will have been intimated by the 'author's biography' on the jacket of this book (and indeed, by even the most cursory of Google searches)[1] I now ply my slightly suspect trade as a writer and broadcaster. I'm not sure what led me down this path, apart from an inability to do pretty much anything else with any degree of success and though my dad still bemoans my lack of anything resembling an actual 'skill',[2] it was he who inadvertently fired the (thankfully metaphorical this time)[3] starting pistol.

As I grew up, my mum, being a nurse, would often work nights. During the day, when Dad was at work, she looked

---

1 If you do ever google 'Jon Holmes' take care to spell it correctly. This isn't me being some kind of egomaniac, it's simply a warning that if you search for '*John* Holmes' and you have safe-search turned off, you're going to get more than you bargained for. John Holmes was a noted star of a selection of adult leisure films that have titles such as *Naughty Girls Like It Big* and *Saturday Night Beaver*. He is, as far as I know, no relation. Although given how little I know about who my real dad actually is, I suppose he could be. He certainly seemed to put it around a bit.

2 See Chapter Three, in which I go to work with my builder dad and fail to be any use whatsoever.

3 See Chapter Five.

after my sister and me, and then at night, because they needed to make ends meet, she went off to work leaving my dad in charge. On any given night, she would put me to bed, and then from my bedroom window, through a gap in the curtains, I would watch her walk up the road to catch the hospital minibus that would ferry her to work. She went, safe in the knowledge that I was tucked up in bed, ready for school the next day. And more often than not, I was. Except for when *Monty Python's Flying Circus* was on.

The original run of Python ended with series four in 1974 when I would have been five, so I can only presume that I am remembering repeats. As soon as my mum left the house, my dad would pop upstairs, rouse me from my slumber, usher me downstairs, give me a cup of hot milk and let me sit with him to watch Cleese, Palin, Jones, Idle, Chapman and Gilliam hit each other with fish and argue about having an argument. I had absolutely no idea what was going on and did not understand a word of it, but over time this became a thing that Dad and I did together. He would laugh heartily at it, so I did too, and a bond was formed over comedy. He would also play me his Goodies' albums and Peter Sellers' monologues that he had on vinyl, but it was Python that had me hooked. With my armchair psychiatrist's hat back on,[4] it was probably this that made me associate all the best comedy with breaking rules; just as Python were pushing the boundaries with sketches about throwing up into graves or cannibalism, so too was my dad bravely trampling all over my mum's strict bedtime instructions. Somewhere in my

---

4 See also Chapter Four: Here Be Spiders.

head I equated the two, and that's probably why I still hold the record for the largest fine ever in British Broadcasting history for taste and decency offences,[5] so it's all my dad's fault. If he'd got me up at night to help him build a house, maybe my career would have taken a very different turn. It would also explain why my parents were called up to school to explain to my teachers why I'd written a story which was essentially an adult version of Enid Blyton's *The Folk of the Faraway Tree*, which I had recently read and subsequently decided that it would be a whole lot more entertaining if the children characters, rather than buy into the whole 'mystical wood' shit, had set about killing the tree's occupants with weapons. It was like *The Hunger Games* meets the 'Teddy Bear's Picnic',[6] and had worried a teacher.

'I think it's a cause for concern,' Mrs Gibson said to my mum and dad. She pointed at the exercise book that was open on her desk. 'In this bit, one of the children beats a fairy called Silky with a rock. There's also cannibalism.'

'Mmm,' said my mum. 'I'm not sure where he gets this from, are you, Les?' looking at my dad.

'No idea,' he said. And shifted uncomfortably in his chair.

*

---

5 I also present stuff on the radio. In 2001, I invented an on-air game for my late-night show on the then Virgin Radio called 'Swearing Radio Hangman For The Under 12s'. When a caller (nine-year-old Katie) came on and spelled out the phrase 'Soapy Tit Wank', it's fair to say that Ofcom didn't find it nearly as funny as I did. It cost the station £150,000 in fines, a financial punishment that was halved when Virgin agreed to fire me. I think it's still a record, although Ofcom didn't give me so much as a certificate.
6 Which, actually, is a bloody good pitch. Hollywood – call me.

Years later, with these stories of dead pixies on my CV, stints on the radio, some television appearances and a couple of Radio 4 comedies under my belt, I found myself being paid to write for Graham Norton. It was 2002, back when he had a five-nights-a-week chat show on Channel 4 called *V Graham Norton* and, with two or three other writers, it was my job to co-write his opening monologue at the top of the show, while the other part of my job was to find increasingly innovative ways for him to show a dildo to Westlife.

It seemed to me at the time that Westlife (who were a sort of Tesco value-range Boyzone)[7] were on every week. In reality they probably weren't, but it certainly felt like it. We would arrive at the office near London's fashionable South Bank where Graham's production company was based, at 10.00 a.m., and be presented with a list of the chat show guests. Graham was obviously going to talk to them, but the question was 'what else should we do with them?'. The answer was often a series of novelty props and odd items that we'd been sent by desperate marketing companies, and more often than not, given Graham's 'saucy' reputation, we would be inundated with sex toys. There was a tall cupboard in the writers' room that was full of them; from vibrating love eggs to anal beads, in fact, we'd pretty much got a whole branch of Anne Summers in the corner and, on a regular basis, something from this cupboard would be employed to embarrass Westlife. In fact, it probably only happened once but I remember thinking (for this was quite early on in what passes for my career) that being paid to sit in a room with

---

7 Who themselves were a sort of Aldi to Take That's Morrisons.

a range of vibrators, genuinely trying to decide which was the funniest one to give to a boy band on the television, was a fairly odd job. It wasn't the oddest thing that happened during my time on *V Graham Norton* though. Yet this one didn't involve dildos, but rather a pencil, a pair of scissors, a disabled toilet and an Oscar nominated screenwriter.

There were two of us writing the show that day: myself and a writer called Simon Blackwell. Simon has since gone on to great things; he's written episodes of *Peep Show* and *The Thick of It*, is a writer-producer on the Emmy Award-winning *Veep* for HBO and was nominated for an Oscar as one of the writers of *The Thick of It* spin-off film *In The Loop*. Back in 2002 though, he was sitting next to me trying to think of jokes about the contestants in the *Big Brother* house. When it began in 2000, *Big Brother* quickly became a ratings juggernaut and, because it was on Channel 4 each night before we were, we were tasked with referencing it as much as possible. So there we were, chatting idly about stuff and doing a thing which comedy writers in comedy writing rooms do – which is being as absolutely offensive as possible about something[8] in a form which could never be broadcast under any circumstances whatsoever,[9] when for some reason, as we were both leafing through the morning's papers in silence, I idly stuck the end of a pencil in my ear.

---

8 In this case Jade Goody.
9 A writer who shall remain nameless once came up with a joke in a writers' room that stunned even other comedy writers into a momentary silence. I can't even bring myself to write it down here, but if you ever meet me, ask me what it was and I'll tell you.

To this day, I don't know why. It was a sharp pencil with a rubber[10] on the end, the kind that sits in its own metal cup and is deployed by turning the pencil upside down to rub out any mistakes incurred with the pointy bit. And it was this rubber end that I was lazily twirling in my auricle to pass the time. And then it came off. Suddenly the rubber, still inside its metal mount, came away and lodged in my ear. My first reaction was to jump slightly, which was a problem, as this only served to shove it further into my ear canal with the rest of the pencil. It went in, and it wedged there. Firmly. It had locked itself in place with no room to move in any direction, except deeper. Who knew that the rubber at the end of a pencil is exactly the same size, shape and circumference as a human ear canal? It was a perfect fit, it was painful, I'd gone deaf, and I couldn't get it out.

Simon was engrossed in the day's big tabloid *Big Brother* story, which was about contestant Jade Goody giving another housemate 'PJ' a 'BJ', so he had understandably failed to notice that I'd tilted my head on one side and was desperately trying to get the pencil to reconnect with its errant end. By this time, I had started to panic a bit. What if it went into my brain? Obviously the rational side of me was telling me that it wouldn't go into my brain, but hang on – what if the rational side of my brain was the very bit of my brain that it had gone into, thus rendering my rationality moot? I would die a slow, lingering, pencil-related brain death. I needed help.

---

10 If you are an American person, I mean an eraser, rather than a condom. We didn't have pencils with condoms on, even in Graham Norton's office.

'Simon?'

It was my voice, but it was all muffled in my head on one side like I was talking at him under water.

'We could do something on Robin Gibb,' he said, seemingly proposing a joke on that morning's death of a Bee Gee,[11] which was also big news.

'Yes,' I said, and immediately started thinking of sick, unbroadcastable ones. I may well have had a pencil lodged in my ear, but a comedy writer is never off duty.

'I wonder if you could do me a favour?' I said.

'Mmm?' he said, not really looking up.

I didn't really want to say 'I've got the rubber off a pencil stuck in my ear' because that would sound weird and embarrassing in an office situation. So because of this I instead opted to say:

'Could you come with me a minute?'

I had reasoned that I was going to need help, and that getting out of the office and to an area with more privacy was crucial. Otherwise I'd come across like a bit of a twat. The sort of person who stuck a pencil in their ear.

'What for?' said Simon, not unreasonably, and looked up from the news of the deceased falsetto with suspicion.

'Just a . . . thing.' I said, entirely unable to adequately explain.

He stared at me. 'What thing?'

It was a fair question. We were friends and colleagues, but

---

11 This was done. And the joke duly went into the programme, angering a surviving Bee Gee to the point of apoplexy. The resulting fallout of complaints even gets a mention in Graham's autobiography.

as I'd never asked him in hushed tones to accompany me anywhere before, we were now in uncharted territory.

'Come with me, I'll explain.' I realised I was sounding like a paedophile trying to entice a child into his car. I may as well have been offering him sweets.

'I'll give you sweets.'

'What? What for?'

'I was joking. Just come outside into the corridor.'

He took a last glance at dead Robin Gibb, and stood up.

'This is weird,' he said, which, to be fair, it was.

He followed me into the corridor, and looked around expectantly.

'So?' he said.

'Not here,' I said. 'In here.' And I indicated the slightly ajar door of the disabled toilet.

He looked at me like things had just got even odder, which they had.

'No.'

'Please . . .'

'I am not going with you into a disabled toilet.'

'It's nothing weird,' I said, when it obviously was.

'What the f—' he began.

'I've got the rubber off the end of a pencil stuck in my ear and I need your help to get it out,' I kind of blurted at him, showing him the end of the pencil where the rubber now wasn't.

'Oh. OK. Fine,' he said.

We went into the disabled toilet and locked the door.

'Look, in here,' I ventured, and tilted the side of my head in his direction. He peered at the proffered lobe.

'You're right,' he said. 'How did you . . . ?' He tailed off, unsure of – well, probably everything at this stage.

'Doesn't matter. Can you get it out? I've tried and I can't.'

He squinted.

'It's quite far in,' he said. 'I'm going to need something to get it. Tweezers or something.'

Simon's career has soared to great heights, but I doubt it's ever bettered this moment.

'Have you got any?'

'No,' I said.

'Right.' There was a silence, as we appeared to be formulating a plan. I caught sight of us in the mirror. I saw one man deep in thought and another, half-deaf one, with his head cocked to one side. We looked stupid.

'I've got an idea. Wait here.'

He unlocked the door and disappeared back into the office. I waited. To pass the time I came up with three more unbroadcastable jokes about the dead Bee Gee. I also re-locked the door in case anyone else came in. No one tried. Shortly, he was back.

'Open the door, it's me.'

I did, and he was holding a pair of scissors.

'What the fuck are you going to do with those? Cut my head open to get it out?'

'No, I'm going to use them to grip it and pull it out. Funnily enough, being a writers' office, pliers are in short supply. And you're the idiot who got yourself into this so be quiet and assume the position.'

I hoped to God no one was listening to this conversation at the door. Especially not Graham Norton. I re-cocked my head and, with the precise skill of someone who had never had to perform a procedure like this before, he gingerly put the pointy scissor blades into my ear.

And pulled it out. With no fuss whatsoever. He'd just gently opened the blades, gripped it and pulled it out.

I was standing in Graham Norton's disabled toilet while a soon-to-be-Oscar-nominated screenwriter was trying to get the end of a pencil out of my ear with a pair of scissors. And again I don't care how many memoirs you read in your life, I think I can pretty much guarantee you'll never find another sentence like that.

We went back to the office and looked at some dildos.

There is a term, well used by anyone except possibly astronauts or anyone who's ever watched anything with Keith Lemon in it, that claims confidently that 'worse things happen at sea'. There are also worse – or at least more embarrassing – things that happen than getting the end of a pencil jammed in your ear next to a cupboard full of sex toys in Graham Norton's office, and one of them almost certainly involves my 2003 self-assessment tax form and a sexually repressed old lady.

I couldn't say for certain, but I'd be willing to bet that there also aren't many memoirs that contain details of a meeting between the author and his or her accountant, on the occasion of handing in a tax form largely because if one is charged with recalling riveting anecdotes from one's life for the purpose of storytelling, an accountant and a tax form are not necessarily where one would begin. But then again, I can't imagine what happened between us, in a stuffy office one January, has happened to that many people.

Marion was the accountant in question. She was in her fifties, and gave the impression of being a stern, sour-faced, by-the-book financial advisor, because that's exactly what she was. She was in my employ simply because I don't understand self-assessment tax forms, and become easily confused by maths. My patronage certainly wasn't because I was seeking to put money into a Chris Moyles, Jimmy Carr or Gary Barlow-style tax haven, partly because I don't have the income of Chris Moyles, Jimmy Carr or Gary Barlow, but also because it simply wouldn't be an option. Marion was the sort of person who, if I'd even mentioned the phrase 'tax loophole', or anything like it, would have pulled me out of my chair by my ear, marched me to the bathroom and washed my mouth out with bleach and ethics. Her approach to my form was one of peering at it over her half-moon spectacles and pointing out that, while it could be argued that I did need to clean my teeth in the morning before going to work, attempting to claim 'toothpaste' as an expense was a criminal act, punishable by death. She was thorough, and would countenance nothing short of absolute scrupulous neatness in the form of forms. And that's what made what happened in her office all the more horrific.

It wasn't quite her office. That was an inner sanctum I never got to see. I secretly imagined it to be a spinster's cave, full of china cats and abstinence; a throwback to an austere time when rationing was all the rage, men would politely wear dinner jackets and belts and braces in the bath and nice ladies had cobwebs over their vaginas until they were married. Marion was just one accountant at a small firm of them; she'd been assigned to me and, as the rest of their clientele appeared to consist of small local companies and successful regional businesses, to be honest, I think the fact that I was on the radio and wrote jokes about dildos for Graham Norton completely confused them. We would annually convene, Marion and I, in a meeting room with wood panelling, nice paintings on the walls, and a large central table, a beautiful mahogany behemoth that was steeped in the history of accountancy. If tables could talk, the tales that this one could tell of the great and the good of Canterbury Window and Door Replacements Ltd discussing the finer points of employee pensions, would literally not be worth repeating.

As usual, an assistant showed me into the room and then left me on my own. To pass the time, I took my completed self-assessment tax form out of my bag. I had also brought along a shoebox with jumbled receipts in it, because I have the filing nous of an idiot. And, true to form, I had left it all until the last minute and had only self-completed the self-assessment tax form the night before, lying on my bedroom floor studiously ticking boxes with a biro and writing the word 'toothpaste' in the appropriate place. I placed the document (eighteen pages) on the table and it wasn't long before Marion swept in. She was the sort of person who sort of made you want to stand to attention on her arrival, so I did.

'Jonathan Holmes,' she said, peering at her austere pad that she'd written my name austerely on with an austere pen.

'Hello, how are you?' I ventured. 'Nice to see you again.'

'Mmm,' she said, suggesting that the feeling wasn't mutual and indicated with an austere wave of her austere hand that I should sit down.

'You've left this late haven't you?'

It was 12th January, so yes. Accountants can never understand why, given that the previous tax year ended in April, we self-employed human people leave it until the following January to do anything about it. Consequently, an accountant's January is a shitstorm of shoeboxes and they hate us for it.

'Is this your . . . form?' She paused before she said 'form', to indicate her disdain, almost sneering the word and looking at it as though I'd written my tax assessment on a turd and had shat it out in the middle of the table.

'Yes. I think I've filled it in right.'

'I very much doubt it,' she said and slid it towards herself, while simultaneously giving my shoebox a glance which, had it been a flower, would have caused it to wither and die.

'Mmmm,' she said slowly and opened it. She ran her eyes over the first page: 'Interest and Dividends from UK banks, building societies, etc.'

'Mmmm.'

She flipped some pages. She ran her eyes over page eight, 'Employment. Hmmm.'

We'd graduated from Mmmm to Hmmm. This was a Good Thing. She glanced over at a separate page I'd handed to her marked 'Expenses'.

She crossed something out. I was on the other side of the table so I couldn't see what, but I was guessing at 'toothpaste'.

And that's when it happened. She went back to the form, turned the page and looked down. I followed her gaze and that's when we both saw it. Right in the middle of Page Eleven somewhere between 'Tax allowances for vehicles and equipment (capital allowances)' and 'Calculating your profit or loss', lay a pubic hair. There was a real life honest-to-goodness pubic hair, one of mine, sitting in the middle of my self-assessment tax form and we were both looking at it.

I'll be frank, if there is a protocol to follow when this happens, I didn't know it. And neither did Marion.

It was Nietzsche, in his work *Beyond Good and Evil*, in a section entitled 'Epigrams and Interludes', who said that 'when you look long into the abyss, the abyss looks also into you'. Well, replace the word 'abyss' in that sentence with the word 'pube' and that's what was happening. The pube was looking at us, taunting us, gazing into our souls. It's a cliché to say that the silence in the room was deafening, but it was. All senses were numbed. Everything became meaningless. There was nothing else, only pube. It was like a black hole singularity; everything in that room in that moment suddenly and without warning condensed down and focused in on one solitary groin hair. You might be thinking 'well, surely it could have been passed off as *any* hair; a head hair, maybe, or a stray one from a much loved pet?' Alas, no. There was no mistaking it. It was a pube. A dark, wiry it-really-could-only-be-one-thing pube and it was obscuring 'Goods and Services for your own use'. In fact, from the angle I was at, its position had almost turned a number '4' into a number '8', making my year-on-year profit far more impressive than it actually was.

What seemed like minutes passed. If there had been a clock in the room, it would have ticked, loudly. Both of us were staring at the violated form, yet neither could mention it. It was clear that someone had to do something about it. And that someone was me. So I took the only option available to me – I resolved to subtly try to blow the pube away. At this point, the form was about three feet away on Marion's side of the table, and I reasoned that, if I spoke breathily, perhaps I could blow it off the table before she realised what it was. The rational part of me knew that it was already too late for this, but I was clinging to the hope that Marion had almost certainly never been this close to another person's pube in her whole life, so maybe she wouldn't recognise it.

She'd recognised it. I don't know if you've ever tried to speak breathily enough to blow a pubic hair off a tax-assessment form at a distance of three feet across a table,[12] but in case you haven't let me be the first to tell you that it's very, very difficult. You have to get a lot of 'f's into the sentence and the odd plosive 'p' and you have to say them quite hard in order to force breath out of your mouth seemingly naturally, but with a force roughly equivalent to that which you'd get if you flapped a newspaper at a wasp, or idly used a magazine to waft away a fart.

'The Form is Filled in using a Pen. I wasn't Fortunate enough to use a Printer.'

That would have been the ideal sentence to try, but what was the point? By the time I'd formulated a string of words that could begin to even slightly work in this context (the

---

12 I'm just guessing here, but probably not?

immediate ones I'd come up with were 'it's a _fucking_ _p_ube') the hair was out of the bag and we had to deal with it, together. So we did what anyone would do in this situation: we ignored it. Marion ran her finger down the list of 'Goods and services for your own use' and simply diverted her finger around the wiry curl, giving it a wide berth. She came to rest on some expenses.

'You're claiming for travel,' she said, staring at some numbers, while I continued to stare at the hair.

'Er, yes. I travel a lot. On the train. To work. In London.' I added for clarification. 'I have to travel to places to write about travel.'

She harrumphed as though this was the most ridiculous thing she'd ever heard and the finger began to move again, like a witch's digit tracing instructions for a spell. And every time she swerved the pube, I winced and continued to mentally weigh up whether or not to actually mention it and explain how it had got there.

'Yes, sorry about the pube but I filled the form in lying on my bedroom floor so a stray one must have just sort of crept in. Off the carpet, I mean, not from my groin. I haven't . . . I mean I don't . . . masturbate while filling in my tax form . . . Although it would make it a bit more enjoyable I suppose? Haha.'

Fortunately I thought better of saying this out loud and instead considered a new option, Option B, which was to reach across the table to indicate something on the form with a flourish, and thus sweep the pube away.

'And see where I have left the allowances on sale of cessation of business use blank,' I would have said, while simultaneously brushing it aside, but she have known what I was doing, because now the pube wasn't so much the elephant in the room, as the great hairy mammoth in the room and we were both in its thrall. Maybe I could style it out.

'Any income from property?' she said.

'No,' I replied, weakly.

I failed to style it out. In the end she shut the form, sealed it in an A4 envelope, pube and all, and put it in the out tray to post to the Inland Revenue. They probably thought it was a protest and have now flagged me as a troublemaker to rank alongside Starbucks and Vodafone.

I know they say that tax doesn't have to be taxing, but that meeting bloody was.

NINETEEN

. . . in which I am threatened by a man with two names,
one of which is 'Chuck'.

I do travel, and sometimes a bit further than to London on the train. It's fair to say that I have the travel bug. Given that, other than the Holmes' family sacking of a rooftop bar in Athens, most childhood holidays were to North Wales I'm unsure as to where I picked it up. Nowadays, if I don't fly off somewhere to look at a remote corner of the world on a semi-regular basis I get a bit twitchy, an itch that is only alleviated by walking a previously unopened trail through the Himalayas or diving on a World War Two battleship in the Red Sea. Among other things, I have been lucky enough to stay in a remote cabin in Alaska, photograph jaguars in the Panatanal, lie on my back on a frozen lake watching the Northern Lights on an archipelago off the top of Norway, and become hospitalised by sea urchins in the waters of Puerto Rico, many of these experiences as a sometime travel writer for the *Sunday Times*[1]. But the travel bug was

---

[1] In the past year or two, my travel writing trips have become far less far-flung and considerably less frequent. This has been due to having a) two young children and b) a proper job, presenting a radio breakfast show. It's difficult to fly to the forests of St Lucia to eat hallucinogenic bark when you've got to be up at 3.00 a.m. to play Arcade Fire songs to a predominantly ABC1 audience of indie music fans. Plus, the best trips are the ones that come with an inbuilt level of potentially deadly risk, which tends to annoy loved ones.

already biting as soon as I was old enough to go it alone. Although the first time I did, I came close to being abducted by aliens.

It happened deep in a remote part of the Blue Ridge Mountains, on the border of Tennessee and North Carolina, and I had an experience that simply could not be explained by any rational means.[2] It was 1991 and I was on my first ever road trip across America with my friend Graham. We were fresh out of university, and had decided to spend our student loans on flying to the States, living for three months in a car. Inspired by Kerouac, our plan was to buy one and drive in a zigzag fashion across the country, attempting to visit every landmark we'd ever heard of or seen in a film along the way. We were starting in June in New York City and our only appointment was with our flight home from Los Angeles at the end of August. And once we'd paid for the tickets, and organised our wheels, we had precisely eight hundred dollars to live on, which worked out at around eight dollars a day. What could possibly go wrong?

Quite a lot, as it turned out. First, we'd bought the car from an unscrupulous friend of a distant cousin of an American relative of Graham's dad. Even though Graham had never met him, 'Chuck'[3] had arranged for his 'buddy' Hank to sell his 've-hicle' to us for just a few hundred dollars, and so when we picked it up, we weren't expecting much, although in 've-hicle' terms, we were expecting more than we got. I can't even remember what kind of car it was, only

---

2 Until it was.
3 This was, apparently, his nickname. His real name was Gary.

that it was broken and rubbish. There was a distinct lean to it that, despite my lack of any kind of mechanical training and/or knowledge, I knew it looked odd. One wheel seemed wrong, what passed for an exhaust pipe was held on with tape, and there was a crack across the windscreen so large that it would have served – if it ever got us that far – as a kind of heads-up display map of the Grand Canyon.

Back then, many US states didn't have any kind of equivalent of an MOT test like we do in the UK. Here, it's a byword for automotive safety, and if your car is three years old or more, then the annual test is a legal requirement that your vehicle must pass. In America they don't need one because if you buy a car and it crashes into something or kills anyone, then the correct thing to do instead is sue the 'ass' off of everyone concerned. But what they did have was a 'State Inspection', a test carried out when cars change hands (rather than every year) which is why, on Day 2 of Jon and Graham's American Adventure, we found ourselves queuing in a state building on the outskirts of Queens, waiting to hear the verdict on the accident-waiting-to-happen we'd bought from Chuck's buddy being passed down by a recalcitrant Vehicle Inspector.

'Are you the new owner?' he grunted through a grille. His name badge implied that his name was Bobby-Joe. This was amazing; we'd been in the US of A less than forty-eight hours and already we'd met a Chuck and a Hank and a Bobby-Joe. It was everything we could have possibly dreamed of.

'I am,' I said, proudly, and in the best English accent I could muster.

'You Australian?' he said.

'No. English,' I said, 'British. From the United Kingdom.' I used all three of our identifiable landmass handles to help Bobby-Joe along.

'Car's busted,' he said.

It turned out that our 'ride' had been pimped, but only in the way that a pimp might beat up one of his prostitutes, causing her so much damage that she wouldn't ever work again. Chuck had sold us what was, to all intents and purposes, an undriveable shitbox. The 'leaning to the left' issue, which my keen knowledge of all things engine based had detected, was irreparable and the windscreen was illegal.

'Fail,' said Bobby-Joe, and stamped our paperwork accordingly. 'Where did you get this heap of crap?'

Chuck's buddy Hank had much to answer for, but that was going to have to wait because the immediate problem was that, because it had failed, we now were not allowed to drive it back to Chuck's house, where we were staying. Our road trip wasn't off to a great start, given that we couldn't currently take a trip on any actual roads and were now just the proud owners of some metal. We called Chuck. I suggested to him, not unreasonably, that we should ask Hank for our money back. Chuck reacted like I'd kicked him in the throat.

'Fuckin' what?' he said, with, frankly, an air of incredulity that belied the situation. 'No fuckin' way.'

'What do you mean "no fucking way"?' I said.

'But he sold us a car that doesn't work,' said Graham. 'It's failed the inspection.'

'Sold as seen,' said Chuck.

I got the distinct impression that Chuck and Hank had split the money and had already spent it in a bar.

'But we're going on a road trip,' argued Graham. 'We need a car.'

'You gotta car,' said Chuck.

'No, what we've got, you stupid, fucking, thick, American-fraternity cockhouse, is the automotive equivalent of your stupid, fucking, thick, American brain in that it fucking doesn't fucking work properly.'

I said this, but only silently in my own head.

What I said out loud was this: 'Chuck, I don't mean to be rude, but you're being a little unreasonable. I have to say that I've got a problem with this.'

'Yeah? Well I gotta gun,' said Chuck.

I'll be honest; our relationship with Chuck had deteriorated. This was Monday and we were due to leave on the Friday, four days later. Graham and I had had a plan; this, the first week of our trip was to be taken up with sightseeing in New York and sourcing a car, and then we'd be off, carefree, with only the open road ahead. Except now we were a bit buggered, especially when, later that evening, I went back into the room that Graham and I were sharing at Chuck's place to find my trip diary[4] open on the bed at the previous entry, in a place and position that I distinctly hadn't left it.

To be fair to Chuck, he had been more than hospitable; we were, to all intents and purposes, complete strangers, yet on some kind of tenuous family connection with Graham,

---

4 Yes, I wrote a trip diary. Once a writer, always a writer.

Chuck had put us up. We were his guests so I guess he had every right to look at my trip diary that I'd left closed in a bedside drawer that was also closed inside a room with a closed door. The issue now was that the entry that Chuck had uncovered had detailed in no uncertain terms not only exactly what I thought of Chuck, but also what I thought of his 'buddy' Hank and their second-hand car business. It *may* have contained the occasional historical swearword of Anglo-Saxon derivation and *perhaps*, when viewed objectively, one could perhaps be forgiven for perceiving the entry to be ever-so-slightly demeaning to our American cousins. The United Kingdom of England, Scotland, Northern Ireland and Wales may well enjoy a special relationship with our 'buddies' across the water, but I'm not sure that the thoughts I'd committed to paper were going to be used as some kind of Anglo-US treaty of friendship anytime soon. Basically what I'd written was that Chuck was a cunt. And so was Hank. And so was their car.

Looking back, maybe I had overreacted. Chuck had put a roof over our dumb student heads, two, in fact, if you also count the one with three workable wheels, the dents in and the broken windscreen hanging off it, and we were grateful. It's just we were now screwed, penniless, and our American dream was turning into a nightmare. Chuck had read my diary and to prove it, below my ranting entry, in scrawled handwriting, Chuck had written four simple words. Four words that made a bad day worse. Much worse. And this was before I'd even remembered that Chuck had a gun.

*

Much has been written, many hands have been wrung, many teeth have been gnashed and numerous voices have been raised for and against gun ownership in the USA. The pro-gun lobby are vociferous in their defence of their right to bear arms, and are a frightening bunch for the politicians and the anti-gun campaigners to take on, partly because they are powerful, well-organised lobbyists and also because, y'know, they have guns. Piers Morgan tried to take them on once, and he ended up having his CNN chat show prised from his cold, dead hands. Americans like guns; it's as simple as that. It's not something we really understand in the UK, because we don't have them, or rather we do, but they're usually the type owned by farmers and no one looks cool packing heat on the street when the piece you're burning is something that is ordinarily used to fire pellets at rabbits. This isn't the time or place to write an impassioned call to arms[5] for anti-gun legislation and there are strong arguments on both sides, but every time a geek with a grudge wanders the hallways of his high school offloading his teenage angst into his classmates, the sight of grief-stricken parents and bloodied pupils hugging each other is enough to make you want guns gone. On the other hand, say the powerful National Rifle Association, 'guns make the United States of America safer, yessir! And that's because if some 'goddam bastard done comes to shoot you with his gun, you can dang tootin' shoot that sonofabitch with your gun first' which is an argument, certainly, but one that misses the basic unilateral nature of the whole 'no guns at all' thing. In Switzerland,

---

5 Yes, I know, bad choice of phrase.

the NRA are fond of saying, 'everyone has a goddam gun[6] and there ain't be no gun crime, you bet your goddam ass, so how can guns be bad?' How indeed? Yet if they're not, this only leads us to the inevitable conclusion that it's Americans who can't be trusted with guns, so the point about taking them off them before they do any more damage stands.

Here's the difficulty, though: I'm willing to bet that most people who are anti-gun have probably never fired one. The majority of people who don't like them and want them banned have probably never even held one in their warm, alive hands; yet if they had, they'd realise in a heartbeat what the problem is, which is that guns are cool. A steady diet of films, television and computer games has conspired to make us clinically obese with gun fun. Put it this way, what would you rather see, Bruce Willis tackling terrorists on top of the Nakatomi building with a flower, or with a gun? No need to answer, because it's a gun. What would you prefer, Clint Eastwood arriving as a strange man in a strange town and cleaning the place up with a flannel? I don't think so. For a few dollars more he could've bought himself a gun. And what the hell was Sarah Connor supposed to have held off the Terminator with, a measured argument?[7] Guns look great and that's part of the problem. And what's more, if you hold one, and then shoot it at something, it feels fucking fantastic.

---

6 Apparently, Switzerland has one of the highest gun ownership rates in the world. It's right up there with ownership of cuckoo clocks and Nazi gold.

7 Yes, I'm being facetious. So shoot me.

The first time I held a proper, real-life loaded gun was in (yes, obviously) Texas. It was a Glock 17, gun fans, and the clip (as gun people say) was fully loaded with seventeen bullets. It was a simple process: I handed over some money, and a man put it in my hands. All at once, in that instant, I was Bruce Willis. Clint Eastwood, Sarah Connor and (weirdly) Deputy Dawg all rolled into one. Or at least I would've been, had I not practically shit myself. As I took it, held it, and turned it over to look at it, I started shaking uncontrollably. Whether it was excitement or nerves I don't know, but it was an utterly odd feeling. I'd had no inkling that holding a gun might affect me like this, but it did, because I was suddenly aware that I was holding something that I could kill someone with right there in that room with just one twitch of the finger, and it scared me.

'Let's go into the classroom,' said the man.

It wasn't a high school, and I wasn't attending a massacre. Instead I was in Dallas at an indoor firing range and I was being taught how to shoot. I'd gone there simply because I'd always wanted to fire a gun, because, yes, I thought it would be cool, and also because I had reasoned 'when in Texas, you might as well do as the Texans do', which is mainly to shoot at things all day.

'This here is a Glock 17,' said the man, whose name, disappointingly, was just Jim, as he gingerly took it out of my hand.

'You bain't[8] never handled no gun before have you?' he drawled.

---

8 This is not a typo. He said 'bain't'.

I confirmed his suspicion that I was a gun virgin, something he'd cleverly deduced from the look of terror on my face. My accent had done the rest.

'Australian, right?'

'No. British.'

'Don't matter either ways. Welcome to your first gun lesson, son,' he said. I wanted him to add a 'yee-ha' but he didn't. Instead, he sat me down and gun school was officially on.

We spent half an hour talking about safety catches and how they work. He was very big on gun safety, was Jim, At first it seemed a bit odd to hear him go so very big on the 'how not to shoot it' side, given that we were surrounded by racks and cabinets of the weapons that were for sale to anyone with as little as sixty dollars and a cursory background check. He showed me how to load, unload and aim and then we were ready.

'Now let's go shoot some shit up,' said Jim, and I followed him through a blank door.

On the other side was a shooting range. An indoor shooting range of the kind you've seen in a thousand films from *Lethal Weapon* all the way through to *Lethal Weapon 4*. There were ten booths, all facing a wide open warehouse along which ran wires that held clips into which you put a bit of a paper with the outline of a man drawn on it. You pressed a button and then, with a crunch of gears, the papery chap was sent off down the other end of the warehouse. Ear defenders were distributed and then, suddenly, it was time to shoot real bullets. I found myself shaking again, so much so that I was fairly convinced my first shot would go wild, rebounding off something and killing me in the face.

'Take your time,' said Jim. 'The trick is to breathe out slow and easy as you pull the trigger. DON'T POINT IT AT ME!'. He was yelling now, which I thought was because of the ear defenders but it wasn't, it was because I'd turned the gun over to have a look at it and it was now aimed at him, fully loaded. He took it off me.

'Only ever point it down the range, son,' he said, quite rightly.

'Sorry,' I mumbled.

'Now I'm gonna take the safety off. And that means this gun is good to go.' He said it nonchalantly, like the gun was a burger, or some completed dry cleaning, rather than what it was, which was quite literally a piece of death metal. He handed it back, carefully, like an adult handing a child some scissors, and manually steered me round so that I was facing the range. I brought the gun up and the shaking became worse.

'Aim at the target, slow, deep breath, and take your shot.'

It was terrifying. I can't explain exactly why, but it was one of the most nerve-wracking moments of my life. And then I pulled the trigger.

Reader, I wanted to marry that gun. It was fantastic. The sound as it went off, the recoil, the feeling, the power, the danger, the edge, the sudden rush of adrenalin and the feeling that I was invincible. I fired it again and again and again. Sometimes slow, sometimes rapidly. The shaking had stopped with the first shot and all of a sudden not only was I Bruce Willis, Clint Eastwood and Sarah Connor, but I was also Mel Gibson and Arnold Schwarzenegger and Bruce Willis again. It felt Godlike. I felt alive. Guns were cool.

After that, you couldn't stop me. I'd paid for two clips' worth of caps (I was even getting the lingo) but I immediately bought more. I was really getting into it, firing shot after shot down the range at the target, and on occasion I even hit it. With another nod to Clint, I tried it every which way; two hands, one hand, kneeling, standing, hiding round the side of the booth as though I was a maverick cop with one last job to do before I retired, and then I got cocky. I turned it sideways. I'd seen it in films. The gangsta with his piece, holding it to a rival's head but turned through ninety degrees. I was throwing the sort of shape I'd seen rappers do in a million music videos. The sort of horizontal gun angle that made it perfectly clear to anyone in the vicinity that I was one badass motherfucka who was to be feared amongst my homies in the hood. Grinning like a dickhead, I pulled the trigger.

The shock of being hit in the face was almost immediate. What I had completely failed to realise, even though I'd been doing it for the past ten minutes, is that when you fire a gun what happens is that while the bullet leaps out of the muzzle, the bullet casing ejects sideways as the slide kicks back, and does so with quite some force; something you can't fail to notice when it hits you in the eye. I was wearing safety goggles, but still the impact was enough to make me think I'd shot myself. I screeched and Jim was immediately at my side, taking the gun away from me for the third time.

'What happened?' he asked.

'Bullet. Gun. Eye.' was all I could manage.

He looked at me. 'Did you fire it sideways?' he said.

'Yes,' I replied.

'Like a gangsta?'

'Yes.'

'You know, one of the first lessons is that films aren't real. The reason we hold guns up the way God intended them to be held up is because they're designed to work the right way up. See here this?' He indicated the ejection port.

'Yes.'

'That's where the shell case comes out when it's fired. Hold it up the right way and it flies out on to the ground. Hold it like you did with the ejection port facing upwards, and it'll come right out into the air and be apt to hit you in the eye. No one holds guns like that. People come in here be thinkin' they're Bruce Willis or Clint Eastwood or some shit and that's why films are bullshit. Did you think you were Bruce Willis or Clint Eastwood, son?'

'Of course not,' I said, indignantly.

'Fuckin' Australians,' he said.

'I'm not Aus—' I began.

'Do you want another clip?'

'Shit, yes!' I said.

Guns are cool. That's the problem. Little wonder that Rob the basketball coach from my childhood had been waving his starting pistol around in the garden. I totally got it now. It felt brilliant to fire a gun. I'd have probably bought one as a souvenir if I thought I could've got it back home on the plane. What's more, I've kind of wanted one ever since, but we don't have Glock 17 firing ranges in the UK and clay pigeon shooting doesn't have quite the same appeal. Be honest, when was the last time you heard Ice-T rapping about that Sunday morning he spent in a pair of wellies popping a cap into the ass of an airborne disc?

Back in New York, Chuck-whose-real-name-was-Gary didn't look like he'd ever even heard of a clay pigeon. He was in his basement garage, working on his own car when I found him and I was holding my trip diary open at the page that had become a battleground. You'll remember that he had written four words beneath the bit where I'd insulted him, his friend Hank and a car. In an angry scrawl, just below where I'd called him a cunt, he had left the message 'Be gone by Tuesday'. And Tuesday was tomorrow. And we had nowhere to go. Chuck was wrathful, and rightly so, but because of the car debacle so was I, and we needed to clear the air.

'Hey, Chuck,' I ventured.

Chuck must have known I was there, standing in his garage doorway, but he was busy using an oxy-acetylene torch although, I was pleased to note, on some metal, rather than a person. He didn't respond and carried on furiously burning something. I moved into his line of sight and, being careful to stay out of his reach, I took a cursory look round for his gun. It was nowhere to be seen, so I sort of hovered until he couldn't realistically ignore me any longer. His torch stuttered to a flameless halt.

'Fuck you want?' he said.

'Pardon?'

'You heard me.'

'No, I really didn't,' I said. 'Welding mask.'

He took it off. Beneath it, he looked really cross.

'I'm sorry about what I wrote,' I said. 'But I was a little snippy because we're now stuck with no car. I appreciate your help in getting the car, but you must see that we don't really know what to do next. All we want is our money back so we can hire a car and then we can be gone by tomorrow. Please don't shoot me.'

He put down his mask and torch.

'Been thinkin' 'bout this,' he said.

'Shooting me?'

'Nah. Wouldn't waste the bullet.' Then he grinned. 'The car's a piece of shit and I figured maybe I'd fix it up for you,' he indicated the welding stuff and some spanners, 'but you're right. I'll get you your money. And you can stay 'til Wednesday.'

Because he'd cheered up a bit, I thought about telling Chuck that it was wrong to go through people's bedside drawers and open their diaries and read them, but thought better of it.

'Thanks. We really appreciate it. We appreciate what you've done for us and I'm sorry about . . .'

'Nah,' he said. 'But next time, you shouldn't leave your book open on the bed where anyone can walk in and see it.'

'Did I?' I said, the vague memory of *not* actually closing the diary and putting in in a drawer beginning to stir somewhere at the back of my mind.

'Uh huh. On the bed. I only saw it cos I went in to open the window.'

Later, over beers in the pool, he said we could stay until Thursday.

On Friday morning, Graham and I hit the road in a rental. Cracks in Anglo-American relations had been smoothed over and our trip had begun. We'd mapped our route to include everything from Niagara Falls to Miami on one side, to Vegas, the Grand Canyon and the weird stone tower in Wyoming that Richard Dreyfuss sculpted a replica of out of mashed potato in *Close Encounters of the Third Kind* on the other.[9] It was a road trip of over thirteen thousand miles and we would do it living in a car. The car was our house, and roadside rest areas became our bathrooms, where we would attempt to wash ourselves in sinks, much to the consternation of any number of vacationing American families. We lived solely on a diet of cheap packets of bologna, which we would attempt to make more interesting by adding complimentary sachets of relish that we stole from petrol stations who actually only offered them complimentarily when you bought a burger, which we didn't, because we couldn't afford them. All of what little money we had went on petrol, which became the most important commodity of all; every mile scrutinised carefully as we journeyed from outpost to outpost. It was like the plot of *Mad Max*, except with more stolen mustard. Twenty-two years old, and we were journeying into the unknown, which is why one night we found ourselves miles from anywhere in the forests of the Blue Ridge Mountains on the border of North Carolina and Tennessee. We were

---

9 Technically this is more Midwest, but we wanted to see it.

driving the Blue Ridge Highway, five hundred miles or so of incredible views en route to Florida down from the Big Apple via the even bigger Appalachians. We hadn't seen another car for miles and it was dark, so when we saw one of the infamous rest areas – really just a small car park and some picnic benches in the trees – we pulled over and made our plans for sleep.

In 1994 the Swedish pop band Roxette tried to have us believe that 'sleeping in a car'[10] was a sexy thing to do, but they clearly never tried to do it in a white Geo Metro, which, if you're unfamiliar with it, can best be described as a less roomy and sporty Suzuki Swift. It was all we could afford, which is why it was not only our car, but also our apartment. Roxette had suggested that if 'the moon is all right' and 'the freeway's heading south' then your heart would 'go boom with a strange taste in my mouth'.[11] They further posited that upon sleeping in your car, there was every chance that you would be 'caressed' and 'possessed', and before long it was fear of the latter that came to haunt this night in the mountains.

Our sleeping arrangements consisted of reclining the two front seats and taking one each, in sleeping bags. I took the driver's seat,[12] with Graham as passenger and, after a few weeks of this, the car had begun to smell a bit like we had died in it. This was, for the most part, due to not being able to have the windows open as we slept, something we

---

10 Written by Per Gessie. Performed by Roxette. EMI, 1994. Quite shit.
11 That would be the pilfered burger relish.
12 Graham had argued, successfully, that my legs were shorter and would be less encumbered by the pedals in the footwell.

discovered somewhere in New England when we'd woken to find ourselves the edible centrepiece of an all-you-can-eat breakfast buffet for insects. Tonight, the windows were safely wound up, the doors were locked and we'd each eaten a yellow-paste-smeared slice of pink meat, so we made ourselves as comfortable as possible on the impossibly un-comfortable seats and turned off the interior light.

I was the one to glimpse it. At first, so the cliché goes, I thought I was seeing things. We were alone in a pitch-black forest, the only sound the occasional call of an animal, wind in the trees and Graham's hideous, hideous snoring. In fact, it was the latter that had awoken me, or at least that's what I thought. Naturally, I very quickly deployed the time-honoured method of quieting a snorer – I reached over and punched him hard on the arm.

He made a noise, failed to wake up and turned over, the movement giving both me and the quiet stillness of the Great Smoky Mountains a moment of respite. I turned over too, but then something outside the car caught my eye. I saw it suddenly in the wing mirror; a momentary flash of light, then nothing. Naturally, my immediate thought was that it was lightning, except the problem was that whatever had flashed hadn't been the colour of lightning; it had been the colour of blood.

I sat up, peering out of the window into the dark. Ob-viously I'd imagined it. There was no such thing as red lightning. Nothing moved, and it didn't come again, so I lay back down, one eye on the wing mirror, but just as I began to get comfy, it came again, longer this time, not a flash at all, just an eerie glow coming from the trees behind the car. I sat up and whirled round to look out of the rear window – to see nothing. I checked the doors were locked. There was definitely somebody or something out there, and whatever it was, I didn't want it to get in here. I sat there for probably ten or fifteen minutes and, when nothing appeared, I decided to try to sleep again, secure in the knowledge that if I had my eyes shut, I wouldn't see it anyway, and therefore whatever it was couldn't kill us. It's the same logic that says a duvet pulled over your head will make the psycho killer's axe bounce clean off your body without harming you. I lay down again. It was reassuringly dark outside.

And then it wasn't. As soon as I'd got comfortable, the whole of the forest behind us lit up a bright and vivid red that seemed to radiate from the trees. It was then that I knew it was a UFO and that we were going to be abducted, which is why I woke Graham. As I did so, the light blinked out again.

'I wasn't snoring,' said Graham, irritably.

'There's a light in the trees,' I said. 'A red light that keeps going on and off.'

'Dreaming,' said Graham.

'No,' I hissed. 'It's there. It keeps flashing on and off and every time I turn round to look it vanishes.'

'Bollocks,' he said. 'No, there isn't.'

'There IS. Just watch.'

He sat up. There was nothing. We were alone in the woods. Graham moved his eyes around the inside of the car.

'When did it happen?' he said. 'Was it when you were lying down and going to sleep?'

'I wasn't dreaming,' I insisted. 'I was fully awake and I saw it. And it was irregular. Sometimes on, sometimes off.' Graham hadn't seen it, but I had, and its other-worldly eeriness had convinced me that this was a close encounter of the shit yourself kind.

'Did it come on when you lay down and then go off when you sat up?' asked Graham.

'Yes!' I said. 'It's like it knew.'

'It's the brake pedal,' said Graham.

'What?'

'You had your foot on the brake pedal. When you lay down you were pressing it, and when you sat up you weren't. Brake pedal. Try it.'

I did, and the forest lit up red.

'Twat,' said Graham, and pulled the sleeping bag over his head.

We lay in the dark.

'You *were* snoring,' I said.

TWENTY

... in which I accidentally become a wanted felon in the State of Texas

Just for the experience, everyone should aim to be arrested at least once. I've actually managed it twice, once in the UK when I surrendered myself at a police station and again in America, at gunpoint. (There was also a 'thing' involving the US military and the perimeter security of an American airbase, but let's not get ahead of ourselves.) To be fair to me, none of this was my fault – well, the arrests were, but the gun thing wasn't. Well, it was, but the whole gun thing had really only come into play because I had broken the law in Texas.

Somewhere, in a dusty filing cabinet in a sheriff's office in a tiny hick town in the Lone Star State, there's a list of America's Most Wanted that has my name on it, instructing any state trooper that's ever been within earshot of a gunshot to hunt me down and throw me in a county jail. Or at least there was, for about five days, until I bottled it.

For nearly a week I, much like John Dillinger, Bonnie and Clyde and Osama bin Laden before me, was on the run; wanted by US Law Enforcement and yes, I realise that this requires an explanation. In America, you see, I committed a crime, a crime for which I was splayed across a car while

251

a policeman drawled into his radio, alerting headquarters to make some room on the bunk next to his last prisoner, the notorious horse-botherer Billy-Jo Inbred, whose brains were made of corn.

I should stress from the outset that, up until this point in my life, I had never committed a crime on American soil; I had not previously inappropriately touched a horse, nor had I ever robbed a local bank, shot a man in Reno just to watch him die or ever played Giant Jenga with some aeroplanes and the sticky-up bit of Manhattan. No, compared to that terrible tally, I'm afraid my crime was a bit rubbish, even if Sherriff Roscoe P. Hardass's demeanour said otherwise.

So let me take you by the hand and lead you through the state of Texas. It's 2004, thirteen years after my first US road trip and the sun is beating down on my friend Alan and I driving our open-topped car across America like we were Thelma and Louise, except male, and with no real plans to drive off the edge of the Grand Canyon.[1] We were Men; two young guns, carefree, laid back, on a road trip from Las Vegas to Houston, in our thirties but pretending we were in our twenties again, with just miles of empty blacktop between us and the heat-hazed horizon; two cowboys riding our steel horse beneath a cloudless American sky with the wind rushing through what remained of our hair. And, on the radio, country music that was interrupted every five minutes with alarming warnings to watch out for a 'dangerous statewide plague of black widow spiders' that they said the hot weather

---

1 Spoiler alert. Sorry.

had made extra bitey. Out here, we were the only car on the road and hadn't seen anything else moving for miles (apart from a spider that we'd stopped to peer at, and my bowels, when it scuttled towards my face) so, when the DJ played Tom Petty, I turned up this amplitude of Americana, put the cliché to the metal and turned our afternoon into a scene from *Smokey and the Bandit*.

The first we knew we were in trouble was when, in the distance, we saw sunlight glinting off glass. Instinctively I slowed, knowing it was Smokey Bear, but it was too late because instead of the regulation 55 mph, his radar had already clocked me doing 115, partly because it was fun, but mainly to get away from the poisonous spider.

I can tell you now that trying to coax sympathy out of a Texan state trooper is only marginally less difficult than struggling to lure a tapeworm out of a dog. In Texas, speeding is a serious crime, up there with cattle rustling or being a vegetarian, so we pulled over and nervously watched as Buford T. Justice walked towards us with his hand on the butt of his gun. When he arrived at the car, I looked him straight in the sunglasses and tried to explain that on an empty road with not another car in sight, surely a small burst of speed couldn't hurt? And it hadn't hurt, but what did hurt, was my head being pressed on to a hot bonnet while I was frisked for weapons. Then he took away my passport.

'Australian?' he asked.

'Er . . .'

He opened the passport.

'English?' he asked in perfect redneck.

'Yes,' I said, and to prove it began to stutter and stammer like Hugh Grant may have done, on being caught with that prostitute that time.

'When y'all flying home?' he barked.

'M-M-M-Monday,' I said.

'Don't think so,' he said. 'Judge don't get into town 'til Thursday and y'all be in jail 'til then. You, son, are under arrest.'

Then we stood together, silent in the sunshine; me with my face on a car and him weighing up the paperwork involved and noisily chewing tobacco. This went on for what seemed like an age.

'I'm gonna let y'all off with a fine,' he said, eventually. 'But if y'all fail to pay it by tomorrow, y'all become a wanted felon in the State of Texas.'

I'll be completely honest; I thought this was the coolest thing I'd ever heard. I immediately resolved not to pay it and, as we drove (slowly) off, I imagined going home an outlaw, pursued by the cops, hunted by the Feds, a desperado with a Texas price on my 'ass'. I would be the envy of my friends, a legendary folk hero staying one step ahead of justice like Billy The Kid or the Dukes of Hazzard. It was then that Alan reminded me that if I was a bandit on the run, then next time I wanted to come back to America I wouldn't be able to, because I would be on file, and they would shoot me or deport me as soon as I landed. Thus I bottled it and meekly paid the one-hundred-and-eighty-dollar fine at a post office. My crime spree was over. At least until the next one. And this time, the US military became involved.

*

The lure of Americana proves irresistible to me, and if you've never experienced an American road trip then I urge you to do so at once. There was a time, before children, commitments and holding down anything approaching an actual job, that I would save up and go as often as I could, picking an area, hiring a car, and seeing where the road would take me. Once, though, I picked an area that wasn't there, via a road that didn't exist and where it led was straight to my second 'Fox Mulder' incident. And despite the first one turning out to be based on nothing more alarming than an idiot flashing the brake lights of a small car at a forest, I still wanted to believe.

From 1993–2002 *The X-Files* was a TV institution, running for almost ten years and, somewhere in the midst of this, as a fan, I decided to channel its blend of conspiracy and cover-up by proving, once and for all, as fact, the existence of aliens. I was dimly aware that deep in the deserts of America there's somewhere that doesn't appear on any maps, isn't mentioned in the official guidebooks and there's no real road to speak of that will get you anywhere near it. The US Government even say it's not there and that they've never heard of it, yet if you know where to look and which bit of remote desert to point your car at, you'll find something vast and sprawling, hidden behind the hills 133 km north of Las Vegas. It has no official name and is referred to mainly by a number and yet, conversely, is America's worst-kept secret – if you discount that thing about that actor. And that other thing about that music industry boss. Welcome to the legendary Area 51, and a welcome is exactly what you won't receive if, like me, you set out to try to find it, then actually *do* find it, and then get intercepted by unmarked helicopters and men driving trucks with blacked-out windows, wearing mirrored sunglasses and toting guns.

Area 51 is a military base and airfield attached to the Edwards Air Force Base, buried deep within the four thousand six hundred and eighty seven square miles of the Nevada Test and Training range where Harry Truman tested his new nuclear toys back in 1951, promptly giving ten and a half thousand Americans living downwind of it radiation poisoning. Funnily enough, they don't much like to talk about that either, and it's thanks to all the secrecy and (radioactive) smoke screens, that Area 51 has become the go-to place for conspiracy theorists and UFO enthusiasts worldwide. Which is why, on one hot day, I decided to try to find it.

The base has long fallen into the realm of mythology. This is because nutters remain resolute in their belief that extraterrestrials from crashed UFOs have been taken there and chopped up, so that scientists can peer into their space guts. Not only that, they are adamant that this is where alien saucer technology has been reverse engineered for the benefit of humankind, although given that all this supposedly originally took place in 1947, after the 'Roswell Incident', it's a bit of a mystery why humankind then went on to develop, say, the Toyota Yaris instead of hover boards. It's just one more mystery piled on all the other mysteries, which is why 'Dreamland' (as other nutters call it) has been namechecked in any number of films from *Independence Day* to the most recent Indiana Jones movie *Indiana Jones and the Not Very Good Adventure*. Does Area 51 exist? Well, like Fox Mulder, I wanted to believe, even though I didn't.

Now I should confess first of all that I'm not really an *X-Files* or *Doctor Who* style 'superfan'. For a start, I don't travel to comic conferences dressed as a sonic screwdriver (in fact, I don't travel to comic conferences at all) and have also, on occasion, (as detailed elsewhere in this book) seen a real-life naked lady. But if someone (in this case the US Government) tells me something is off limits and isn't even there, then I definitely want to go and have a look, which is why in 2006 I found myself searching various websites which promised directions to the place that didn't exist. Very quickly, I found detailed and comprehensive instructions about how to travel north from Vegas and find the desert road that leads to the dry river bed that indicates a turn-off that passes the mysterious 'Black Mailbox' that pinpoints the vicinity of the dirt track that leads to the perimeter of the base. The game was on.

If you go, take water. And sunscreen. Temperatures out here can reach 110F in summer so it's advisable to drink both. It takes around two and a half hours to get to the middle of nowhere from Las Vegas and, thanks to my spoddy website map, it wasn't long before I found the infamous 'Black Mailbox', about which the first thing to note is that it's white. And it really is just a mailbox. An all-American mailbox standing alone by the side of the dark desert highway, cool wind in its hair. If it had hair. Which it doesn't, because it's a mailbox. But, crucially you see, this mailbox is important because its location marks the best place to come at night to 'watch the skies'. It's mailbox Mecca for UFO spotters, and they come here with their flasks and tents, camping under the stars and staring through the flaps into the airspace directly above where Area 51 officially isn't. And sure enough, out here in the middle of nowhere, there was a man sitting by a tent, sipping from a thermos. I pulled over.

'Are you here for Area 51?' I asked him.

He was possibly in his fifties, and looked like he'd been sitting out here since his twenty-first birthday. He was weather-beaten, certainly, but had a face that suggested that during that beating, various other chaotic phenomena had joined in. He looked at me as if to say, 'Why the hell else would I be out here, you moron?'

'Why the hell else would I be out here, you moron?' he said.

We chatted a while longer and soon got to the point, which was, he said, because 'the night sky over yonder' (and he nodded to indicate the distant low hills, beyond which Area 51 was said to sit) 'is filled with strange lights that move unlike any other aircraft.' I pointed out that given that Area 51 is supposed to be an experimental aircraft base where they make experimental aircraft, it stands to reason that experimental aircraft may move around 'unlike any other aircraft'.

He fixed me with a hard stare.

'Unlike ANY other aircraft, including them ones,' he muttered, and then went into his tent to experiment with his flask. I turned and, for a while, watched the skies myself, but I couldn't see anything in them so I got back in the car and consulted the paper Geek-Nav.

Groom Lake Road, the unmarked dirt track, little more than some ruts in the sand, that lead to the base, was ahead and within another twenty minutes I was quite literally on its trail, with nothing to stop me. Except for what did, an hour or so later. The entrance to Groom Lake Road is unremarkable. I swung off the main highway and rattled and thumped my way over lumps and ruts, idly wondering if my Collision Damage Waiver also waivered me for colliding with big rocks and it's then that I noticed that the track was now running between two high ridges, and high on those ridges were what looked like antennae; white, complicated-looking aerials sticking up from the dust, themselves looking fairly alien out here. There were also what could have been cameras half hidden in the brush; I got the occasional glimpse of bits of electronic kit presumably designed to watch whoever is watching the skies. Obviously, this was all quite exciting because it was a clear indication that *something* was ahead, so I ignored them and carried on. By now I had been off-roading for just over twelve miles and had just one more to go before I could prove with my own eyes that Area 51 was real and would become the first human to prove to the world the existence of extraterrestrials.

At mile thirteen the road narrowed as it disappeared around a corner and then, behind another ridge, it dipped slightly and veered off unseen to the left. Except there was something in the way: a signpost, all on its own, standing stark against the sky, much like the Black Mailbox. And also like the Black Mailbox, the sign wasn't black either, it was red and white but it's what was written on it that made me stop.

'Warning' it announced, 'Restricted Area' (Oh, so there *is* an 'Area' is there? In your face Government.)

'It is unlawful to enter this area.' (Ha. There it is again. The Government are idiots.)

But then came the (buttock) clincher. 'Use of Deadly Force Authorised.'

Oh.

There was no fence, no gates, nothing to prevent me from driving on past the sign, except for the advice on the signpost that if I did, I would be killed. I got out of the car to take a photograph, which is when I noticed another sign under the first sign that said 'Photography is Prohibited'. Still, I reasoned, I'm thirteen miles from a main road and there was no one about so what's the worst that could . . .

Up on the ridge to my right, there was now a truck with blacked-out windows. It was some distance off, totally in-congruous all the way out here (as was I, in my bright blue Chevrolet) but I could see it clearly enough to know that it wasn't there a minute ago, and that if trucks could look in any way pissed off, then this one certainly did. And then, as if to prove its point, the doors opened and two men with guns got out.

I like to think I can read a situation, and this one was now reading like a novel in which the protagonist is left for dead in the desert. The men were dressed in black army fatigues, wore sunglasses (of course) and their guns were large assault rifles which I presumed was the deadly force which, I was quick to remember, round these parts was 'authorised'. They were staring back at me, one through binoculars, so I put my camera away and decided that the best course of action was to stand and read the sign for a bit as if to say, 'Hey, I took a wrong turn back there, roughly thirteen miles ago, and have just seen your sign pointing out my mistake. I had no idea there was an Area out here. There isn't, you say? No Area? OK. Whatever you say, you're the one with the M16.'

According to the warnings I'd read posted on websites by other searchers for The Truth, I should, as I got closer to the base, also be prepared to be 'buzzed by black helicopters'. These unmarked machines apparently patrol the perimeter of the base to warn people away and are, according to my tented friend from earlier, 'associated with cattle mutilation'. Not being a cow, but still fearing that I might get mutilated, I stood debating with myself as to what to do next. And that's when the helicopter arrived. It swooped in low overhead, black and unmarked, exactly as promised. What would Fox Mulder do in this situation? He would make a run for the Area, determined to prove the existence of beings from other planets and the Government's attempts to hide their knowledge of them. He would think nothing of sacrificing his own safety, leaving his car and running for cover in the scrubland, engaging in a deadly game of cat and mouse with the helicopter and the mysterious gunmen.

However, when the helicopter made its second pass, the only thought I had, briefly, was one of waving, but then I thought better of this too and so, under the watchful eye of Tweedlegun and Tweedledeath, I got back in the car and went back the way I'd come. In the end, I didn't see hide nor hair of an alien base with my own eyes, but I'd seen enough to know that something approaching The Truth is out there, in the Nevada desert.

At the highway end of Groom Lake Road, there was a police car marked 'Nevada Highway Patrol' waiting for me. It was no coincidence that he was parked up here.

Waving me down, the very polite officer asked me where I'd been.

'I went to the Area. To see the base.'

'The military base?'

More proof! He'd just told me with his own official Government employee mouth there *was* a military base! The authorities and their anonymous drones were fools!

'Er, yes.'

'It's restricted.'

'Yes.'

There was a pause. 'Is that because they have aliens there?' I said.

I couldn't see his eyes behind his sunglasses, but I'm sure they flicked nervously upwards into the sky behind me. There was silence. The only sound that of the late afternoon desert wind picking up, and rolling sand across the road. And the distant noise of a man who wants to believe, unscrewing his flask.

'You should be on your way, son,' he said. 'Before I arrest you.' And that was that.

Later I solved the mystery of the Black Mailbox that wasn't black. Apparently at one point it was black but now it's white, because a UFO geek nicked the black one as a souvenir. You can't trust anyone.

TWENTY-ONE

. . . in which I am arrested, again. And then attacked with raw mince.

Despite being arrested almost twice, I have only once been imprisoned. I was young, I didn't know any better and I got caught; banged up doing bird in chokey for a stretch, a bit like Ray Winstone's character Carlin in *Scum*. But where Ray Winstone's character Carlin in *Scum* was doing any number of years in Borstal for taking the rap for his brother stealing scrap metal, I was put in a police cell for almost an afternoon for hiding a sign behind a couch. There's only one thing worse than being put in a police cell after you've been arrested and that is being put in a police cell after you've been arrested while the officer in charge is laughing at you because your crime has been so pathetic.

It was a Friday night, and because I was a student in Canterbury the decision amongst my peers was taken to spend the day in nearby France. From Canterbury it was a simple trip on the ferry.[1] It was inexpensive and you could drink beer on the crossing, which we duly did. The trouble was,

---

1 Or on the Eurostar now. But this was 1991, and though the holes that had been dug simultaneously from Dover and Calais had met in December 1990, the tunnel wouldn't open until 1994.

we also drank it *en Francais*, and then even more of it on the way back, so by the time we disembarked in Dover to catch the train back to Canterbury not one of us could really walk properly. There were four of us: my housemate Nic, fellow-student Graham (with whom I was later to live in that car in America) and my friend Gary, who wasn't a student, but was visiting from Nuneaton, where we'd been friends growing up. And now all four of us were drunk, which is why, on our walk back up the hill from Canterbury station to our house in Cherry Garden Road, we decided it would be a good idea to collect all the Bed and Breakfast signs that we could find. The road up the hill was one of the main routes into Canterbury, a road that runs all the way to Whistable, past the university and St Edmunds Private School, through the village of Blean and out towards the coast some eight miles away, and it's fair to say that it had more than its fair share of comfortable accommodation for the discerning, yet budget-conscious traveller. In fact, there were precisely eleven B&Bs on our route back and I know this because once we were back home with all their signage around us in the lounge like the spoils of war, I counted them. We'd taken them off walls, from hanging chains, from atop posts in gardens and, in one particularly tricky manoeuvre worthy of a Black Ops unit breaking into a high-security facility, from the roof of a porch. Somehow, between us, we'd got our haul home and then we simply went to bed and forgot about it.

The next morning, I had a job interview,[2] so it was while

---

2 This was at the then local radio station Invicta Radio. I'd submitted a demo tape and had been called in to meet the programme controller. I didn't get the job.

wearing my best (only) suit that I came downstairs, remembered the signs and joined the others in stacking them behind the sofa or moving them into the downstairs toilet where they would be (kind of) out of the way. Except for two of them. Graham was off to visit his parents in Hertfordshire so one we loaded into his car as a trophy, and another we wrapped in a black bin liner so that Gary could take it back to Nuneaton on the train as a souvenir. And then I went off for my interview, oblivious as to how the day was about to unfold. The only other person in the house on the fateful night was Jane, Nic's newly qualified teacher girlfriend, who had been asleep when we'd arrived home and, upon waking to a houseful of broken wooden contraband, gave us a look of disdain and went off to work, leaving Nic alone in the house. Which was when the police arrived.

Nic answered the door in his pants. He was not one for dressing early, and so he sat in them in the lounge as three police officers questioned him as to what he might know about a number of Bed and Breakfast signs that were now absent from their rightful place outside the guest houses of Whitstable Road. Nic, thankful that we hadn't left the evidence scattered around the room, denied all knowledge of the crime.

'We know you took them,' said the first one. 'Just tell us where they are.'

Nic's dad was a solicitor, so Nic believed – and erroneously continues to do so – that he could handle himself in an argument. Despite sitting on the sofa in his underwear, his long curly hair, unkempt beard and cigarette making him look like Brad Pitt's stoner character in *True Romance*, he mounted his case for the defence.

'I don't know what you're talking about,' he said. 'I was here all day yesterday. Didn't go out.'

It wasn't much of a defence, since even the most cursory check on his whereabouts would have revealed that his passport had been to France and back. But the police didn't need to go down that route, due to Nic's stupidity.

'Who said anything about yesterday?' said another one.

Nic thought about this, and took a drag on his cigarette.

'You inferred it,' he said. 'You being here this morning would indicate that a crime of some sort has been reported overnight which leads me to the conclusion that the crime aforementioned was committed sometime in the past twenty-four hours, a time during which I have been here and so cannot be placed at the scene.' To be fair to him, this wasn't a bad save.

'You *were* placed at the scene. A man matching your description along with . . .' And here he consulted his notebook, 'Along with a short man with dark hair (me), a man with big ears (Graham) and seemingly a young boy (Gary). I have you down as . . .' he looked at his notes again, '"long hair, beard, scruffy looking". Now, where are the signs?'

'Circumstantial,' said Nic, without really knowing what that meant.

The policeman ignored him. 'Where are the signs?' he repeated. 'They're in the toilet,' said officer number three, having come back from a number one.

'And over here,' said the other one, who'd just looked behind the settee.

'You're under arrest,' said the first one.

*

It turned out that we'd been seen, and reported on, by a diligent member of the Canterbury neighbourhood watch scheme. *Ocean's Eleven*, this was not. An old lady had seen four people staggering up the road clutching various Bed and Breakfast signs between them and had called the police. Realising that this wasn't exactly the stealing of the crown jewels, the police had waited until morning, visited the pensioner's bungalow and asked her to point out the house that the perpetrators had gone into. And so here they were in the lounge, and here we were bang to rights.

From the police station Nic was allowed his one phone call and used it to call his dad, the proper solicitor, who lived in Peterborough. His dad advised him to admit nothing and then he (dad) called Jane, Nic's girlfriend, to find out what the hell was going on. I arrived home post-job interview to find Jane at home (it was lunchtime by now) and in a state of panic.

'What are you doing here?' was my first question. My second was, 'Why are you hitting me?'

'You stupid, stupid, *stupid* fucking idiots!' she was saying, although at this stage, I had no idea why.

'What? What? Ow!'

'Nic's. Been. Arrested. That's. What.' She punctuated each word with a slap to my head and/or body.

'Stop hitting me!'

She did.

'You were seen stealing those stupid fucking Bed and Breakfast signs,' she said. 'And the police were here and everything.'

I glanced behind the sofa. The signs were gone.

'Ah.'

'They want you down at the station.'

'Pardon?'

They want you at the station. The police.'

'Wait a minute, how do they know I'm involved?'

'Nic gave them all of your names.'

Oh great. Mr play-it-cool and I-know-how-to-handle-myself-in-an-argument had caved at the first instance of interrogation and grassed us all up. So much for honour among Bed and Breakfast Sign thieves.

'I'm not going down there,' I said. 'Are you mad?'

'Get fucking down there and sort this out,' said Jane, through furiously gritted teeth. It's worth pointing out that I was scared of Jane, everyone was, which is why she's gone on to make an excellent teacher. I got fucking down there.

The police station was on the other side of the city, on the ring road, and it's fair to say that I walked there as slowly as I've ever walked anywhere. I was aware that I was essentially going to be 'handing myself in at a police station', a sentence that can often be heard on the news. It's a phrase that I've never really understood; given that I'd always thought that, given the choice, and knowing that you are in trouble for something, surely 'running away from a police station' would be a more preferable option. But here I was, doing exactly that, because I was frightened of Jane. By the time I got there, however, my gait had changed from that of a condemned man to that of someone who had had an idea. I walked through the door into reception, and, ignoring what appeared to be a homeless man slumped in a chair in the corner, I gave the desk sergeant a wide smile. I had reasoned that if I could pass the whole thing off as an amusing student prank (which surely was all they could be treating it as?) then we'd all be OK.

'Good afternoon, officer,' I said, still smiling.

'What can I do for you?' he said.

'I understand you are holding one Nicolas Peters in custody,' I said, trying to speak the lingo, which I had heard being spoken on *The Bill*.

He looked me up and down. Let us not forget that I was still wearing my suit.

'Are you his solicitor?' he said.

This was interesting. I briefly considered my options. By replying 'yes' I could potentially get away with not being arrested like Nic, but this relied on Nic not grassing me up (again) by shouting 'that's not my solicitor, it's one of my accomplices' the moment I was ushered in to 'advise' him. Realising that this was the most likely scenario, and unsure as to whether impersonating a solicitor was a crime and would therefore only delay the inevitable and make the inevitable worse, I decided to come clean.

'Er, no,' I said. 'I'm his accomplice.'

The desk sergeant stared at me. Even the homeless man looked up, surprised.

'Are you handing yourself in?' he enquired.

I cleared my throat.

'I don't know,' I said.

'Wait there.' And with that, he disappeared into the office behind him.

The homeless man was still staring at me, so I gave him a friendly nod as if to say 'there's been a terrible misunderstanding but don't worry, I'll have it all sorted out in a jiffy'.

'Fuck off,' said the man.

'Be quiet you,' the desk sergeant told him, as he came back. 'Now,' he said to me, 'If you'll just go through that door, someone will meet you.' He pressed a buzzer and I went through. On the other side a sour-faced, uniformed automaton was waiting for me.

'This way,' he said, and led me down a corridor and into a room where two men in rolled-up shirt sleeves and ties were waiting. I was steered towards a chair and a wave of a bare lower arm indicated that I should sit down.

'Name?' said the first man.

'Jon – Jonathan – Holmes,' I said.

'Do you know why we're here, Mr Holmes?'

I resisted the urge to reply with something deep and philosophical.

'Is it to do with Bed and Breakfast signs?' I said.

There followed an hour or so of questioning. They genuinely played Good Cop, Bad Cop too, Bad Cop telling me that what I had committed was the crime of theft, which carried a maximum sentence of seven years, and Good Cop asking me how long I'd been a student, what I was studying and what I planned to do as a career. I replied that I'd like to work in radio. This was Bad Cop's cue to pounce.

'Oh yeah? Well, I wonder how the radio industry would look upon employing a criminal?' he said.

Given what we now know of Operation Yewtree and what had been going on at Radio 1 for all those years, I personally can't imagine anyone would have batted an eyelid over the theft of some signs, but of course all of those particular revelations were years away. In 1991, Dave Lee Travis was still just regarded as faintly amusing. Although Jimmy Savile was definitely weird from the off.

'We've counted the signs,' he said. 'There are two missing.'

I wasn't about to grass up Graham and Gary, so I said nothing.

'Your friend Nicolas says they're with two people called Graham and Gary,' he said.

For fuck's sake, Nic.

'Here's what's going to happen. You are going to be released on police bail, pending our investigations. You will contact your friends and have them attend this police station, with you, in one week's time. They must bring with them the missing Bed and Breakfast signs. If, by then, we think there is enough evidence to charge you, that is what will happen. Are we clear?'

I wasn't clear as to how much more evidence they needed, given that Nic had already been arrested and charged with the crime, (after he'd been found hiding the evidence in a toilet and behind a settee) but nevertheless I was sent home to make some calls. I don't know if you've ever had to telephone friends to tell them that they have to return to somewhere in order to be arrested and charged with a criminal offence, but it's a tricky conversation.

'So you want me to come back to Kent and hand myself in at a police station?' said Graham and Gary separately, yet more or less word for word.

'That's the gist of it, yes.'

'No.'

'The police said that the alternative was that they will come round to your parents' house to recover the property and arrest you there.'

There was a pause.

'When do we need to be there?' they said.

Without telling their parents, they both came back a week later, the Bed and Breakfast signs back in the car boot and on the train, respectively. After the longest week of my life, in which I genuinely believed I was going to prison and that I would get a criminal record rather than a job, we all, Nic included, went back to the police station at the allotted time. As we walked through the door the same desk sergeant looked up. This time, he knew who we were.

'Well, if it isn't Al Capone and his gang,' he said. 'Committers of the Crime of the Century.' I got the distinct impression that he wasn't taking this seriously.

The homeless man was back in the corner. I don't know if he'd ever left. He, too, eyed us with suspicion. I glanced at him.

'Fuck off,' he said.

'Be quiet you,' said the desk sergeant.

And then we were back in the room, or rooms, given that we were taken away to be questioned separately. And then the bombshell:

'I am arresting you on suspicion of theft, you do not have to say anything but it may harm your defence if you do not mention when questioned something which you later rely on in a court of law.'

Shit.

Then there were more questions (most of my answers consisted of words like 'drunk', 'France', 'stupid' and 'sorry') and then I was photographed, fingerprinted, had my shoe-laces and belt taken away[3] and then I was locked in a cell.

With nothing else to do, I contemplated my future behind bars. All of us, with the exception of Nic, whose solicitor dad (to teach us all a lesson) had told the police that they could do what they wanted, were yet to tell our parents. I was going to have to use my one phone call to tell my mum and dad that they had adopted a criminal. Out of all the children that they could have chosen at the Mother and Baby home in Stratford-upon-Avon, they had picked one that was destined to lead a life of crime. They would be disappointed. They would be heartbroken and would probably disown me, wishing that this errant child hadn't ever come into their lives and would immediately make plans to go back to Stratford and pick a new one.

Two hours later, shoelaces and belt in hand, we were released with a police caution. We were reminded that our crime, despite being pathetic, was still a crime and that it would stay on our record for a number of years. We were also instructed to go and personally apologise to the owners of the eleven Bed and Breakfast establishments and com-pensate the proprietors for the repairs and damage, which we dutifully did.

---

3 Presumably they either thought I might hang myself or fashion some kind of rudimentary rope for escape. They weren't hedging their bets with the latter; there wasn't even the slightest sign of a poster of Rita Hayworth.

Eventually, some days later, I finally plucked up enough courage to phone my parents to tell them the whole sorry tale.

'Idiot,' they said. And that was that.

Until that is, some years later when Graham was engaged to be married to the daughter of the Chief Constable of Hertfordshire. The reception was held in the local police social club and, as best man, I told the story in quite some detail, embellishing Graham's role in the affair as seemed fitting for the occasion. I spoke of his arrest, his questioning, the removal of anything he could have used in either a suicide or escape bid, and his criminal record. I thought the whole thing doubly relevant and amusing, given his father in-law's position and our auspicious surroundings. The trouble was, he'd never ever told his parents, let alone revealed his criminal past to the Chief Constable of Hertfordshire, whose face was like thunder, particularly when Nic, Gary and I also chose the moment to present Graham with the Bed and Breakfast sign we'd bought him as a wedding gift.

This time, we'd legitimately paid for it.

When he wasn't in trouble with the law, Nic was more often than not in trouble with his girlfriend. Jane (who, you'll remember, we were all frightened of) had a temper like a war and not only did not suffer fools gladly, but, if she caught a fool would gladly make him suffer, which made the fact that she was going out with Nic all the more of a mystery. Particularly after Nic, following a can or two of strong continental lager, announced to everyone that tonight was the night that he was going to cook an 'endothermic chilli'.

A decent chilli is, of course, a student staple. Mince, kidney beans, onion, tomatoes, celery, bacon (if you're being fancy); it's pretty much the budget culinary gift that keeps on giving. Cook enough, it'll last you for a week – three, if you're Nic and you heave it into the fridge by the bucket load. Chilli was his speciality, but one night, one terrible, memorable night, he outlined his new recipe and commended it to the house.

'I'm going to cook an endothermic chilli,' he said, bringing science to the kitchen, years before anyone had heard of Heston Blumenthal. 'It is a chilli. But it is a chilli that is so hot that it COOKS ITSELF!'

Obviously he didn't say this in capital letters, but he was so proud of his idea that if he could've done, he would have. Nic's plan (which as far as I know had never been done before or since)[4] was to take the hottest chillies known to mankind, (or at the very least, to Sainsbury's) add them to all the rest of the ingredients and then simply flash-fry the lot, believing that this process would let the latent hot power of the chillies out which, in turn, would heat everything that they were sharing the pan with to edible temperatures. It was, of course, bollocks and what he was really doing was creating food poisoning in a pan. However, we were students, so we all agreed that it was an idea worth trying.

So much so, we made a night of it. It was deemed 'Mexican Night' and one or two of us were dispatched to buy tequila,

---

4 Probably because it doesn't work.

nachos and more tequila from Sainsbury's, and we returned to something that was less a kitchen, more a laboratory. Nic had been planning this experiment for a long time and had stockpiled a good number of chillies of mass destruction. He had habaneros, a handful of Prairie Fire chillies, even a mighty Scotch Bonnet, and he confidently topped this off with more than a few drops of Mad Dog Ghost Pepper Hot Sauce and just the right amount of chilli powder – all to make a sauce so powerful that just one shot of it (to badly paraphrase Johnny Cash), if given to a man in Reno (or anywhere), would have almost certainly have resulted in watching him die. We drank tequila and Mexican beer while Nic carefully and painstakingly chopped and grated his deadly vegetables into infinitesimal pieces, incorrectly reasoning that the smaller the slivers, the better they would infiltrate the dish and thus cook it from the inside out. And the more tequila we drank, the more it seemed like a good idea that might just work and, by mid-evening, even scary Jane was up for it, her mood buoyed by the fact that the following day was an inset day, and thus she had time off from terrifying the children that she was in charge of.

Finally, with table set, more tequila poured, nachos chucked in a bowl in the middle and Herb Alpert's Tijuana Brass on the stereo, it was ready. I should add at this point, that halfway through his experiment (and with some input from us, staring into the pan) Nic had admitted that hot though the chillies were, they were never going to cook mince to anything approaching an edible standard, so there had been a longer flash-fry to turn it brown and now we were sitting down to a meal that was now one part tepid beef to eight parts red hot chilli pepper. It was the hottest thing I have ever eaten. It burned with the heat and ferocity of Hades, but Hades after its radiators have been turned up full by Satan, and then the whole place set on fire by arsonists wielding flamethrowers using the molten core of a volcano and the nuclear reaction at the centre of the Sun as an accelerant. The pain that the possessed child Regan felt in *The Exorcist* when doused with Holy Water by Father Damien Karras, was as nothing compared to what was going on in the mouths of those who would dare to approach this malevolent meal.

'It burns! It burns!' each of us screeched after more or less just one tentative taste as we writhed on the floor, because the power of pepper compelled us. Nic, the culinary cleric and architect of our oral destruction tried to claim he was enjoying the demon dish, eating two forkfuls before he too was defeated by it, for it was truly evil. Naturally, then, the evening was deemed a complete success, partly down to the tequila but mainly because it proved Nic (who never likes to be wrong) to be wrong. Later, after eating just rice and discussing whether or not NHS dentists perform skin grafts on tongues, everyone went to bed, retiring to our rooms and bidding each other goodnight through horribly inflamed lips.

It was but twenty minutes later when the silence of this recumbent, slumbering, recovering house was shattered by a scream. It was a scream followed by a screech and then a sort of pained, strangled gurgle. If you've ever heard foxes copulating in a garden after dark, it was kind of like that but higher pitched. It's true of houses to say that, if you've lived in them long enough, you get to know their quirky sounds, their creaks and groans; the settling of the floorboards or the water in the pipes. After The Night of the Long Chives, I can now say with some confidence that I will henceforth always recognise the noise of someone on the receiving end of a boyfriend who has chopped raw chillies of an evening, has forgotten to wash his hands and has then gone to bed and manually pleasured his girlfriend. Though we were all in separate bedrooms, we also each recognised the sound of Nic and Jane's bedroom door, later agreeing that no one could recall it ever before slamming open with enough speed and force to ram its handle through the plaster of the adjacent wall. We also all correctly identified the sound of the bathroom door being opened at a similar speed, the light going on, the extractor fan kicking in and then the noise of the shower being switched on and set to the highest pressure. And while this was going on, there came the sound of some-one else padding downstairs, going to the fridge, opening it, and rattling around with the ice cube tray. The footsteps came back upstairs, the bathroom door opened again, we all heard a whimper, and then it closed. It then went silent, apart from the continuous drone of the shower and, eventu-ally, the running of what we subsequently found out to be a cold bath, which lulled everyone off to sleep. We only woke up again, a few hours later, when Jane finally emerged from the bathroom, went back into the bedroom containing her sleeping boyfriend Nic and detonated her anger bomb.

The elusive and mythical endothermic chilli may well remain the holy grail for any student chef who is also an idiot, but if there is any such thing as an endothermic temper, then Nic was, pretty much single-handedly, the catalyst.

TWENTY-TWO

. . . in which I am rendered half naked in front of my elderly relatives.

Somewhere around this time, I celebrated my twenty-first birthday and, because I was away at university busy being arrested and bearing witness to the notion that Hell Hath No Fury Like a Woman Who's Hoo-Ha is On Fire, it proved impossible to get back to Nuneaton to see the family Holmes on the actual date, so it had to wait a few weeks. Mum had promised a party – relatives old and young all invited – and she'd also called upon two of my oldest friends, Woody and Gary,[1] to attend by way of a surprise, although in the event, it really wasn't Woody and Gary that surprised me. And it wasn't just me that was awkwardly surprised by the other surprise as it also surprised Woody, Gary, my dad and my two sisters, along with various elderly great-aunts and uncles (all in their seventies and eighties) and a couple of Mum and Dad's friends who'd been invited along for both good measure and a glass of wine. This Event Of The Year in the Holmes' calendar was to take place in the most auspicious of venues – my mum and dad's lounge – and was scheduled for a Saturday night, with friends and family arriving around

---

1 He of 'gang of hardened criminals responsible for the Great Bed and Breakfast Sign Heist' fame.

six for a 'special buffet tea',[2] followed by what transpired to be the most uncomfortable evening that I have ever spent.

The first surprise – that of the arrival of Woody and Gary – came as no real surprise at all. They were the two friends from home that I'd kept in touch with the most after I'd made the long journey south to spend three years getting drunk on snakebite and black. Woody, or Darren Wood, was my old school friend who had been given his inventive nickname by the very same playground genii that had come up with mine of 'Holmesy' – yet his had followed him into adulthood, for reasons that are unclear. Gary, for his part, was a friend from church youth club, and it was his elder sister, Deborah, who had been partly responsible for Fat Kev's nickname of 'Octopus'. Gary, who remains a good friend, doesn't like to be reminded of Fat Kev sexing his sister, which is why I still like to bring it up even now, twenty-something years later. In short, we'd shared many moments together, but tonight was to be one of the most bizarre.

Before long, the Holmes clan had gathered, all squashed into my parents' living room. The youngest was my sister Vicky, joint eldest were Great-Auntie Sylvie and Nana Holmes (Dad's mum), who were well into their seventies, sitting awkwardly on dining-room chairs that had been

2 This would have included the Holmes' family party buffet speciality – a frozen King Prawn Ring, from Iceland. If you haven't had the pleasure, it mostly consists of a circle of prawns, arranged around a dip. And that's it. I wish there was more to it, but there isn't. Quite how this says 'party' to anyone other than someone who's never actually ever been to any kind of party, I don't know but I guess if you regularly shop in Iceland, anything that isn't an act of wilful suicide seems like fun in comparison. My sister Kelda likes them, so Mum has to make a special trip.

positioned around the room facing the middle, so that everyone could enjoy chit-chat, warm Hofmeister that my dad had inexplicably bought for the occasion, and a glass of Asti Spumante, 'because we were celebrating'. It was early, only about half past seven, when it happened. We hadn't even had the buffet yet. The frozen party treat that was the King Prawn Ring from Iceland had barely even defrosted and twenty-five elderly people hadn't yet needed the toilet, when the doorbell rang. My mum went to answer it. When she came back into the room, her face was grave.

'Jonathan,' she said, 'it's for you.'

Naturally I assumed it was someone else she had invited to the party, though I didn't know where they were going to sit because the small lounge was full up.

'Who is it?'

'I think you'd better go and see.'

I stood up, handed my Hofmeister to Gary, and went to the front door. I don't know who I was expecting, but it certainly wasn't the police.

'Jonathan Holmes?' said the lady officer at the door.

'Er, yes?' I said, desperately trying to figure out what I'd done recently that could warrant arrest. Any Bed and Breakfast signs were all accounted for, and I hadn't been recently speeding through Texas.

'Is it your birthday?' she said.

I began to answer, which is when I noticed her partner. If he was also a police officer, then he was a slovenly one. His attitude to his uniform could best be described as 'half-arsed' and he appeared to be wearing trainers. His jumper, while dark blue, didn't seem right and his helmet looked distinctly like a toy one. I looked back at Juliet Bravo. She was wearing way too much make-up, and now that I thought about it, her skirt was too short. She also had terrible, terrible teeth, was well into her forties and wasn't exactly what a sexist man would refer to as 'a looker'. Now, I'm certainly not suggesting for one moment that any these qualities should in any way affect her ability to do her job as a policewoman, but as a stripper it was a positive disadvantage.

I find the whole 'stripper' thing a bit peculiar, strip clubs in particular. Not the reason they're there, that much is obvious – they fill a hole for lonely businessmen, stag-night organisers and Capital Radio Breakfast presenters just coming off their shift – but inside they're a bit odd. I have been to precisely three strip clubs; two were on stag nights and the other while recording a documentary about the industry for BBC 5 Live. They strike me as soulless, entirely unsexy places, even more so backstage where women share a room and get changed out of jeans or jogging bottoms into lingerie and heels with all the enthusiasm of someone turning up to work to enter data into a computer at a boring pharmaceutical company. Of course there's no reason on Earth it shouldn't be like this – stripping is a job, just like any other (except with fewer clothes) and the job is to go out there and sell the notion of sex to idiot men. Or women on a hen night, if you're a male one. It's performing, and many of the girls I spoke to for the documentary were completely matter-of-fact about it; many following the familiar route of doing it to earn fees to get them through university, others just for a good income. The arrangement seemed to be weighted in the clubs' favour, however, because like hairdressers renting a chair at a salon, they had to pay to be there and their income comes from the dance fee and the tips – after the club had taken a cut of this as well, of course. But they all seemed perfectly happy in their work and were happy to chat.

On the other side of the curtain, chat isn't really what anyone is in it for. The first time I went was when I was around twenty-two, on my friend Jonny's stag night and no one had told me that that's where we were going, so when we walked into what, from the outside, looked like a per-fectly ordinary pub in Shoreditch in East London, I got a bit of a shock. I headed for the bar and, as I did so, noticed that everyone was facing the other way. I turned round. Not five feet away was a totally naked girl seemingly perform-ing a gynaecological examination on herself. Two things immediately occurred to me: first, we were either in a strip club or a quite off-the-wall STD clinic that also doubled as a bar – although given that we were in Shoreditch, the latter was entirely possible. Second, if this *was* a strip club, it was a steep learning curve, because I had had no idea strip clubs were this explicit. In my strip-club virgin head, I'd assumed that the ladies in question just faffed around on a pole for a bit, disrobed, paraded around the stage, waved at the customers and called it a night, but what was going on here was bordering on a medical procedure. Naturally then, we bought beer and went down the front to see what all the fuss was about. I was standing next to my friend Mike who wears glasses and now works for BBC Radio Devon, although these two things aren't related. We were watching, open-mouthed, as this naked girl, who can't have been any older than we were, opened and closed more or less anything she owned with impunity, often only centimetres from our faces. And then she spotted Mike.

Mike is one of my best friends, we share a love of radio, too, but, with the best will in the world, Mike is a geek. This is a man who once rebuilt the engine of a Fiat 126 using parts of an old fridge, made a bomb in childhood that, when detonated in the sewer outside his house, blew all the manhole covers off within a half-mile radius and who, to this day, likes nothing more than to hang around boot fairs buying bits of old wires and metal in case they're useful. Once, when we lived together as students, he brought home a large, heavy Banda copier of the type used for printing in schools in the 1970s. It required two people to lift it, and an ill-fated attempt to move it through the house resulted in its hitherto-unseen reservoir of thick ink pouring out and gushing down the stairs in a torrent of black oil. As if this wasn't bad enough, Mike insisted that he'd read somewhere that the best way to clean up thick oil was with petrol. He then disappeared to the twenty-four-hour garage and returned with a couple of litres of unleaded that he began to rub into the carpet. Obviously it didn't work at all and simply resulted in us spending three days and nights with all of the windows open and the electricity turned off at the mains lest someone forget and accidentally flick on a light switch and blow the house up. Our housemate who smoked simply moved out for a week. He was Jonny, whose stag night we were now on.

The friendly naked lady approached Mike slowly. He looked like he didn't want her to, but he was trapped, penned in by the rest of the audience. What happened next

I can safely say I had never seen before and certainly never have since; she lay down on her front, bottom in the air, so that she was level with his face, gazing directly into his eyes, eyes that were clad in his statutory geek-issue glasses. And as we watched, she reached out and took them from his face. Sans specs, Mike can see very little so he had to mostly rely on eye-witness testimony as to what happened next. With his face furniture in her hand, our new friend (who we were by now all fairly intimately acquainted with), spun around so that she was on her back. She then opened her legs, raised her buttocks up like someone preparing to do some yoga and, in one swift movement, ran Mike's glasses, lenses first, down and through her own lady's hoo-ha, like someone swiping a credit card.

To this day, I don't know whether it was supposed to be sexy or not but I do know that it was weird. It was also hilarious, especially when she then popped the specs back on Mike's face and (forgive me this, I'm just relaying the facts) the lenses were so smeared that Mike couldn't see out of them. After this, she carried on her dance, but Mike missed it. Afterwards I asked him why he didn't wipe them clean. He said she might have thought it was rude.

Shortly after this 'dance' I went to the toilet, only to see an old man, erect penis in hand, ejaculating into a urinal. It was time to leave.

In context then, strippers make me feel a little uncomfortable. Out of context, for example in your parents' own lounge which is full of Asti Spumante-fuelled old-age pensioners and two of your friends drinking tepid lager, it's fucking horrific.

'Happy Birthday!' grinned the toothless police imperson-
ator at the front door, and that's when PC Trainers pressed
play on his ghetto blaster and they pushed me back into
my own house. It was 1990, carrying around music on your
mobile phone – and indeed having a mobile phone – were
firmly in the future. If you wanted to be wired for sound in
1990, your choices were the ever-dependable personal Sony
Walkman, that reliable cassette-tape playing behemoth, or
the ghetto blaster. Back in the glory days, if you wanted to
share your vibes with anyone in as wide a radius as possible,
you didn't impose your shit music on strangers through the
shrill speakers of the as-yet uninvented smartphone, but
rather through the bass-heavy boom box of the shoulder-
mounted radio cassette player. And it was one of these, now
playing 'I Was A Male Stripper In A Go Go Bar' by Man 2
Man Meets Man Parrish at full volume, that accompanied
me as I was pushed into the lounge by a fake policewoman
who had already begun to disrobe.

No amount of descriptive passage or turn of phrase on the
page can even begin to describe this situation. All I can do is
remind you that we were now standing in a small Nuneaton
living room in the middle of a circle of chairs; chairs that were
occupied by some friends, yes, but mostly by great-aunts
and uncles with a combined age of around five hundred and
seventy-eight. To say my mum had massively misjudged this
birthday surprise would be to grossly undersell the moment.
While all of my ancient relatives looked on, I was sat down
on one of the chairs (which had been hastily moved to the
middle of the room by my confused dad, after Sergeant Toy-
helmet had indicated that he should do so) and my hands

were handcuffed behind my back. Between each flourish (that consisted mainly of making a big show of putting the key to the handcuffs in her bra) the lady I now knew to definitely not be a genuine policewoman, removed an item of clothing. And not just from herself, either, also from me. As she danced in front of me, I caught sight of Woody and Gary's horrified faces and knew that they were reflecting my own. My sisters were wearing similar expressions, and even Kelda, whose gerbil I had accidentally squashed all those years ago, was looking at me with pity in her eyes. My mum, for her part, still hadn't properly grasped the situation, and was clapping along to Man 2 Man vs Man Parrish like there was no tomorrow. She certainly wasn't expecting what came next. First, with my hands cuffed behind me, WPC Stripper undid my shirt. It was a smart shirt – it was a party, after all – and she undid it from top to bottom. Then she realised she couldn't get my arms out, what with them being chained together behind me and all, so she just pulled it off me as far as she could. Her ghetto-blaster friend just looked on, his job to ensure the music flowed and that no one touched the girl. Given that the majority of her audience would have taken ten minutes to get up out of their chairs, his job that night was an easy one. And to be fair to him, even he was looking uneasy; when they'd been booked to perform their routine at a twenty-first birthday party, I'm not sure he was expecting to be greeted by the cast of *Cocoon*.

But, ever the professional, if she thought it was odd, the stripping policewomen didn't show it, and was by now undoing her blouse. We all knew where this was heading, and we were powerless to stop it. The rest of it went by in a kind of blur. Her blouse came off, the skirt was removed, stockings and suspenders were revealed, and out came the whipped cream. Somewhere in the midst of that, the music had changed to 'Touch Me (I Want Your Body)' by Samantha Fox, which she took as her cue to spray the stuff on my chest and lick it off. When she was done with that, she turned round, put her back to me, and took off her bra. This was, of course, meant to be teasing and sensual, yet as she was now fully topless and directly facing Great-Aunt Florrie, this rather took the edge off, and besides, I was busy willing her with all my might not to reach over and take Great-Uncle Ken's glasses off. She didn't, thank Christ. Instead, she turned round to face me, all sagging, naked breasts and with one final shake of her drooping dairy arrangement, she squirted the cream on to her own tits and shoved my face into them.

That done, the music stopped, she picked up her clothes, and within moments she and her friend were gone. I was left handcuffed to a chair, squirty cream dripping from my face and chest on to the carpet, in silence. A silence amplified tenfold by the fact that seconds earlier a man in a toy police helmet had been blasting out stripping anthems on his portable stereo.

We all sat there, unsure of what to do or say next. Even my mum looked hesitant, which she had begun to right around the time the bra had come off. It was seventy-two-year-old Uncle Ern that saved us. He bent over and picked up the handcuff keys from where they'd dropped out of the bra and on to the floor.

'That was brilliant,' he said. 'Is there any more Asti Spumante?'

TWENTY-THREE

And now the end is near.

So here's the thing.
I'm going to die.

TWENTY-FOUR

Not immediately though, I hope. Don't worry; this isn't a surprise 'misery lit' ending. What I mean is, we're *all* going to die at some point, but I don't know whether or not I'm carrying something medical that might just do it sooner rather than later. And, as we established just over eighty thousand words ago, neither do my young daughters, as I can't pass that knowledge on to them. All I can pass on is this book. Although if you've reached this point, you'll probably agree with me that they should never ever be allowed to read it.

But what have we learned? More importantly, what have *I* learned? What has been handed down to me and forged me into the shape of a man who appears to have just written an entire book based on teenage sex fumbling, not being very good with hammers, accidentally filling tax forms with pubic hair and an elderly man's sweet, sparkling-wine-fuelled love of a stripper?

Way back in Chapter Two, I posited that when you are adopted, a family formally agrees to take you on as a child to raise as their own, but of course when they adopt you, you sort of adopt them, too. This inevitably means that whatever baggage *they've* been carrying through the years becomes yours and, if there are any skeletons in the closet, then their bones automatically become those of your ancestors, if not by blood, then certainly by default.

It's fortunate, then, that Uncle Paul isn't a blood relation to any of us. He married into the Holmes family late on, the second husband of a second cousin. I saw him irregularly, perhaps only at Christmas or the odd wedding, and gave him little or no thought over the years. Not until he did what he did to Millie. I'm going to reiterate here that despite knowing him as 'Uncle Paul', he was nothing of the kind. His name simply appeared on gift tags, written and attached to festive wrapping by Auntie Christine,[1] and I remember that he had a moustache. Other than that I had had no real cause to think about him for nigh on thirty years, not until what happened, happened.

I first found out about it at the Christmas dinner table. It was 25th December 2009, and I was back to visit the family. My sister Kelda had long since moved out (and had two children of her own), other sister Vicky was still living at home but not for long, and Mum and Dad had both retired. We gathered together with our respective partners and soon all talk turned to reminiscences of Christmases past. Over

---

1 She isn't actually my aunt, either. This was one of those things that families do – take someone who might be a cousin or even a very close family friend and affix the prefix 'Aunt' or 'Uncle' as a sort of catch-all. As mentioned earlier, Mum and Dad were only children, so my sisters and I got a lot of Aunts and Uncles foist upon us who were nothing of the kind. Great-Aunts (who were actually my mum or dad's aunts) became simply Aunts, as did second cousins who were my mum and dad's age. It's confusing and I feel for you trying to follow this. I've known them all for years and, for the most part, I still don't have a clue exactly how we're related.

Mum's turkey, pork, sprouts, several different kinds of stuffing and cracker jokes, we chatted of this and of that (and the fact that every Christmas, Mum forgets to serve something that she's left in the oven) when suddenly, during a natural lull when I poured more wine, Mum said brightly:

'Do you remember your Uncle Paul?'

I think now that Dad knew what was coming, because he stopped chewing.

'Which one's he?' I said. I often have trouble with Mum's conversations that begin 'Do you remember . . .?' followed by someone's name because a) I invariably don't remember them at all and, b) she will carry on telling me her story about them whether I remember them or not. Once I sat though a half-hour-long, quite detailed anecdote about 'Mrs Bennett' who had taken ill while on holiday.

'You remember Muriel Bennett?'

'No.'

'She was taken ill on holiday.'

'Right.'

'They had to fly her home.'

'OK.'

'You remember. Muriel Bennett? She had that son who you were at playgroup with.'

This was a playgroup that I attended forty-three years previously.

'I don't remember.'

'Anyway, I often see her at the shops and she said that she'd been taken ill on holiday and that they had to fly her home. You remember Stephen? He went on to be a holiday rep, which is ironic.'

And so on. This happens a lot, and I never really have any idea who she's talking about. And now it was Uncle Paul.

'Is he the one married to Auntie Tracey?' I said, trying to keep up.

'No. That's David. Paul is the one married to Auntie Christine.'

'Is she an Auntie?'

'No, she's your second cousin, and Paul is the one she married after her and Graham split up. He's got a moustache.'

'Paul or Graham?'

'Paul.'

'OK,' I said, not really any the wiser.

Vicky decided to help. She's pretty much an expert on how the family works. Whether this is because she's genuine Holmes family flesh and blood and thus finds it easier, I don't know. Either way, she's my go-to when I lose track.

'Uncle Paul's had sex with a dog,' she said.

For any dinner table, this would surely be a revelation; here was an area of family disclosure that even the scriptwriters of the Christmas Day edition of *EastEnders* would've thought twice about, and it knocked the twenty-first birthday family stripping debacle into a cocked bra. So many questions regarding Uncle Paul, so many queries in my mind, all of which seemed wholly inappropriate to ask over so many different kinds of stuffing.

'What the fuck?' was more or less all I could manage.

'Jonathan!' said Mum. 'Language.'

We were talking about a relative shagging a dog, yet she was worried about the F-word.

It unfolded over the turkey that 'Uncle' Paul had filmed himself having proper penetrative sex with his Old English Sheepdog called Millie and, following a tip off from a neighbour,[2] the tape had been found by the police, who had turned up to search his home. There was a forthcoming court case, an impending divorce, and for the dog at least, a long period of counselling. It was genuinely the most bizarre family Christmas dinner I have ever sat through, discussing the ins and outs of bestiality with my parents while helping ourselves to pigs in blankets with all the trimmings. And reader, we found ourselves laughing. Yes, it was an horrific situation – awful, for those involved, especially the dog – but, as a family unit sitting, late in the afternoon, around the centrepiece of a home-made cotton-wool snowman full of sweets that had traditionally come out after the Christmas pudding dishes had been cleared away since we were children, it was the right thing to do. Laughing *with* your family *at* your family is what your family is for, whoever they are.

I include this awkward, bizarre and frankly peculiar tale of our familial dog-botherer simply to illustrate that families are awkward, bizarre and frankly weird. But the thing is, whatever they have attached to them, by dint of birth, marriage, ancestry or adoption, you are part of them, and they you. Nature may certainly bestow her gifts, but it's nurture that goes quite some way in turning you into the person you eventually become.

I looked round the Christmas dinner table at my family – my two sisters Kelda and Vicky (Kelda adopted, like me,

---

2 The mind boggles as to how this came about.

Vicky not) and at my mum and dad laughing at the fact that, post-pudding, Mum (as usual) realised she'd forgotten one of the stuffings and had left it in the oven, along with the peas. Though I didn't know it at the time, we were less than twenty days away from the (early) birth of my first daughter and I looked at my heavily pregnant wife, and at the growing bulge in her belly that was a child, rather than Christmas pudding, and realised that very soon, this new baby – the next generation of Holmeses – would also be related to our familial dog-botherer simply because, forty years previously, my mum and dad had walked through a door in Stratford-upon-Avon and chosen to take home one particular baby. Christ, life is weird.

They say you can't choose your family, but mine chose me.

And I wouldn't have it any other way.

ACKNOWLEDGEMENTS

I'd like to thank everyone I've mentioned in this book for inadvertently contributing to it along the way. I would thank them by name, but I've changed quite a lot of them because I would like to keep (most of) them as friends. People I *can* legally name are my family, my Mum, Dad and sisters for answering my endless questions, the brilliant Amanda Harris, Jillian Young, Leanne Oliver and everyone at Orion, Vivienne Clore and Nick Canham at RSP, and also Tina and Jeremy who conspired to lure me away from my laptop with wine and mad flights over Kent in a microlight – although not at the same time. Any mistakes (and things I've totally misremembered) are my fault.

ABOUT THE AUTHOR

Jon Holmes is an eight-time Radio Academy and double BAFTA award winning writer and presenter. He's worked on some of those programmes that you like, and probably some others that you don't. He's put food into his children's mouths by putting words into the ones of, among others, Armando Iannucci, Stephen Fry, Graham Norton and Harry Hill, with the likes of Bono and Leonardo DiCaprio thrown in for good measure. He co-wrote TV's *Horrible Histories*, co-created the multi-award winning *Dead Ringers*, and is the short one from BBC Radio 4's *The Now Show*. He's been heard presenting on Radio 1, Radio 2, BBC 6 Music and the Xfm Breakfast Show, where he was nominated for Radio Presenter of the Year. He is also an award winning travel writer for the *Sunday Times*. He lives in Kent. You can follow him on Twitter @jonholmes1 or visit his website, jonholmes.net.